A GROUNDED *IDENTIDAD*

A GROUNDED *IDENTIDAD*

Making New Lives in Chicago's Puerto Rican Neighborhoods

Mérida M. Rúa

OXFORD
UNIVERSITY PRESS

OXFORD
UNIVERSITY PRESS

Oxford University Press, Inc., publishes works that further
Oxford University's objective of excellence
in research, scholarship, and education.

Oxford   New York
Auckland   Cape Town   Dar es Salaam   Hong Kong   Karachi
Kuala Lumpur   Madrid   Melbourne   Mexico City   Nairobi
New Delhi   Shanghai   Taipei   Toronto

With offices in
Argentina   Austria   Brazil   Chile   Czech Republic   France   Greece
Guatemala   Hungary   Italy   Japan   Poland   Portugal   Singapore
South Korea   Switzerland   Thailand   Turkey   Ukraine   Vietnam

Published by Oxford University Press, Inc.
198 Madison Avenue, New York, New York 10016

www.oup.com

Oxford is a registered trademark of Oxford University Press

Library of Congress Cataloging-in-Publication Data
Rúa, Mérida M.
A grounded identidad : making new lives in Chicago's Puerto Rican neighborhoods / Mérida M. Rúa.
   p.   cm.
Includes bibliographical references and index.
ISBN 978-0-19-976026-8 (hardcover : acid-free paper) 1. Puerto Ricans—Illinois—Chicago—Social conditions. 2.
Puerto Ricans—Illinois—Chicago—Ethnic identity. 3. Puerto Ricans—Illinois—Chicago—Interviews. 4. Ethnic
neighborhoods—Illinois—Chicago. 5. Chicago (Ill.)—Ethnic relations. 6. Chicago (Ill.)—Race relations. 7. Chicago
(Ill.)—Social conditions. 8. Chicago (Ill.)—Biography. 9. Social surveys—Illinois—Chicago. 10. Interviews—Illinois—
Chicago. I. Title.
F548.9.P85R83   2012
305.868'7295077311—dc23   2011051389

Cherrie Moraga's "The Welder" from *This Bridge Called My Back–Writings by Radical Women
of Color* used with permission.

9 8 7 6 5 4 3 2 1

Printed in the United States of America
on acid-free paper

En memoria de Luis Rúa (1941–2006) y de Petronila Delgado (1906–2006)

I am the welder.
I understand the capacity of heat
to change the shape of things.
I am suited to work
within the realm of sparks
out of control.
I am the welder.
I am taking the power
into my own hands.

— Cherrie Moraga, "The Welder,"

CONTENTS

ACKNOWLEDGMENTS

This project, more than a decade in the making, would not have been possible without the generous support of a number of individuals, institutions, and grants. The list of those who contributed directly and indirectly to this manuscript is lengthy and I apologize in advance to any I may have forgotten. I am deeply grateful and indebted to the Chicagoans who trusted me with pieces of their personal stories and allowed me to follow them about their daily routines. Time and again they made themselves available throughout my field research and allowed me to reenter their lives through follow-up phone calls and visits. It was their commitment to my studies, to me as one of their own, that gave me the strength to pursue and complete this project. The Bishop family deserves a most cherished acknowledgment for graciously accepting to be the subjects of more than a few undergraduate research papers, and what eventually became this book.

Archivists and librarians in Chicago, New York, and Puerto Rico helped me immensely in the acquisition of sources. I thank staff at the Research Center of the Chicago History Museum; at The Special Collections Research Center, University of Chicago Library; Lara Kelland at the University of Illinois Chicago Daley Library, Special Collections Department. At the Archives of the Puerto Rican Diaspora, Centro de Estudios Puertorriqueños, Hunter College, I especially thank Pedro Juan Hernandez; at La Fundación Luis Muñoz Marín, Dax Collazo was a life saver on the copyright front; and, finally, my appreciation to Gloria Arjona, who gave me access to her personal archive in Puerto Rico. The time and resources necessary for research, writing, revising, and editing were made possible by generous grants and fellowships from the University of Michigan, Williams College, and the University of Illinois at Chicago.

The spirit of this book began as a doctoral dissertation under the guidance of Frances R. Aparicio, Earl Lewis, Arlene Torres, and Alford Young Jr. I thank them for their encouragement, intellectual engagement, and true generosity in reading my work. In their own unique way, each challenged me to make my arguments more precise and more nuanced, allowing me to see what could be most interesting for a book.

I am grateful to the many students I have had the pleasure of teaching and learning from; they have made my life in the academy worthwhile. Many thanks to students from Pedro Albizu Campos Alternative High School, Latin American and Latino studies majors at the University of Illinois at Chicago, and American Studies majors and Latina/o Studies concentrators at Williams College, particularly students in my "Chicago" course. A special shout-out to Yamnia Cortez, Priscilla Damaso, Luz Gomez, William Lee, Omar Mendez, Hannah Noel, Cristina Villegas, and, research assistant extraordinaire, Taisha Rodriguez.

For providing a warm and supportive atmosphere that has encouraged and enriched my development as a scholar and teacher, I thank my colleagues in Latina/o Studies and American Studies at Williams College. Two individuals who deserve special note are Carmen T. Whalen and Roger Kittleson, who read many, many versions of various chapters, offering wise council, incisive critiques, and tons of encouragement. I would also like to extend heartfelt gratitude to Linda Saharczewski, Lucy Gardner Carson, and Megan T. Konieczny for the extraordinary assistance they have provided Latina/o studies faculty over the years.

To my morale-boosters–Thank you, thank you, thank you, for listening to ideas and/or reading and commenting on parts of chapters, full chapters, or the entire manuscript: Carlos Alamo, Marixsa Alicea, Jillian Baez, Gene Bell-Villada, Devyn Benson, Magnus Bernhardsson, Leslie Brown, Denise Buell, Mari Castañeda, C. Ondine Chavoya, Maria Cotera, Nicholas De Genova, Zaire Dinzey Flores, Virginia Dominguez, Tyrone Forman, Jennifer French, Lorena Garcia, Jennifer Guglielmo, Tom Guglielmo, Jacqueline Hidalgo, John L. Jackson, Jr., Gaye T. Johnson, Liza Johnson, Regina Kunzel, Aldo Lauria, Amanda Lewis, George Lipsitz, Gretchen Long, Norma Lopez, Alejandro Lugo, Nancy R. Mirabal, Kenda Mutongi, Elena Padilla, Gina M. Pérez, Kashia Pieprzak, Isaura Pulido, Ana Yolanda Ramos-Zayas, Bernie Rhie, Mark T. Reinhardt, Stéphane Robolin, Richard T. Rodríguez, Alberto Sandoval Sanchez, Eiko Siniawer, Lorrin Thomas, Armando Vargas, Kiara Vigil, Javier Villa-Flores, Manu Vimalassary, Steve Warner, Scott Wong, and members of my UIC writing accountability group, the Puerto Rican History working group, and my virtual writing compañeras–Las Profes Online Writing Group. All offered good advice about things large and small, making this a much better book. Special thanks are due to Lorena Garcia, Kashia Pieprzak, and Ana Yolanda Ramos-Zayas for the gift of their friendship and for the much-needed distractions that kept me human and sane.

To Nancy Toff, Sonia Tycko, Lora Friedenthal, and the production team at Oxford University Press, I am grateful for the care with which they shepherded this book into press. Thank you, too, to Sharron Macklin for the amazing maps.

To the late Jeannette Hopkins, I owe a debt of deepest gratitude for her unwavering commitment to this project and to me. She taught me much about the craft of writing, improving every aspect of this book as she relentlessly challenged me (often to a point of great frustration) to find my voice and to write a book that would give readers a reason to turn the page. I hope I've succeeded. To the friends I made in Portsmouth, N.H., David Taylor, George Friese, and Jennifer Holloway, thank you for the wonderful meals and great conversations.

The greatest appreciation, however, goes to my family: my mother, Mérida Maria Rúa Cruz, my sisters Lorraine Rúa-Figueroa and Lissette Rúa, my brother-in-law Richard Figueroa (who by now has accepted that he is a Rúa), and to my nephews Clemente, Ismael Aníbal, and Joaquín. Thank you all for the unfailing love and support that you give me on a daily basis. My father, Luis Rúa, and my *abuela*, Petronila Delgado, nurtured my love of history and my appreciation of everyday life. This book, appropriately, is dedicated to them.

PROLOGUE

Field Trips and Field Notes
Reflections on Memory and Neighborhoods

My sense of narratives of place and community and my first "field trips" began on weekends after church on Sunday afternoons when I was a child in Chicago's Puerto Rican neighborhoods. My father, Luis Rúa, a welder by trade, became tour guide as my mother, my *abuela* (grandmother), my two sisters, and I climbed into our gray Buick Regal for his weekly history lesson and his lesson plan for his daughters' futures. In "site visits" we explored the neighborhoods of his childhood. This book continues that story of Puerto Ricans in Chicago.

Chicago was my father's adopted city. He had migrated, in 1954, at fourteen, with his mother and sister from Patillas, Puerto Rico, to the city's Near North Side, and soon called Chicago "home." He loved the city even when the feelings were not mutual. He was especially proud of his old grammar school, Ogden Elementary, "one of the best schools in the city," so he said, and it was so in the 1980s, if not in the 1950s when he and most other students were children of migrants and immigrants. Places that existed only in his memory he described as he remembered them and they became as real to me as the places I inhabited, my own first "field sites"—St. Sylvester grammar school and church in Palmer Square, the Puerto Rican parade festivities in Humboldt Park, our house on Armitage Avenue (where we lived on the second floor and rented the storefront). After he had driven us to places where he had lived and streets he had played in, we went beyond, to places of his aspirations. We would drive along Lake Shore Drive to see the city's vaunted skyline, and arrive, by one route or another, at one of Chicago's elite campuses, the University of Chicago or Northwestern.

A building we never entered on our Sunday field trips was one I would enter later as a scholar—the pristine, elegantly carved, white marble Newberry Library across the street from the Ogden School. When I became a "credentialed dissertation researcher" at the University of Michigan in 2000, I ventured into the Newberry and approached a research associate about its collection of community histories in search of anything on Chicago's Puerto

Rican community. Nothing there would be of use to me, he said, the subject being too "new." Too "new"? Puerto Ricans had lived near and around the Newberry for a half-century, had walked the very streets yet nonexistent in the Newberry files or on its shelves. Today, a decade later, the Newberry sponsors a seminar in Borderlands and Latino Studies, occasionally on Latinos in Chicago.

As a scholar myself I discovered that the Chicago of most social science scholarship was a white-and-black polarized city, the people whose heritage I shared obscured. I began to feel a responsibility to record their past and their "living" history. But I had, in fact, begun the search earlier by instinct, as a sophomore at Notre Dame High School for girls, when I took part in a Chicago History Fair; I prepared a poster on "Puerto Ricans in local politics," and saved the photographs I took for later use. As a junior at the University of Illinois, I wrote a paper on black Puerto Rican women, and titled it "Triple Threat: Black, Puerto Rican, and Woman." Assigned to conduct oral histories, I interviewed four women I had known as a child in Logan Square: Gina Bishop and three of her daughters, Gini, Becky, and Elsa, the only black family I really knew growing up in a segregated Chicago. For a year after graduation from the University of Illinois, I taught Caribbean history, Latino studies, and mathematics at Pedro Albizu Campos Alternative High School in West Town/Humboldt Park and worked, some evenings, at the Caribe Funeral Home, where, later, in researching this book, I lived in an upstairs apartment. At the University of Michigan, studying for my PhD in American Culture, I wrote an essay about my grandmother, "Tracing Partial Remembrances: The Everyday Politics of Language in the Life of an *Abuela*." And I must have been imagining this book when, as a young adult, I took part in organized protests for better schools, affordable housing, and safer neighborhoods on the streets of the city.

Still, this book is not my personal story but a story of Chicago's Puerto Rican neighborhoods and its people. I chose as "organizing spatial sites for my field research," Chicago's Near West Side and Logan Square, neighborhoods the literature characterizes as "secondary Puerto Rican communities."[1] I was now armed with a detailed plan, my dissertation prospectus, and my "interview protocol," and with an intent to perform as a detached "objective" scholar in search of "hard" data. My "subjects" and "informants" disrupted my careful scheme. I was interviewed by those I intended to interview: "*¿Por qué tu no vives con tu familia?*" ("Why don't you live with your family?")[2] "Why are you asking those questions, you know the answers, don't you?" "What is this research for?" I realized that to some I interviewed, I myself was one of the actors in these narratives of place, memory, and identity. I was *la nena*, the neighborhood girl, who went away to study and now needed help with her homework.

In the position of "native" researcher, I found a Chicago different from my memory but also different from the one I had read about in the scholarship, that city supposedly polarized between black and white. The Chicago I found had far more dimension and depth and complexity. It was apparent that the scholarship needed to be revised to reflect the reality of the lives of Puerto Ricans, and hence of the city itself. This book is part of that revision, a story of the complex ethnoracial dimensions of identity and space and their necessary connections. It explores the multiple meanings of *latinidad* (a shared sense of identity among people of Latin American and Caribbean descent) from a historical and also an ethnographic perspective by examining daily lives in the past and present Chicago. African Americans, whites, and, particularly, Mexican immigrants and migrants, had helped shape the meanings of Puerto Rican identity even as Puerto Ricans created their own identities in the city.

Identidad, complex and fluid, needs to be recognized and explored as "grounded," as rooted in both time and place, and as manifest in everyday exchanges with people within and beyond one's own ethnoracial groups. The second largest population concentration of Puerto Ricans in the United States at the time of this study, Chicago's Puerto Ricans have continually constructed, restructured, and transformed place through discourses and experiences of rejection and belonging, despair and hope, claiming the city even as they sought to negotiate and honor their own distinct identity.

A Grounded Identidad begins in 1946 when two migrant groups in separate but converging streams arrived in the City of Neighborhoods. One was the small group of University of Puerto Rico graduates who had earned scholarships to enroll at the University of Chicago. The other was of contract workers recruited by an employment agency for household and industrial labor. It was the beginning of Chicago's first community of Puerto Ricans, a virtual colony of the United States' Caribbean empire in the industrial heartland. These arrivals laid the foundation over the next half century and beyond as a study of place and identity, of memory and loss and of renewal, of six decades of urban renewal, loss of neighborhoods, emergence of multiracial coalitions, protest movements, and celebrations of life. The story concludes with my reporting back to the community on what I learned. Or at least it is the end of a chapter in the larger story to come.

Puerto Ricans in the United States had come from their island colony not as émigrés but with the status of US citizen. Most considered themselves, and were considered in Puerto Rico, to be "white." And, yet, in the United States their brownness was considered "colored," their citizenship "second-class" and their status "foreign." They discovered that they shared few of the rights other Chicagoans took for granted and wondered whether those of Puerto Rican descent were/are, in effect, historical anomalies of the vestiges of empire, or genuine US citizens. Puerto Rican Nationalists themselves prefer for Puerto Rico to be not a 51st state but rather an independent country. At an early stage of the mass arrival of Puerto Ricans in mid-twentieth century Chicago, legal residence in the city itself assumed more pronounced meaning than simply one of US citizenship. Puerto Ricans were regarded, and treated, as personas non grata. Residence in Chicago has remained a dominant theme of Puerto Rican existence and identity. Their claims to the social benefits of residence were challenged in contests over housing, neighborhoods, and community. For those cast as outsiders and underrepresented in history, residence is both a goal and a trope for belonging.

And what of the ties that bind Puerto Ricans to other Latinos, those who are US citizens and those who are undocumented or documented migrants? Is it only the Spanish language? Or origins in the Caribbean? What about Cubans and Dominicans? What role did race, class, and legal status play? And do Puerto Ricans consider Mexicans their "cultural twins and national others?"[3] I discovered that memory and place, desire and reality, led, inevitably, to explorations of latinidad within and beyond *puertorriqueñidad* (Puerto Ricanness). After all, there had been considerable intermarriage and mixing. Julius Bishop, husband of Puerto Rican pioneer Gina Bishop and owner of the Caribe Funeral Home where I lived while I studied Chicago for this book, was an African American from the Deep South. One of the funeral home's morticians was Mexican. Puerto Ricans took part with Mexicans in a 2001 May Day protest march, in which I joined, with flags and banners to the Near West Side's Union Park to form a 20-mile long human chain of linked hands for amnesty for undocumented immigrants and for peace on the island of Vieques, where until 2003 the US Navy held bombing exercises. Puerto Ricans had marched with blacks in Chicago in the 1960s, and Jesse Jackson now marched with them in a brown and black coalition. Not homogenized, identities and discourses and loyalties, were competing and conjoining together, negotiated in memory and in the living present. Were/are identities distinct, and, if distinct, should they be acknowledged as significant, or neutralized and overcome, and if either in what context?

A Grounded Identidad, a story of many places and people, focuses on the series of neighborhoods Puerto Ricans possessed, in a way, and lost, expelled from Lincoln Park/Old Town by, for example, urban renewal or pushed out by gentrification. And yet some I talked with who were on the way up to secure a middle-class status told me they were not wholly opposed to gentrification, especially if it abetted racial and class diversity of the neighborhood. Mine is a story of places as embodiment and symbol of identity, certain channels more conspicuous than others. I strolled along boulevards on Sundays with sauntering people and traced the shifting neighborhoods. Certain buildings, too, I found central to this living history, as, for example San Francisco de Asís Church on the Near West Side, a historical site of latinidad; the Shakespeare building, once multiracial, now remodeled as pricey apartments rented by young, mainly white, people; and Caribe Funeral Home, the first Puerto Rican-owned funeral home in Chicago.

Inevitably *A Grounded* Identidad is a story of people, among them, these: an Anthropologist-in-training, Elena Padilla, graduate student at the University of Chicago in the late 1940s, who collected testimonies about the working conditions of migrant laborers and distributed a report to the press, engaging in a series of "extra-anthropological interventions" that made an actual difference in peoples' lives; William Rios, with his sky-blue zoot suit, white-brimmed hat, and dazzling salsa moves despite his seventy years, who told me tales about negotiating the City's color line; Ana La Luz, a tiny but hard-edged grandmother, and matriarch (I trace her family's intracity migrations from the 1950s to the present); Cándido Quiñones and Damaris Delgado, an upwardly mobile couple, he a state trooper, she a grammar school teacher, with a home in Logan Square and several properties in Humboldt Park; Bobby Escalas, a talented musician with a warm personality and a quiet charisma, Puerto Rican and Mexican, a quintessential Chicago Latino; Julius Bishop, who played his violin in his basement sanctuary amid his vast collection of books, a living repository of life in Chicago, and whose eulogy I would deliver; and Gina Bishop (née Rios), my landlady and owner (with Julius) of Caribe Funeral Home, high cheek-boned and bossy—a gambler at heart, she served as a sounding board for my research, occasionally asking for favors in return. These were among the living archives, my "interlocutors" and "informants," the Puerto Ricans of Chicago.

In many respects, *A Grounded* Identidad takes up the intellectual challenge for Puerto Ricans that Harriet Jones put before Anthropologist John Langston Gwaltney—to compose a work in which she could recognize herself and the black people she knew as "drylongso": "You know, like most of us really are most of the time—together enough to do what we have to do to be decent people."⁴ My intent became to bring to light those often missing from the pages of traditional scholarship, Puerto Ricans and communities often typically rendered socially and racially expendable, with the "complex person-hood," to borrow from Sociologist Avery Gordon, of populations often reduced to lifeless stereotypes.⁵ History, as this book demonstrates, does not "happen" to aggrieved communities; they take part in making it, but they do not make it alone. I found a powerful sense of loss of place and neighborhood in the shifting ethnoracial landscape of Chicago, but also constant renewal of hope in new possibilities of belonging, and for creating place. Although social relationships and neighborhoods shifted, they were the blood and tissue that held the people together.

This work, therefore, is neither a traditional community history nor a conventional neighborhood ethnography but a blending of historical and ethnographic research that explores the varied ways Puerto Ricans in Chicago came to understand their identities and rights within and beyond the city they made home. In the process of writing, I thought critically about the relationship of scholars to the community of study. What were the community's own views of me as a researcher and as a community member? What are their expectations of my scholarship and me? How did our exchanges shape the theoretical and methodological approaches of this scholarly endeavor? Thus, this book became a means of reimagining the relationship of and the responsibility between scholars, whether we consider ourselves "insiders," "outsiders," or the "outsider within," and communities of study.⁶

A GROUNDED *IDENTIDAD*

1 A FEMALE NETWORK OF DOMESTICS, STUDENT ALLIES, AND SOCIAL WORKERS

"Help available, Puerto Ricans (White), U.S. citizens, male or female," reads the heading of a September 10, 1946, classified ad for general household workers placed in the *Chicago Daily Tribune* by Castle, Barton and Associates, a Chicago employment agency. In accord with the Puerto Rican Insular Department of Labor, the agency signed contracts with 362 domestic workers who responded, the majority single women, some as young as sixteen. It recruited some seventy men for the Chicago Hardware Foundry Company in North Chicago, and another eighty for Inland Steel Company in East Chicago. Daring Puerto Rican women and men, each with a limit of twenty pounds of baggage, boarded Commander Airline and Eastern Airline cargo planes in San Juan bound for Chicago's Midway Airport. Half the cost of "regular" tickets, including one for return, would be deducted from their paychecks. The new arrivals were bussed to the Hotel Lincoln on Chicago's North Side, to be lodged there until work placements were assigned.[1]

Georgina "Gina" Bishop, my landlady during my research, and owner of Caribe Funeral Home, the first Puerto Rican funeral parlor in Chicago, had arrived in December 1950 from Humacao, Puerto Rico. When I asked why she migrated, Gina responded simply, "*a buscar arroz y habichuela*," ("to look for rice and beans"). Her sister Medelicia Rios had come four years earlier, in the fall of 1946, to work as a maid for a Jewish family, and found a factory job instead. She arranged for Gina to be a *niñera* (nanny) for that same family. "*Yo era de la' primera*," ("I was one of the first ones"), Medelicia proudly claimed, perhaps even one of the "recent migration" of domestic workers Elena Padilla, a University of Chicago anthropology student, would write about in her 1947 master's thesis, "Puerto Rican Immigrants in New York and Chicago: A Study in Comparative Assimilation."[2] The labor and social conditions of the recruited low-wage, especially female, Puerto Rican migrant workers in Chicago by Castle, Barton and Associates had attracted the attention of Padilla as a "daring scheme . . . to reduce the domestic wage scale to an all time low."[3]

Padilla herself was part of a parallel, if smaller, migration—of young women and men sponsored by the University of Puerto Rico as part of the island's nation-building project, who enrolled at US campuses, especially Harvard, the University of Michigan, and the University of Chicago.[4] Padilla's mother had died when she was an infant, her father, a businessman, when she was a child, and she spoke of herself as an "orphan." Her godparents in San Juan had raised her. At the International House on the University of Chicago campus, her roommate turned out to be Muna Muñoz Lee, daughter of Luis Muñoz Marín, who in 1946 was president of the Puerto Rican Senate, a poet, journalist, and politician, son of Luis Muñoz Rivera, poet, politician, and founder of the Puerto Rican daily *El Diario*.[5] Muna Muñoz Lee's mother was the poet, feminist, and Pan-American activist Muna Lee. Together the two vibrant young women took Chicago as their duty.

The image that has persisted in the scholarship and in the popular imagination of the Puerto Rican migrants is that they were, mostly, male. However, it was women who predominated in these early migratory flows. More recently, migration scholars have insisted that migration itself is a "gendered phenomenon." The nature of this phenomenon directs attention to the relationship between power and gender in the "politics and governance of migration" and its link to ideologies of dependency and development.[6] The "Chicago experiment," the administrative name for the recruitment, was a prime example of this, intended, in part, as a means of birth control on the island, where a lower birth rate would be expected to reduce the rate of unemployment.[7] In personal letters to Puerto Rican leaders, in the island and in the diaspora, Padilla and Muñoz Lee would point to the racial order of this Chicago recruitment plan: "White" Puerto Ricans were located in the US North and "colored Puerto Ricans [were imported] to work as domestics in the [S]outh" in response to US corporate capital's scheme to reinforce a North/South racial divide of the US workforce.[8] Yet, the migration not only reflected the racial complexity of Puerto Ricans themselves but also prefigured ways in which Puerto Ricans would begin to unsettle polarized US notions of race. The University of Chicago roommates' letters and reports would bring a Puerto Rican social worker to Chicago—probably at the instigation of Muñoz Lee's father—to investigate the matter and improve the daily lives of migrants.

Padilla's master's thesis became the first scholarly work to illuminate the significance of Puerto Rican migration to the Windy City and her investigations of Puerto Rican experiences in Chicago, and later in New York and Puerto Rico, would be reclaimed by a generation of scholars examining racial, class, and gender inequalities in daily life and in the academy.[9] Taken together, the popular configuration of Puerto Ricans as a cheap, and racialized, labor source and, consequently, as a people in need of population control can be understood as a demonstration of the politics of colonialism. Yet, from the perspective of "the girls" (as press described them), the "Chicago experiment," most pointedly, provided a means to take initiative for their own lives. They were the core of what became the Puerto Rican community of Chicago.

The "Chicago Experiment": A Colony of Contract Migrant Workers

"Solving the maid shortage and conducting a social experiment at the same time—this has been the experience of 39 Chicago families and 39 young Puerto Rican girls who are serving as maids for these families." So read the opening passage of the *Chicago American Herald*'s October 5, 1946, feature story, "Puerto Rican Maids—A Successful Experiment."[10] Ana Rosa Garcia, an eighteen-year-old maid in the home of the Harris family in the South Shore area, was "typical" of the thirty-nine girls, according to the article. Initially skeptical of signing on with Castle, Barton and Associates, Mr. and Mrs. Harris were purportedly delighted with their Puerto Rican maid: "Ana is the pride of the household and the envy of the neighborhood." An "accomplished personal maid" (styling Mrs. Harris's hair) and babysitter for the family (looking after four-year-old Veta Lee), Ana spoke "English with only a slight accent" and her cooking was "far from being too spicy." Ana's only misgiving was the prospect of a Chicago winter, but she had a solution: "I'll just stay in the house until it gets warm again."[11] Weeks earlier, a brief news story in the *Chicago Daily Tribune* reported that the "Puerto Rican girls" were not obligated to stay with their new employers, but that Castle, Barton and Associates predicted they would be "well satisfied."[12] An official communication from the chief of employment services of Puerto Rico's Department of Labor to all contracted domestic workers outlined the terms of the contract and described the "migration program"; it suggested that if the experiment continued to be a success, Castle, Barton and Associates intended to hire "a thousand or more workers for domestic services to work in the city of Chicago and its suburban zones."[13] Yet, not long after the first shipment, this enthusiasm for recruited low-wage laborers turned to complaints from both the employers and the workers.

In the light of history it is apparent that ideologies of gender, sexuality, and reproduction, as well as of labor supply, structured early relations between Puerto Rico and the United States.[14] During the Depression years, the failure of the Puerto Rican economy intensified debates about overpopulation, and, by 1940, the fact that women outnumbered men loomed as a significant and troubling trend.[15] Donald O'Conner, an economist for the Office of Puerto Rico in Washington, DC, concluded that, "aside from birth control, the most effective means of reducing the population of Puerto Rico is emigration, primarily of women of child-bearing years."[16] But, wanting to keep such a purpose sub rosa, he issued a cautionary statement: "What need not be made clear, except in executive sessions of the legislative committees, is the demographic effect of female migration."[17] At the same time, migration could also be a low-cost remedy for Chicago's shortage of domestics, since, at the close of World War II, housewives "deprived of the women who parked their mops and took factory jobs, were screaming for maids," as the *Chicago Daily News* put it.[18] Castle, Barton and Associates, with an office in San Juan, saw a unique opportunity to draw on the island's cheap female labor pool, and, since Puerto Ricans did not need entry permits to migrate to the continental US, they could be "brought into the country with a minimum of red tape because they are American citizens."[19] Nonetheless, soon after their arrival in Chicago, the YWCA of Puerto Rico asked the Chicago branch to "look out for the girls"— the new maids who were turning out to be more vexing than convenient.[20]

To assist in proper assimilation of the new Puerto Rican maids, the YWCA's Industrial Relations Department sponsored Thursday Teas in order to provide the maids with "educational and recreational opportunities during their day off from work."[21] It was there that Puerto Ricans in Chicago first came together as a group; otherwise, social relations were almost nonexistent. Puerto Rican women were not fond of "tea time"—they drank tea only when sick and preferred strong coffee with steamed milk. Still, they attended for the conversations, to foster friendships, and to assess and compare work conditions. The women (and men) in households, soon dissatisfied with working conditions and low wages, found the YWCA a space to vent their growing dissatisfaction with fifteen-hour work days, lower wages than their US counterparts, employers' disregard of a day off, and impromptu transfers from homes without workers' consent.[22] If the majority of Puerto Rican men and women who migrated as contract laborers hoped for decent pay and an opportunity for social advancement, they got much less. In North Chicago, the foundry workers' contract provided 88½ cents an hour, forty hours a week with time and a half for overtime, but after various deductions, many workers received less than one dollar for a week's worth of work. Men who fell ill were charged the full amount for their living expenses.[23] For Puerto Rican maids sixty dollars a month was the going wage, of which ten dollars was deducted for travel costs to Chicago and another eight dollars and thirty-three cents withheld by Castle, Barton and Associates until the terms of the contract were met or termination of employment occurred. The young women were left with net earnings of approximately ten dollars per week and without guarantee of standard work hours and tasks or a day off.

A Puerto Rican social worker assisting the YWCA told of a domestic worker who watched her new employer, little by little, drop her other household service workers after she arrived. "Now for sixty dollars, [the Puerto Rican girl] does the work of three people: the nanny, the cook, and the maid."[24] These were the very tasks praised by the Harris family in the *Chicago American Herald* story of their assessment of the "Chicago experiment," in particular, how their maid, Ana, simplified their lives while trimming household costs. Recruited for low-wage work, Puerto Ricans now also generated animosity among their North American counterparts, according to a December 1946 headline in *El Imparcial*, a newspaper in Puerto Rico: "Boricuas in Chicago Considered 'Undesirable' Due to Their 'Disloyal Competition.'"[25] The Household Employees League of the YWCA, an organization of domestic workers "who agree on certain minimum standards of pay and working hours for their household services," announced an extensive waiting list of employers prepared to hire maids "at the minimum pay of $25 per week, eight hours of work, and 1-½ days off." Despite the scarcity of household help, many employers were willing "to hold to standards such as those set forth by the Household Employees League of the Y.W.C.A."[26] The League "consider[ed] it unfortunate that so many of the Puerto Rican workers (who were serious minded and responsible workers) came to work in Chicago under a contract which was unfair to them."[27] With unfair working conditions, 142 of the 362 women brought to Chicago in fall 1946 left their employers within five months, becoming "floaters"—that is, they took a job elsewhere. Thirty others returned to Puerto Rico within their first several weeks. Their departure left 142 disgruntled employers "out the $210 they had paid to obtain the girls' services."[28]

The Industrial Department of the YWCA now began to sponsor tea in the homes of a few employers to discuss the girls' and employers' concerns. A representative from Castle, Barton and Associates noted that, "all employers understood that the girls were untrained and spoke little, if any English."[29] Still, their grievances were many. Employers complained of girls who drank too much and consorted with men, and of women with possible disease— including one who had had gonorrhea for more than a year. One employer criticized her maid as "extremely slow in her work," after which the maid admitted that she "took her time just for spite" because she was not paid enough.[30] Apparently, few girls were actually "the pride of the household and envy of the neighborhood."[31] A Mrs. Jackson was one of few employers "well satisfied." The rest "wanted no more Puerto Rican maids." Some household employers had come to the tea social for the purpose of recruiting others to organize against the employment agency. Other employers had taken their complaints to the Chicago Better Business Bureau,[32] which had, in turn, advised media outlets that the "advertising of Castle, Barton & Associates" was "not in the public interest."[33] The agency spokesperson told a *Chicago Daily News* reporter that "those families who got good ones got jewels, and those who got bad ones got lemons. . . . Puerto Ricans aren't of the nature that you can overwork."[34]

Some workers said they were told the police would be called if they broke their contracts, others that they "were threatened with 'deportation' if they complained."[35] Since the US citizenship of this unique labor pool had been touted to employers, the most attractive aspect may have been elimination of red tape in hiring cheap labor, and the laborers' status as persons subject to deportation. Puerto Rican workers who wanted to leave their jobs were often threatened in ways that denied the full protection accorded to US citizens. Some "spoke of sending letters to the press and to legislators."[36] Elsa Rafaela Charneco, in December 1946, wrote to the director of *El Imparcial* in Puerto Rico detailing harassment tactics. Upon her arrival in Chicago, she had been taken to the suburb of River Forest. Unhappy with the location, though relatively content with her employer, she asked to be reassigned. The day after she was placed in another household, she was taken back to the agency and informed that "she would be returned to Puerto Rico." While waiting, she was assigned to a family who gave her the "totality of household tasks," apparently to serve as maid, nanny, and cook, and when she refused, Miss Mason of Castle, Barton and Associates, explained once again that if she did not comply, she would be sent back to Puerto Rico. When the ultimatum failed to persuade her, Miss Mason threatened that "no longer were they going to send her to Puerto Rico but to jail." Charneco fled to friends in Chicago.[37] Another woman "wrote to the President of the United States [President Truman] in January, complaining that she wanted to return to

Puerto Rico on account of the serious illness of her mother"; her letter was sent on to the regional consultant of the State Department of Labor, Women's Division, and from there to the YWCA.[38] It came full circle. As a domestic worker confronted by poor working conditions, she and others found allies among the University of Chicago students, and a particular advocate, a Puerto Rican social welfare official, Carmen Isales, hired temporarily by the YWCA of Chicago.

Puerto Rican Graduate Students Taking Up the Cudgels

Elena Padilla, nineteen at the time of graduation from the University of Puerto Rico and too young for medical school at the University of Michigan, gained a fellowship from her alma mater to the University of Chicago to study the "Great Books" through the university's famed Chicago Program in Social Thought, directed by the president, Robert Hutchins, and the noted Philosopher Mortimer Adler. Through this renowned program, Padilla met Sol Tax, a specialist of Native American cultures, and Robert Redfield, an authority on folk culture, and, as she told me in 2005, "became captivated by anthropology," renounced her plan for medical school, and enrolled in Chicago's graduate program in anthropology. When Jaime Benítez, chancellor of the University of Puerto Rico and alumnus of the University of Chicago, had decided to sponsor some of his students for graduate study at elite US institutions, the largest number became a cadre at his own alma mater.[39] From 1944 to 1947, Padilla conducted fieldwork among the Winnebago in upper Wisconsin under the direction of Sol Tax and served as a research assistant for famed urban sociologist Louis Wirth on the Committee on Interracial Relations (Wirth, along with Tax and Everett C. Hughes, supervised the university's Committee on Interracial Relations of the Division of Social Sciences).[40] Two compatriots, Muna Muñoz Lee and Ricardo Alegría, the latter later to lead the Institute of Puerto Rican Culture and the Center of Advanced Study on Puerto Rico and the Caribbean, joined Padilla in anthropology. It was a talented group, some eventually joined the faculty at the University of Puerto Rico, among them, Ángel Quintero Alfaro, secretary of education in Puerto Rico in the 1960s, and Milton Pabón, political scientist.[41] Yet others became scholars in the US, among them Elena Padilla, the spirited fledgling of the talented 1944 group.

Padilla, with some of her compatriots, now honed her analytical tools in order to gain access to prominent scholars and institutions, for the purpose of investigating the importation of Puerto Rican contract workers. What can be described as Padilla's "extra-anthropological interventions"—efforts to move beyond mere research to help individual workers, to illuminate their plight, and to produce changes in policy on migrant workers—reflected her refusal to accept the social abandonment of destitute migrants by both the Puerto Rican and the US federal government. In September 1946, dismayed by Castle, Barton and Associates' "help available" posting advertising for the services of "white" Puerto Rican workers as "maids, kitchen help, porters, elevator operators, housemen, etc.," she and Muñoz Lee rode to the North Side of the city, site of Castle, Barton and Associates and the Hotel Lincoln, temporary lodging of migrants, to speak with workers, and then to North Chicago to speak with men hired by the Chicago Foundry Company.

On October 3, Padilla dispatched an impassioned letter to New York's Jesús Colón, a labor activist, communist, and public intellectual, about the precarious state of these Puerto Rican workers.[42] They were benefiting neither from minimum wage legislation nor from union membership that could defend their rights as workers. Even more troubling, Padilla had learned through her fellow anthropologist-in-progress, Ricardo Alegría, that the Department of Labor of Puerto Rico had sanctioned the migration plan from the beginning. She wrote to Colón that she would pay him a visit but not until she had "done something to abolish the importation of Puerto Ricans who head straight to their own demise as well as contribute to the poverty and hunger of other workers."[43] Two days later appeared, in the tabloid *Chicago American Herald*, the story touting the "successful" Puerto Rican maid experiment, with a full-page photograph of the "accomplished personal maid," eighteen-year-old Ana Rosa Garcia, "pride" of her employer's household.[44] Padilla, utilizing her credentials as a University of Chicago graduate student, interviewed representatives of Castle, Barton and Associates, and drew on her social position as a Puerto Rican student-migrant to gather data on her working-class compatriots' experiences.

On November 25, 1946, Padilla and Muñoz Lee issued a report, "Preliminary Report on the Puerto Rican Contract Workers in the Chicago Area," with the help of other University of Chicago students, and circulated it promptly among persons of influence.[45] It told of foundry workers, among them Leonides Algarín and Miguel Rivera, whose handwritten testimony reported "being forced to work Saturdays to pay my debt during the time I was ill."[46] It also discussed an October 21 letter from Mr. Enrique Baiz Miró, a foundry worker, to Puerto Rico's Commissioner of Labor Manuel A. Pérez, signed by forty-six Puerto Rican workers who were protesting working conditions, wage deductions, and the inadequate meals served at The Chicago Hardware Foundry.[47] An employment agency official in charge of domestic worker recruitment and placement later admitted to a reporter for the *Chicago Star*, a new weekly backed by progressive organizations, that "the contract these people signed, which binds them to work for a year with employers, wasn't worth the paper it was written on."[48] The "Preliminary Report," written both in English and Spanish, was signed by Padilla and Muñoz Lee, by a Spanish instructor, and by four other University of Chicago graduate students,[49] and distributed to the local press, to presses in New York (*La Prensa*) and in Puerto Rico (*El Imparcial*),[50] and to insular, state, and federal government officials, including the commissioner of labor in Puerto Rico. It went to organizations, too, such as the Welfare Council of Metropolitan Chicago and the Immigrants' Protective League, and, several weeks later, to prominent individuals within and beyond Chicago, among them, Sol Tax, Padilla's advisor at the university; Jesús Colón in New York; and Luis Muñoz Marín (Munoz Lee's father and president of the Senate of Puerto Rico) in San Juan.

Three days later, on November 28, Thanksgiving Day, Puerto Rican graduate students, among them Elena Padilla and Muna Muñoz Lee, and members of the United Students Progressives and the Workers' Defense League joined Puerto Rican maids on a picket line. More than fifty maids, on "their semi-day off," picketed the downtown offices of Castle, Barton and Associates demanding "a day off, a raise, less work hours, etc."[51] The *Chicago Defender*, the largest and most prominent African American weekly newspaper, covered the maids' protest and their contention "that certain provisions in a binding labor contract between their government's labor department and Castle, Barton had been violated." They had forwarded their complaints to the Puerto Rican Department of Labor, the paper said, but "no immediate action had been taken," other than assurance that the department would notify Castle, Barton and Associates of the workers' charges.[52] Coordinated letters dated December 9, by Padilla and Muñoz Lee were mailed to Jesús Colón in New York and Muñoz Marín in San Juan with news of the protest picket line: "The demonstration was impressive: it looked like a CIO line with how well it was organized," Padilla wrote to Colón. "On Thanksgiving Day the maids refused to work or to speak English."[53] Muñoz Lee wrote her father, "People with vast experience in workers' organizations assured us that even in veteran workers' struggles they had not observed more order, or more enthusiasm on a picket line."[54]

Except for the *Chicago Defender* and the *Chicago Star*, newspapers in Chicago, at first, ignored the students' report and the Thanksgiving Day picket line. Two weeks later, however, the *Chicago Daily Tribune* produced a re-buttal story, "Plight of Hired Puerto Ricans Starts Dispute, 'Deplorable Conditions' Denied by Employers," about the "360 Puerto Rican men and women . . . living and working . . . in the Chicago area." The *Tribune* chal-lenged the findings of the students' report, citing a survey of its own among the young women; it had "found them pleased with their food, clothes, work, and employe [*sic*] relationships."[55] A few days later the *Tribune* published an editorial, "FREE PUERTO RICO." It cited the charges of exploitation of Puerto Rican contracted workers in the report of the students at the Univer-sity of Chicago, and sought to defuse the charges: "An investigation by THE TRIBUNE indicated that the charges are overdrawn, to say the least, but the incident does demonstrate the wide gap in living conditions and economic status between the citizens of continental United States and the Puerto Ricans, who are by act of congress our fellow citizens."[56] The editorial was debating, once again, the island's fraught political relationship with the United States, an issue it had raised a few months earlier, suggesting Puerto Rico be granted independence rather than statehood: "Whereas we have no right to run their lives, they are not qualified for a voice in running ours, which they would have if granted statehood."[57] Moreover, the *Tribune* now asserted, "We doubt that the people of the United States are willing to as-sume the burdens that would have to be assumed if the island were admitted as the 49th state. It is doubtful also whether the two societies are mutually assimilable."[58] The editorial echoed debates from the turn of the century on whether the United States should make Puerto Rico an American colony.

In Puerto Rico, government officials were responding defensively to the students' report. Commissioner of Labor Pérez warned the Senate president, Muñoz Marín, "I am afraid that these kids' activities, as well intentioned as they may be, can be obstructive to the migration programs that have begun to develop rather satisfactorily."[59] One of these "kids" was Muñoz Marin's daugh-ter, Muna Muñoz Lee. In a December 17 letter to her in Chicago (carbon-copied to her father), Pérez asked the students to send "all of the evidence you have concerning contract violations, signed by the workers, and the mistreat-ment that, allegedly, they are receiving from their employers and from the employment agency." He wanted a lot more—the names of the workers, their employers or ex-employers, and postal addresses, plus the average salary and work hours for maids in Chicago, and a copy of the document or statute reg-ulating household labor or establishing a standard that would substantiate the complaints of workers the students had recorded. He would also appreciate the student committee's proposed alternatives, reminding them, all the while, of the poverty and unemployment in Puerto Rico. Why had not a single one of the female picketers spoken with a representative from the Illinois Department of Labor in a position to assess, and likely to be "of great assistance in all things related to the well-being of our compatriots"?; Pérez found such reticence inexplicable in light of the domestic workers' denunciations. His office had received no reports of interviews with foundry administrators, representatives of the employment agency, or employers of the household workers. "It would have been useful and fair to hear from all parties before formulating the complaint." "Nonetheless," Pérez concluded, "I hope you continue studying the situation, bringing to light all the factors and circumstances, keeping in mind the unemployment rate level in the island and with an eye to the best labor opportunities you can suggest for our compatriots over there."[60]

Pérez had enclosed in his letter of reply to Muñoz Lee a scathing editorial from the island's daily newspaper *El Imparcial*, "bringing to light all the factors and circumstances" in the debate and perhaps to show the political uproar the students' report had generated in the island. *El Imparcial* had forcefully criticized Pérez for seeming to side with the Illinois state government and business interests rather than supporting "our migrant workers." An Illinois official, Frank Graves, had downplayed the protest, insisting that "there were few female workers" on the picket line, mainly "sympathizers recruited from other places," and adding that "the group of Puerto Ricans who channeled the protest . . . [were] 'small and petty.'" The employment agency representative had accused the students of "falsifying the facts" and of "trying to organize all the girls we have brought from Puerto Rico." *El Imparcial*, on the other hand, charged that Pérez had tried to undermine the student's organizing efforts, treating the report as "sloppy and unfounded" and as "trying to create difficulties for the Insular Government." Its editorial said: "The accusations made in this case are too serious for anyone—including the Commissioner of Labor of Puerto Rico [Pérez]—to presume to be false rumors, let alone an attempt at sabotage against the Insular Government. It is not about minor differences between employers and workers that can be easily resolved. It is about fundamental violations of the rights of our migrant workers, violations that have all the marks of outrage and abuse." To the contrary, said *El Imparcial*, the students were "patriotically assum[ing] the task of organizing and defending . . . their humble migrant compatriots." It was the newspaper's stance that the Puerto Rican Department of Labor should "do something more than publish biased letters" to justify its own position.[61]

Padilla and Muñoz Lee, in turn, responded to Pérez's questions and accusations with a letter to the editor of *El Imparcial*. Pérez and Frank Graves were "very naïve" if they "sincerely believed" that Puerto Rican maids interviewed by Graves would "confess to questions [of the Illinois state official] that they were being mistreated" in their employers' homes. Further, most of the maids who joined the picket line did so "fully recognizing that their protest was because of the contract's conditions." "Other Puerto Rican maids, satisfied with their situation, joined in solidarity as did a group of Puerto Rican students, and an even larger group of American students and representatives of the 'Workers' Defense League.'" Padilla and Muñoz Lee challenged Graves's claim that the maids had refused to let him interview them at the picket line. Muñoz Lee, they said, had phoned his office to set up a meeting in which students and workers could participate. When Muñoz Lee identified herself as Puerto Rican to an Illinois state official, he, "assuming that he was speaking with one of the protesting maids," reprimanded her: "If you did not like the contract, why did you sign it?" "Commissioner Pérez knows well," the students' rejoinder said, "that no such law exists in the State of Illinois for the protection of domestic service. And so, what legal guarantee could the Department of the Labor of Illinois offer them?" [62]

In her master's thesis of 1947, Padilla would refine her initial effort to investigate "processes of acculturation and assimilation" of Puerto Rican identity and community formation in the United States, with a comparison of the New York and Chicago populations.[63] Her thesis made evident the diverse ways in which migratory experiences, racial classifications, color, class, language, and other racializing practices shaped Puerto Rican identities in Chicago. She identified two distinct groups of settlers there: "old migration" and "recent migration." Members of the "old migration" were mostly individuals who had lived in other US cities before settling in Chicago, or if they had come directly from the island, university students who established themselves in the city. Padilla divided the old migration into four groups: "white" Puerto Ricans fluent in the English language and from a well-established socioeconomic background, usually accepted into white society and maintaining ties with other Latin Americans of similar professional and business standing; "white" Puerto Ricans fluent in English, but of more modest backgrounds, living among "other white ethnics and Americans"; "white" Puerto Ricans from working-class and poor origins, not fluent in English, living in Mexican neighborhoods; and "very dark skinned" Puerto Ricans, able to speak English, living in neighborhoods within the "Negro Belt."[64] Settlers of the old migration developed adjustments "to reduce conflicts with their host society."[65] One "informant" told Padilla he had chosen to live in the Midwest metropolis because he "knew that only selected people could come to Chicago, neither laborers nor Negroes from Puerto Rico could come."[66] Some Puerto Ricans had more in common with Mexican residents, others identified with, or were identified with, African Americans, still others with "white" ethnics, or "mainstream American" culture. Padilla's "recent migration," referred to the recruited contract laborers hired to remedy, on the cheap, the domestic worker shortage as well as a "manpower" shortage at a foundry plant.[67] Some "recent" migrants, discontented with their labor conditions, had breached their contracts and searched for factory or service work instead; others opted to try their fortunes elsewhere, migrating to New York or returning to the island. Those who left the jobs they had been recruited for but resolved to stay on in Chicago found temporary quarters in transient hotels in the Loop or in the homes of Mexican friends.[68] Padilla's study shed light on, and compiled a record of, pioneering Puerto Rican workers who might otherwise have remained in the shadows of history.

Although only graduate students, and in their early twenties, Padilla and Muñoz Lee already had a network of contacts and relationships that carried clout. They understood the political world of Puerto Rico and the importance of working with social and political activists in the diaspora to reach a wider public. Still, they were limited in the assistance they could generate for aggrieved individual workers. They did help women, especially, dissolve abusive contracts. "Munita and I are operating a non-profit employment agency to find them factory jobs and rooms to live," Padilla wrote to Colón. "Many want to leave for N.Y. and we plan to do what is possible so that the women can achieve their objective. Our poverty prevents us from doing something [more], but that is no reason to be discouraged."[69] In a later biography, *Ricardo Alegría: Una Vida*, Alegría, their housemate in the International House at the University of Chicago, recalled that Padilla and Muñoz Lee "were aware of the growing influence of Puerto Rican migrants to the city." Of the young women recruited as maids who had problems with employers and were either thrown out or ran away, Alegria said Muñoz Lee "picked them up and would take them to her room in International House without permission to do so." They "had created a commune with those girls," five or six sleeping on the floor in the room Muñoz Lee shared with Padilla. The consequences, he claimed, were "problems with the administration."[70] In October 2008, at the Eighth International Congress of the Puerto Rican Studies Association held in San Juan, Alegría referred to a near expulsion of his classmates. Padilla told me in 2005 that she and Muñoz Lee did bring to International House girls who had nowhere else to go, though less frequently and more spontaneously than Alegria's recollection suggests. "We were not going to leave anyone out in the cold. It was more accidental than routine."[71]

Padilla wrote to Colón in New York in an effort to help workers who wanted to move to that city in order to find sponsors there, also asking him for application forms for the US Merchant Marine. Colón, in turn, opened his Brooklyn home to, as one example, Evangelina Serrano, a young domestic to whom Padilla and Muñoz Lee had lent a hand, inviting her to address a radio public about the situation of domestic workers in the US industrial heartland. Serrano wrote to Muñoz Lee: "Don Jesús wants me to talk on the radio on the Puerto Ricans in Chicago and I'm writing to see if you can send me some details about how they are being treated so that I can complete what I'm going to say."[72] Another worker, a Mrs. Pilar Cruz de Ortiz arrived on Colón's Brooklyn doorstep with a note of introduction from Padilla, who explained that she came "in search of better life and work opportunities—and I have asked to her to go to you, who I am certain will help her carry out her wishes."[73] Letters to Luis Muñoz Marín from his daughter Muñoz Lee updated him about her educational, social, and political activities, but their purpose was larger than personal. Surely the president of the Puerto Rican Senate would want to weigh in on the situation of contract workers, considering his own political aspirations for higher office and in light of pending US congressional approval of legislation for the first popular election of the island's governor.

In view of his own political influence and ambitions, Muñoz Lee assured her father, she had made no promises in his name to the contract workers, though she *had* committed herself to relay word of their circumstances to him. She urged him as president of the Senate to take immediate measures to improve the conditions of Chicago's labor migrants.[74] According to Padilla, Muñoz Marín now used the pretext of a late 1946 visit with his daughter to look privately into the matter.[75] The Puerto Rican workers had already aroused resentment within their North American counterparts, accusing them of being "strike-breakers," but his daughter insisted that, in principle, the group was not against migration as a strategy to alleviate Puerto Rico's problems, and thus any information to the contrary in the island press had not come from anyone connected to the report. The contracts, however, did not protect workers' rights and made it impossible to earn a living wage. This was no way to resolve the island's own employment problems and, in fact, it simply created new ones.

Muñoz Lee reminded her father that Castle, Barton and Associates' advertisements had "specified that they only wanted white workers for the area of Chicago." When she and Padilla consulted Chicago sociologist Everett

C. Hughes, president of the Commission on Race Relations and Industry, on the racial implications of selective placement of recruited Puerto Rican labor, Hughes had responded, "The poison of racial prejudice, injected by means of this kind of advertisement, can be tremendously dangerous for the solution of the economic problems of Puerto Rico."[76] US notions of racial inferiority could hamper migration as an instrument for the island's own economic development. Although both Padilla and Muñoz Lee noted the shipping of black Puerto Ricans to the South as especially outrageous, they intentionally omitted this fact from their public report for fear that "the reactionary press would use it to create more diversions" to "stimulate racial divisions among Puerto Ricans."[77] Their omission points to the ways in which the subject of race in Puerto Rico has been glossed over with the pretext of not transporting or confounding US racial ideologies to the island.[78] It also reflects the difficulties faced by scholars committed to a social agenda.

US racial ideologies generally hampered political affiliations among workers of color. Padilla had noted in her thesis:

An attitude of dislike is indicated by verbalizations against American Negroes. A member of the new [Puerto Rican] migration said "not even Negroes were getting as low wages as the Puerto Ricans in Chicago." Another migrant claimed "that American Negroes were not like Puerto Rican Negroes because in this country, Negroes just were not equal to white people," so she would not even think of speaking to an American Negro.

This attitude toward the American Negro probably stems largely from the fact that the recent migration of Puerto Ricans theoretically only included white workers. Among the workers who came, nevertheless, many of them would be considered Negroes in the United States, but were considered as white by the Puerto Ricans.[79]

In her December 9, 1946, letter to Colón, dispatching the "Preliminary Report," Padilla wrote, "I am prepared to write however many articles you like, in English or Spanish—let me know how you want them."[80] In an earlier letter she had referred to the recruitment of Puerto Rican workers to Chicago as a "scandalous act," "one of the greatest betrayals" of the Puerto Rican people by their government.[81] "The bewildered Puerto Ricans are not entirely friendless," *The New Republic* reported in an April 1947 article on the "Maid Problem." Puerto Rican students from the University of Chicago "took up the cudgels" and had joined the workers' cause.[82]

Most of the students and protesting workers were women. These actions challenging conditions they considered unjust and providing the support for Chicago's Puerto Rican community, and for the diaspora in general, have often been ignored in published accounts and in the scholarship. Ricardo Alegría, a fellow student, described Muñoz Lee as "shy, she didn't participate in groups," "at the margins of [her] father's public life," overlooking Muñoz Lee's solidarity with workers, the leadership she demonstrated in the struggle, and her interventions with her father, though Alegria would not have known of her daughterly influence.[83] Muñoz Marín responded by proposing legislation on migration, writing to his daughter, "I will send you a copy for your comments before action is taken on the issue."[84] Despite their dependence on the financial sponsorship of the Puerto Rican government for study abroad, neither Elena Padilla nor the other Puerto Rican student leaders at the University of Chicago deferred to or endorsed the Puerto Rican government policies that they considered unjust in treatment of the poorest of their fellow citizens.

"Look Out for the Girls": Puerto Rican Workers and a Puerto Rican Social Worker

In early December 1946, Carmen Isales, another island compatriot, would become an advocate for contracted domestic workers and would confirm the findings of Padilla and Muñoz Lee. Isales, chief of the Office of In-Service Training, Division of Public Welfare, Department of Health of Puerto Rico, arrived in Chicago on vacation, or ostensibly so. A graduate of the University of Chicago's School of Social Service, she was well aware of the situation of Puerto Rican migrant workers, perhaps apprised of the situation by Muñoz Marín, though the available record does not say. Could Muñoz Marin have suggested, even arranged for, a timely visit and a stay-over, perhaps to substantiate his daughter's letters? Whatever the impetus, Isales promptly offered her assistance to the YWCA, interviewing thirty or so women at the weekly social gatherings, and went to the foundry to talk to Puerto Rican men living in the "train wagons." She wrote a first report in December to the Puerto Rican government: "*Situación de los Obreros Puertorriqueños Contratados por la Agencia de Empleos Castle, Barton and Assoc.*" ("Situation of Puerto Rican Laborers Contracted by the Castle, Barton and Associates Employment Agency") (another report would follow three months later) confirming the conditions exposed by the University of Chicago students.[85] She then contacted the Social Service Department of the YWCA, at the suggestion of the Council of Social Service Agencies. In January 1947, vacation forgotten, she was hired "as an official non-paid member of the staff, on a [three-month] leave of absence with pay from the [Puerto Rico] Division of Public Welfare." In that role she now compiled extensive information for a second report, "Report on Cases of Puerto Rican Laborers to Chicago to Work as Domestics and Foundry Workers Under Contract with Castle, Barton and Associates, Inc.," distributed that spring to US officials and Puerto Rican policy makers and politicians, its findings based on Isales's interviews with laborers, communications and interviews with employers, discussions with Castle, Barton and Associates, and interviews and conversations with employment officers of hotels, factories, and hospitals, and local social service agencies.[86]

Puerto Ricans' status as nonresidents of Chicago (though US citizens), perceived as "immigrants" or "foreigners" and as second-class, made them ineligible for public services, thus transferring nearly all of the responsibility for social needs to the shoulders of private agencies, most of whom found the needs "extremely varied" and requiring "not only our own activity, but also a pooling of all the resources available in the community."[87] Meetings of private social service agencies, held at the Chicago Council of Social Agencies, tried to cope with a matter of great concern: "which governmental agency is responsible for the protection of these people?"[88] One particular situation presented to the agencies involved a stranded sixteen-year-old girl who had been placed with a family in the suburb of River Forest for seventeen days. Unhappy with her placement, the girl was transferred to another home and, after a day, transported by Castle, Barton and Associates back to the Hotel Lincoln, the temporary housing reserved for recruited workers without assignment. Because she was a minor, a social worker at the juvenile court was notified, but, since the court's involvement might send an unfavorable message if "a newcomer [were] to be put . . . in the Juvenile Delinquent Home," the social worker approached the Illinois Children's Home and Aid Society about placement in a foster home, meanwhile housing the girl in a Salvation Army Emergency Lodge. United Charities was asked to look after her while the Family Service Bureau tried to reach her family in Puerto Rico with the possibility of repatriation. When Miss Skinner, a representative from the US Children's Bureau, Child Labor Division, called the Immigrants' Protective League office to discuss the case, the League told Miss Skinner it would be interested in the case should repatriation be considered appropriate, "even though this young woman is not an 'immigrant' in the ordinary sense. The fact that she speaks only Spanish, would make the League anxious to assist," despite her being a US citizen, not a foreigner.[89] The true meaning and rights of Puerto Ricans' US citizenship confounded the various US social service agencies accustomed to foreign immigrants or continental migrants.

Carmen Isales, in her continuing role as consultant, unpaid and on leave, now called into question employers' impression that the Puerto Rican workers were indebted to them, citing workers' rights to decent wages and conditions. She reported in March 1947 that domestic and foundry workers' most common complaint of mistreatment was "that the employers refused to consider the worker's demands for better working conditions on the basis that they should be grateful for the protection they had received inasmuch as they had been starving in Puerto Rico." Yet weekly net earnings of ten dollars did not provide enough for the maids in Chicago or their families on the island.[90] Isales had seen one weekly check from the Chicago Hardware Foundry Company of sixty cents and another of eighty-six cents, and a foundry worker told her that on "receiving a check worth 26¢ he ripped it to pieces." His foreman had smirked, "You could have bought a package of cigarettes with that," though "in Puerto Rico he didn't have money to eat much less for vices."[91] Workers worried about offending the agency thought of other ways to resolve conflicts. One suggested "she would work for a few more months to permit the agency an earning of $8.33 monthly," after which she could abandon the job without causing problems. "*Bendito* [poor things]," she reasoned, "they spent money to bring me here." Carmen Isales, dumfounded by the worker's concern for the "poor things," exclaimed in her report, "¡*bendito! Quiere darles un poco mas de ganancia.*" ("Poor things! She wants to give them a little more profit."). The employment agency itself had earned a minimum of $150 for each domestic worker, that is, $60,000 for every 400 Puerto Rican workers it imported.[92] (For the 512 imported in September 1946 this would have yielded $76,800.)

At the "Y," Isales now spoke to Miss Mason, director of the Department of Contracts for Castle, Barton and Associates, about working together to improve the workers' situation, but the agency never fully cooperated, attributing the tense relationship "to the difference in purpose in our work." Domestic workers had signed contracts with employers, not with Castle, Barton and Associates, and the agency maintained that, when a domestic worker "escaped," the $210 for transportation and other fees was the employer's cost. In consequence, employers would resort to tracking them down to demand repayment, some seeking to garnish their workers' wages from their new, often factory, employers.[93] Isales explained the dispute to factory employment officers, with one refusing to give Miss Mason the names and addresses of thirty female workers for her to release to ex-employers seeking recompense.[94] Isales also arranged for girls and women to gain access to the courts, with the assistance of social agencies, to challenge employers and to assert their rights as workers and US citizens. Six such cases were referred by Isales to the Legal Aid Bureau of the United Charities following employers' refusal to return workers' personal belongings after they abandoned their jobs. In March 1947 Isales attended court with a Miss Quiñones, who was being sued by her ex-employer for $180 for breaking her contract. The Legal Aid Society lawyer representing Miss Quiñones had countersued for $450 of unpaid wages, and for an additional $1,000 for slander, since the employer had denounced the maid to the police as a thief who had "escaped" from the home. Astounded by the countersuit, the ex-employer and their lawyer sought a continuance to study the counterdemand, Isales noting, in a confidential (and "extra-official") letter to Muñoz Marín: "They thought that the girl was going to go there like when she came to see me for help that first day—she looked like a beaten dog begging for mercy."[95]

"The difference in purpose in our work" between the YWCA and Castle, Barton and Associates escalated at a court proceeding of March 10, 1947, involving five Puerto Rican girls. The employment agency's Miss Mason had accused Isales and the YWCA of encouraging female workers to break their contracts and advising them to lie about their age. When the judge told Miss Mason the employment agency itself should be investigated, an incensed Miss Mason said YWCA officials and the Legal Aid Bureau had engaged in "subversive activities." Isales rebutted Mason's accusations: "The professional nature of the work we undertook, of course, was in itself a denial of her statement. Besides, we [Isales and the YWCA] had worked previously in Chicago and were known to many officials in agencies of the community. Had it not been for this, we might have found a less receptive attitude in our effort to help the P[uerto] Rican group of laborers."[96]

A number of maids and ex-maids were becoming more assertive, with assistance from various social agencies, while others asserted their independence from the very agencies that helped them. One such young woman, who had attended YWCA activities, had planned to leave her job for employment in a factory so as to earn more money working fewer hours. In conversations with YWCA staff, however, it came to light that she had not had a contentious relationship with her employer. With the girl's permission, the employer was then asked about the situation. "The girl was slow," the employer said, but, overall, "satisfactory"; she hoped to keep her on as a maid though she could not afford to give her a raise, but only an end-of-year bonus of fifty dollars. The girl, skeptical about the plan, returned to the employer's home to consider her options, but in a meeting a week later, repeated her intent to leave as soon as she found a suitable place. Once again, the YWCA staff consulted the employer, who, certain the girl would remain, said the YWCA's services were not needed. At a further meeting, the girl was still intent on departing "but had let the matter go until her employer lost her suspicious attitude, which had arisen by the fact that [the YWCA] had called her once and informed her of the girl's plan." She was apparently annoyed by the Y's continued interference and "avoided too much questioning or advice." She was on her own thereafter.[97]

Puerto Rican women objected not only because of what they were denied but because of what they had expected—better wages and reasonable working hours. Factory work seemed to offer more benefits than household labor to thirty young women who took jobs at the National Biscuit Company: "They earn $39 a week which is about $36 net pay," said Isales's confidential letter of March 11, 1947, to Muñoz Marín in San Juan. "For that $5 is deducted for general rooming and from $7–$10 for meals. They have about $20 left over, even if they have less left over, that means 8-hour workdays, medical protection, union and time and half pay for overtime." Isales wrote to Muñoz Marín, "I don't know how they found out about that work, but the case is that it satisfies them."[98] In an unrelated instance, Isales's YWCA staff overheard two young women tell another of a plan to break their contracts. When the staff interviewed them, the two, while expressing appreciation for the staff's advice, remained firm in a decision to leave their jobs, and refused suggestions to the contrary. Both now had jobs at higher pay, one in a private home at thirty dollars a week, room and board included, and the other in a factory, also at thirty dollars a week.[99] Both had negotiated ably for better working conditions and had developed effective social networks of their own.

In that same confidential letter to Muñoz Marín, Isales reported that, by early March 1947, she was already handling seventy-four cases, nine of them minors and the majority of them women, including a few who had been taken to court and charged with prostitution.[100] "60 Puerto Rican Women Hunted by Vice Squads," read the headline of a March 5, 1947, news story in the *Chicago Daily Tribune*, reporting that the police commissioner's office and the detective bureau were searching for women and girls who had "disappeared after leaving their domestic jobs." Seven were arrested on soliciting charges and more were likely to fall into prostitution "because they were unable to find suitable living quarters."[101] A group that called itself the "committee of 15 against vice," working for four decades to "aid authorities in combating organized prostitution," had determined to make an example of another group of thirty women, some of them minors, who lived with a variety of men in hotels in dead-end areas.[102]

The policing of gender norms, specifically ideas about female respectability, made evident the internal class differences among Puerto Rican women. Isales suggested that some of the women had migrated to Chicago to escape undesirable personal circumstances in Puerto Rico, but, experiencing treatment as "*burras de carga*" (work mules) in the homes of employers, had "escaped" again, with few lodging options other than in questionable areas. "All said and done, for many of them, it is much easier to live with a man who will provide for them," Isales wrote matter-of-factly to Muñoz Marín, adding that some young women "with a craving for beautiful clothing find it hard to get along on their earnings."[103] Some employers, recognizing that the services of the young domestics were worth more than the sixty dollars a month stipulated in the contract, raised their pay, one employer going as high as twenty dollars more per week. Even so, these earnings were below the standard of the YWCA's own Household Employees League. Of the girls under twenty (approximately 40 percent or more), Isales concluded, immaturity was the reason why "most of them were unable to adjust to a working situation or to work out satisfactory arrangements with the employer concerning hours of work and other working conditions." One "16 year old girl constantly cried because she missed her mother."[104]

Beyond providing assistance to domestic workers and documenting conditions, Isales, like Padilla and Muñoz Lee, had clearly become a strong and persistent advocate for the workers. Even as she roundly criticized efforts to improve their lives in Chicago, she took prudent account of the political implications of her criticism on the political party in power in Puerto Rico, a party she supported. In her confidential and "extra-official" letter of March 11, 1947, to Luis Muñoz Marín, head of the Popular Democratic Party (*populares*), which supported change of political status from colony to unincorporated dependent territory (not to statehood), she told Muñoz Marín she had more than enough evidence "to discredit the Puerto Rican government," but, because of her loyalty to the *populares*, she was addressing him directly.[105] In another letter a few weeks later, enclosing her official report of March 1947, she wrote to him: "My only intention in reporting this situation is so the errors are corrected to avoid future migrations from having the undesirable results that this one has had."[106] Both letters expressed concern that the *populares* had been implicated, in view of the claim by Castle, Barton and Associates that it had the approval of the Puerto Rican government. She offered her opinion that "there were good intentions but a lack of vision" in the contracting out of Puerto Rican migrant workers and had explained publicly, "until her throat hurts," the feats of the Popular party, keeping to herself her opinion of certain party leaders who "have betrayed the best interests of the people."[107] She supported the populares' economic development efforts and opposed neither birth control nor migration nor industrialization: "Migrations, which can be one of the most feasible means to solve our problem, deserve the same dedication [as studies of industrial development], because the errors that are committed fundamentally affect the hegemony of the party. The frustrated worker who returns to the country without having reached his ambitions is a seed of displeasure and distrust of the party." Inadequate attention had also been paid to the impact of the influx of Puerto Rican workers on other US workers: "A group of foreign laborers willing to accept work conditions below standard make an excellent weapon against American workers. Unscrupulous individuals and organizations try to offer work opportunities in the United States to thousands and thousands of Puerto Ricans, meanwhile the greater the number of imported workers, the more debilitated the position of the American worker. . . . It is obvious that there will not be an attempt to protect the rights of those workers, but rather to keep them at the lowest level possible. For precisely these reasons, the migration to Chicago has been a failure."[108]

Just as Padilla and Muñoz Lee had combined scholarship with advocacy, so, at the institutional level, a skilled professional social welfare official was no disinterested bureaucrat but an involved observer and advocate as well as researcher and analyst. The Chicago experiment was certainly in serious need of corrective intervention. The YWCA itself, intended as a benevolent assimilating agent, was trying to "look out for the girls," to police morality and proper feminine behavior, but the "girls" were "looking out" for themselves, gaining influential allies in the process, as they also experimented with labor activism and community formation.

"Knowledge . . . [for] More Skillful Living and Human Understanding"

Puerto Rican female workers, graduate students, and social workers together had employed their limited resources to "direct the men in their communities and the affairs of those communities," as historian Earl Lewis had noted of African Americans in another context.[109] Elena Padilla and Carmen

Isales applied the professional expertise they developed in Chicago and elsewhere, to making Chicago a pivotal site in the scholarship on Puerto Rico and the Puerto Rican diaspora.[110] In the aftermath of the generally favorable publicity aroused in Chicago and Puerto Rico by the workers' protest of Thanksgiving 1946, three months after their arrival in Chicago, the reports of the Puerto Rican graduate students of the University of Chicago, and the public and private correspondence of Padilla, Isales, and Muna Muñoz Lee, the Puerto Rican Senate was prevailed upon to order an official investigation. Padilla and Muñoz Lee had made strategic use of their academic credentials and personal access to public officials, academics, and activists, and made the Chicago contract labor "experiment" an object of public and private scrutiny and revision. A January 1947 investigation by Puerto Rican Senator Vincente Géigel Polanco, apparently at the urging of Luis Muñoz Marín himself, had concluded that the situation of the workers was fine. A Western Union cable of January 12 by Géigel Polanco to Muñoz Marín read "INVESTIGATION DONE! REGARDING WORKERS FOUNDRY INLAND STEEL MAIDS. LIVING WORKING CONDITIONS PRETTY GOOD. COMPLAINTS UNFOUNDED EXCEPT FEW INDIVIDUAL CASES.WRITTEN REPORT INCLUDES RECOMMENDATIONS."[111] But, Muñoz Marín had trusted the report of his daughter and that of her University of Chicago roommate, Padilla, and the fieldwork of Isales, a trusted confidant, that conditions were *not* "pretty good."

As Clarence Senior, director of the Social Science Research Center at the University of Puerto Rico, noted in *Puerto Rican Emigration*, "Puerto Rican students at the University of Chicago took the lead in giving publicity to the complaints of some of the girls and an official investigation was made."[112] As a consequence, labor migration from the island was temporarily suspended until the Insular Legislature could adopt a new policy to regulate migrant contract labor.[113] A revamped program, supervised by Puerto Rican government specifically to train women for household employment, was developed with "improved contracts and no deductions; the girls would be more carefully 'screened.'"[114] Castle, Barton and Associates opted across the board "to stop importing girls for housework."[115] Before that triumph, no government or business bureaucrats in the United States and in Puerto Rico, and certainly no scholars at the University of Chicago, could have imagined that unprotected migrants, especially women, would have any allies in young students in their twenties, especially female; or that poor women would have any power to affect social change. While scholars since have claimed that, because of their small numbers, Puerto Rican migrants represented no economic threat to black and white workers in the United States, the targeted recruitment of Puerto Rican women tells a different story, of a process that undermined both workers' rights and labor organizing.[116] The migration of 1946 was, in retrospect, a significant event in the history of Puerto Rican labor migration.

Despite this, women's contributions to the migration process, to diasporic community formation, and even to the scholarship about Puerto Ricans, was challenged and, in many respects, marginalized or rendered invisible. Early studies of Puerto Rican migration to the United States clearly had identified women as predominant among sojourners joining the US workforce, a distinctive feature unlike past Puerto Rican migratory flows, although reflecting a general trend since the 1930s.[117] However, according to C. Wright Mills, Clarence Senior, and Rose Kohn Goldsen—authors of *The Puerto Rican Journey*—women were less resilient and less able to adjust to life in the continental United States because of limited exposure to mainstream society. Yet, considering Mills et al.'s own statistical findings, their book's portrait of the Puerto Rican migrant ought to have been presented as significantly female.[118] In the conventions of the era, however, the Puerto Rican migrant as male had been assumed. After all, men were characterized largely as "deciders," in the migration process, women as "followers."[119]

To a certain extent, Padilla herself fell into this conventional trap, concluding that no Puerto Rican colony would be established in Chicago as had been in New York City. Indeed, she suspected that Puerto Rican migrants, mainly women, in that Midwest metropolis would become "Mexicanized" because of their fairly scant numbers and their scattering across the city, infused into majority Mexican neighborhoods, and, most salient, because of the engendering of "mixed" Puerto Rican-Mexican offspring.[120] Thus, if migration "does not increase considerably enough so as to shape itself into a Puerto Rican community in Chicago," she predicted, Puerto Ricans would face a kind of breakdown.[121] Padilla did see relevance in, and was intellectually curious about, topics hitherto deemed inconsequential and unworthy of scholarly or political attention, such as the labor rights and political capability of female domestic workers, but it appears that she was somewhat skeptical of their potential because they were women to sustain a sociospatial community in Chicago. Nonetheless, Padilla has left a foundational—although until recently oft-neglected—imprint on scholarship about Puerto Ricans in Chicago, New York, and Puerto Rico.

After the Chicago contract labor mess, the New York City dailies rediscovered their own "Puerto Rican problem," in the summer of 1947 as newspaper accounts and exposés alerted New Yorkers to swarms of depraved islanders overcrowding slums and overwhelming welfare department offices. The reality was that social service workers and administrators lacked the experience to cope with "the only substantial influx of colored migrants from a non-English speaking culture" entering that city, in the words of C. Wright Mills et al.[122] Jesús T. Piñero, who had been appointed the first Puerto Rican governor of the island in 1946, funded a study by Columbia University's Bureau of Applied Social Sciences on Puerto Rican migration to New York.[123] The findings of *The Puerto Rican Journey*, largely statistical, depicted the "normative" experience of Puerto Rican migrants in New York City, its key objective to discover if Puerto Ricans were following the "classic" pattern of assimilation. It did not examine matters of rights and treatment by employers. Still, the authors concluded that avenues for upward mobility were narrowing, thereby encumbering Puerto Rican prospects and possibilities for assimilation.[124] Puerto Ricans' own perspectives on the assimilation question were not engaged, nor was the model of assimilation itself critically examined. Clarence Senior's preface acknowledged Elena Padilla and Carmen Isales, "whose intensive interviews and close-up memoranda from the field were indispensable to the design and execution of the work."[125] Precisely how their work made a difference in the study remains unclear.

With an MA from Chicago in 1947 and a PhD from Columbia four year later, Elena Padilla got caught in a University of Chicago Columbia University intellectual feud on the development of theoretical paradigms and methodological approaches in anthropology on social change and "cultural evolution" to modern society, as scholars attempted to carry out research in Puerto Rico and on the Puerto Rican diaspora.[126] US social scientists were interested in the adjustment of the Puerto Rican people to the complex industrial order of US society and its colonial outpost, as a means of evaluating investments in modernization, with two strategies predominating: economic development and population control.[127] Policy makers in Puerto Rico cited the studies of US experts to promote migration as a means of reducing both the island unemployment rate and population, which in part contributed to growth of Puerto Rican communities in US cities, among them Chicago and New York.[128] Sol Tax and Everett C. Hughes of Chicago proposed a study building from Padilla's master's thesis and on the attention Puerto Rican contract workers received because of what I call her "extra-anthropological interventions." "The Puerto Rican Immigrants Project," headed by Tax and Hughes sought to "learn much from what happens to them about the process of assimilation."[129] In a memo requesting research funds from the Social

Science Research Committee of the University of Chicago, Tax and Hughes wrote: "The immediate task is to get a file on each of the Porto Ricans [*sic*] containing personal and background information and a chronological record of major activities since coming here. Some of this information is already available because of the activities of a group of University of Chicago students, Porto Rican [*sic*] themselves, who became interested in the condition of the immigrants (see attached report). Through their intervention, the Y.W.C.A. assigned a social worker to them; the social worker has now left the job, but her records are available. In addition, the students themselves have considerable information."[130] In a July 22, 1947, letter responding to Tax's request for assistance from the Insular Department of Labor, Ruth Senior, wife of Clarence, wrote, "It appears that the reason there has been a delay in acceding to your request is the adverse publicity received in the press through the entire affair. The Department wanted to make certain the list would not be used in such a way as to add fuel to the fire. Of course I reassured [the new Commissioner of Labor]."[131] Tax did not receive the background information, and no mention was made of the prospect of a Puerto Rican migration study in New York directed by Columbia University's Bureau of Applied Social Sciences.[132]

As Tax proposed a longitudinal study of Puerto Ricans in Chicago, Padilla completed fieldwork on the Mills et al. study on Puerto Ricans in New York and was preparing to join Columbia University Professor Julian Steward's team of researchers on the first anthropological attempt to study the culture of an entire region, taking into account political, economic, and ecological relationships.[133] In many respects, Steward's study, *The People of Puerto Rico: A Study in Social Anthropology* (1956), was presented as a challenge to University of Chicago anthropologist Robert Redfield's "folk-urban continuum" as a conceptual framework for a study of sociocultural change, specifically Redfield's focus on form over process. Steward was particularly interested in the course of proletarianization (how rapid economic change shaped culture) over time, with an historical cultural approach to social change in an enclosed community. The island of Puerto Rico was considered an ideal "social laboratory" because of its natural boundaries.[134] The study established the Caribbean as an important site of anthropological inquiry. Among the five senior researchers was Elena Padilla (along with Robert A. Manners, Sidney W. Mintz, Raymond L. Scheele, and Eric R. Wolf); Padilla was the only Puerto Rican and the only woman granted senior researcher status.[135] Her participation was riddled with ambivalences. In a January 1948 letter to Sol Tax, she wrote:

It was impossible for me to see you before I left Chicago on the 21st to work with Dr[.] C. Wright Mills in the Bureau of Applied Social Science Research at Columbia on his "Puerto Rican Migration Study." I am doing intensive interviews in East Harlem, but learning very little. The only fascinating thing I see on this migration stuff and ethnic life in American cities is that it strengthens a lot the prediction angle in sociology, which at the same time makes the investigator bored.

By the 23rd I'll be leaving for Puerto Rico and join the Steward-Murra research on Puerto Rican communities. The five Columbia people, Murra and I have been having seminars in order to coordinate the project. My own opinion is that the Columbia people speak another language, specially when I am told such things as "we want to do process," etc. and one wonders how that is done in the field and it is amazing how words can be given more useless content for research purposes. Murra's abilities have shown very strikingly and if he continues with us the project will probably be saved, and instead of more histories of communities, we get useful sociology.[136]

The Chicago-Columbia competition regarding the development of theoretical paradigms and methodological approaches in anthropology, evident in *The People of Puerto Rico* project, was foreshadowed as scholars attempted to carry out research on the Puerto Rican diaspora. Padilla's scholarship portrayed some of the tensions involved in her efforts to enrich the Chicago School tradition in ethnography. She confronted important challenges of studies on ethnoracial relations, the politics of scholarly production on aggrieved populations, and the ambivalence of research of the personal and intellectual politics of a scholar. She attempted to blend the structural process approach advanced by Julian Steward of Columbia with the behavioral and social form framework proposed by Robert Redfield of Chicago.[137] In many respects, hers was a lived experience of negotiation between form and process.

Although Padilla earned a PhD in anthropology from Columbia University in 1951, as of 2011, she has never held an academic position in an anthropology department, but rather in applied fields of administrative medicine and public health.[138] Advocacy and public service are seen by some scholars as contrary to the means and ends of scholarship. Scholars who work to dismantle boundaries they see as artificial or as distorting reality can be disparaged for doing so. Anthropologists Faye V. Harrison and Ira Harrison, writing about black pioneers in anthropology—words also applicable to Latina/o pioneers in the social sciences—characterize as impediment to their admittance to the "fraternity of anthropologists" the "ideologically constructed assumption concerning the necessary distinction and distance between the 'purity' of science and the 'pollution' of the partisan advocacy often embodied in subjugated knowledges."[139] Padilla herself, reflecting on the goals of her own scholarship in a recent essay, has drawn a clear distinction between disclosing the theoretical grounds and results of research experiments, and "doing research to confirm rather than question one's political views."[140] Her 1947 master's thesis at Chicago was her first attempt to influence policy via grounded research and activism; so, too, her book, *Up from Puerto Rico* (1958) illustrates the potential of ethnographic work to shape social policy. In the preface of the book, she wrote: "I have written this book for the people interested in the quiet dramas of anonymous lives. It is neither an apology nor a condemnation. Rather, I hope that it will serve the cause of offering the general public access to the findings of the scientific study of society, with the additional hope that this kind of knowledge may be applicable to more skillful living and human understanding."[141] Understanding is a central purpose of scholarship; it may share that purpose with advocacy. Padilla's *Up from Puerto Rico*, a venture into medical anthropology, connected ways of life and belief systems to health, illness, and medical care practices in the Puerto Rican barrio of East Harlem in New York City. Continuing subjects in her scholarship include the internal diversity of Puerto Ricans, interracial and interethnic relations, and housing, health, and life stresses and the means by which they correlate with labor conditions. Padilla considered evidence other scholarship sometimes rejects, her view of theory and practice (form and process and structure and agency) one that would, by revealing facts, improve the daily lives of communities of study, not by distortion or concealing but by exposure to the light of investigation.

Examining the Chicago experiment today from different perspectives reveals not only the competing interests of government and corporate capital in regulating women's bodies and the role of women's actions in interrupting and in altering those schemes, but also the intellectual rivalries of scholars and institutions in producing gendered and racialized knowledge about migration and modernization. Puerto Rican women were forging a separate and distinct path to ensure their economic prosperity via migration and labor patterns. These migrant-workers and migrant-students were the roots of Chicago's Puerto Rican community, a community of racial boundaries and understandings distinct from the urban center they came to call home. Female domestic workers, graduate students, and a "vacationing" social worker, divided by class and status, discovered that wage labor and workers' rights were a common cause, one that spoke to the intertwining challenges of Puerto Rican migration to Chicago. As the Chicago experience demonstrates, women were not only creating alternative networks but creating a Puerto Rican community as well. The community would continue to grow as a predominantly working-class one in which women played the significant role. The lived experiences of recruited female domestic workers and anthropologist Elena Padilla is a story about colonialism, migration, and labor, a dynamic narrative of women as workers, as chroniclers of history, and as architects of community.

2 "NON-RESIDENT PERSONS"

NAVIGATING THE LIMITATIONS OF US CITIZENSHIP

The question seemed straightforward enough, *¿Y que clase de trabajo hacías cuando llegaste aquí?* ("what kind of work did you do when you got here?") But William Rios, garrulous older brother of Gina Bishop (née Rios), decided on a serpentine response:

> *Yo hice mucho trabajo, y peleé también en muchos trabajos, porque cuando yo vine aquí yo era jovencito, yo era independentista y después cambié. Pues, [el primer] trabajo que pase fue que yo volé a Miami y cogí la greyhoun'.*

> I did a lot of work, and fought in lots of these places too, because when I came here I was a kid, I was an *independentista* [supporter of Puerto Rican independence] and later I changed. Well, the first trouble I had was when I flew to Miami and took the Greyhound.

William used the multiple meanings of "*trabajo*" to acknowledge my question about "work" and "jobs" to then launch into a story that he wanted to tell about the troubles Puerto Ricans faced as they contended with conventions of race and citizenship upon arrival in the continental United States in the mid-twentieth century.

Puerto Ricans, indeed, are US citizens. Nonetheless, in the wake of various 1950s controversies—including divergence on their right to public resources, a dramatic armed attack carried out by the Nationalist Party on members of the US House of Representatives, and subsequent mass arrests of Puerto Rican Nationalist Party members or sympathizers in Chicago—Puerto Ricans were often viewed not only as welfare dependent "nonresident" citizens, but as terrorists. During the 1950s a "Puerto Rican problem" would become a popular research trope for public policy and for scholarship of migration to the United States.[1] Anthony Vega, director of the Midwest Office of the Commonwealth of Puerto Rico Department of Labor Migration Division, wrote in an April 1954 memo to Mary Young, executive secretary of the Division on Family and Child Welfare of the Welfare Council of Metropolitan Chicago: "It is not always necessary to tell a welfare worker that the Puerto Rican migration to Chicago presents a problem. It is usually only necessary to say that Puerto Ricans are here and he assumes that they are a problem."[2] A problem, it was assumed, because of racial and linguistic "foreignness," no doubt, by an "American" population that could not accept them as full US citizens. On their own in Chicago, Puerto Ricans were considered to be a drain on the public resources to which, if in need, they were in fact entitled as economically impoverished US citizens. Puerto Ricans in Chicago struggled to cast off this damaging stereotype and sought simultaneously to formulate a more dynamic and accurate image of themselves, their affiliations with other "Spanish-speaking" communities, and of their rights and entitlements, a more nuanced identity. In the process, they learned to navigate the limitations of their own US citizenship and their rights as US citizens, with both disillusionment and hope.

From Colonial Subjects to US Nationals to Second-Class Citizens

William Rios, spry well into his late-seventies, would often attend prominent Bishop family functions (which were many) dressed to the nines, dazzling everyone with his sky-blue zoot suit, white-brimmed hat, and crackerjack salsa moves. In addition, William was a regular at "*el club de lo viejos*" (the old peoples' club) at Casa Central in Humboldt Park, a social service organization for Chicago's Hispanic population. I was fortunate, in light of his busy social schedule, to be able to arrange a life history interview with him one November afternoon in 2001. (It would take two lengthy sessions.) This is the story he told me about Puerto Ricans as a "problem."

In August 1949, at twenty-five years old, William had begun a three-day trek to Chicago on that Greyhound bus from the rural South to the industrial North. "There was no one in the *guagua* [bus], me by myself. And I sat in the middle of the big *guagua*," he said. The bus from the Miami depot picked up passengers, black and white, along the way. Although the bus was nearly full, no one sat next to William. Then, a white woman boarded and stood in the aisle. "I said, 'Miss, why don't you sit down? There are no [other] empty seats.'" William then motioned to the seat next to his. The woman waited a while, then turned back to speak to the driver, who stopped the bus and announced, "Those of color move to the back." "Driver, what kind of money is this lady giving?" William inquired. While relating the story to me, William confided, "*Yo sabia to' la mogoya* [I knew the whole mess]." He had in fact experienced segregation while in the military but decided to test the limits of the racial order by feigning ignorance. "No . . . you don't understand," replied the driver. "It's that there's a law. Those of color have to move to the back and leave those seats." "I'm from Puerto Rico, I'm Puerto Rican. I don't know that law," William said, adding, "What happens to the colored folks when the bus is full?" "They have to get off," was the driver's response. William asked for a refund for his ticket so that he could immediately exit the bus. "Oh, I can't," said the driver. "Oh, well, me neither," William snapped, returning to his same seat. "You know who made me get up?" he asked me and quickly answered, "Those of color." Each person who passed down the aisle had tapped his seat and advised, "You bette' move back." One warned, "They're going to yank you and get you off." That was enough for William. "I got scared and got up."

By 1954, married with two children, William Rios was living in the Jane Addams housing projects on Racine and Roosevelt on Chicago's Near West Side, within walking distance of his factory job. Although the popular view of 1950s Chicago was one of neighborhoods polarized between black and white, everyday life painted a more multicolored picture. Italians may have dominated the Near West Side—the largest and most renowned of Chicago's Italian neighborhoods—but it was no homogeneous community, also being home to African Americans, Mexicans, and Puerto Ricans. Each understood the boundaries of their community, with Puerto Rican and Mexican communities serving as an uneasy buffer between Little Italy and black neighborhoods.[3] Despite this, in all communities there were friendships and intermarriages between people of diverse backgrounds. Andrew Diamond's comparative ethnoracial history of male youth culture and its spatial practices in Chicago asserts that, "While there is certainly some truth to the contention that the whiteness of working-class European Americans was much more secure by the 1950s, the racial identities of Puerto Ricans and Mexicans within the new racial regime of color were far less certain in this moment."[4] Puerto Ricans were troubling the racial order. "After Loomis [Street], that whole neighborhood was Italian," William told me. "[Every time] Puerto Ricans . . . came through there, [Italians] jumped [them]. But, because I was black, they thought I was . . . African American. I walked all over there and never . . . was I harassed." The darkness of his skin let him "pass" as "African American," dodging confrontations in a space where "Puerto Ricanness" was particularly disadvantageous. Never denying his *puertorriqueñidad* because the question did not come up, William nonetheless understood that, at certain moments, it was more prudent to be silent and assume the identity assigned to him by others.[5] Sociologist Gerald Suttles noted of Chicago of the 1950s and 1960s, "Anyone who lives in the projects is automatically assumed to be a Negro or 'like the Negroes.'"[6]

Erasmo Souchet, an ardent supporter of community uplift who worked his way from factory floor to bank executive, also vividly recalled painful lessons of race and space he learned as a young boy in Chicago's West, the Near West, and the Near Northwest Sides. Erasmo's family had come from Puerto Rico to Chicago in 1954, subsequently experiencing numerous intracity migrations. One particular migration, from a West Side neighborhood, was the result of Erasmo being harassed: After his parents watched in distress from their apartment window as Erasmo was chased down the block by African American youths, one swinging a chain with a padlock, the family made a prompt decision to move further west to a white ethnic neighborhood. But they found no solace there. Erasmo recalled one particular visit to a Puerto Rican family in the Taylor Street area of the Near West Side. As he sat by a window eating *arroz con gandules* (rice with pigeon peas), his hostess urgently asked him to move away from the window. Her fear was that their neighbors, upon seeing him, would immediately discover that the family was not Italian. Erasmo told me he considers himself not "black, but while white, not 'white.'" As a result, he "had problems." His experiences echo Bernado Vega's observations of Puerto Rican life in the continental United States at the turn of the twentieth century: "if anything taught the Puerto Ricans—including white Puerto Ricans—what life was like in the United States, it was the awareness of discrimination."[7] As a consequence, they avoided racial conflict either by moving to another space, or by "passing" as either "black" or "white" if their complexion permitted. Life was more complex than the simplistic black/white binary would attest.

One day, a policeman or an immigration official stopped William Rios during his walk to work from the Near West Side, asking for "papers." William presented an ID card, and also his military ID. "The only thing that bothered me," he said to the man, "is that you came to stop me because you probably thought I was Mexican." For him, the critical distinction was not only one of race but also of US citizenship—undocumented Mexican immigrants and US citizens of Mexican descent had been rounded up and repatriated from the late 1940s into the early 1950s. An October 1953 report on Chicago's Near West Side stated that the number of "illegal Mexican immigrants, 'wetbacks,'" was still rising "in spite of a program to deport" them.[8] In July 1954 the federal government had officially launched "Operation Wetback"—synchronizing efforts to locate and repatriate Mexicans.[9] Hence, it was not uncommon for Puerto Ricans themselves, mistaken as Mexicans, to be stopped and interrogated by local and state authorities. William Rios intended to clarify that he was a US citizen, a Puerto Rican, *and* a veteran; hence, he flashed his military service card. On his trek "goin' to Chicago," he, like other "colored" Puerto Ricans, was compelled to submit to Jim Crow, in the South but in the North as well. Once in Chicago's Near West Side, however, William found the issue involved not merely color, but also the complex matter of Puerto Rican identity's relationship to Mexicanness and to latinidad.

Chicago's Puerto Ricans adopted numerous strategies to deal with the lesson that they did not belong—an understanding informed by the US presence in Puerto Rico and the implications of that presence on their political and social identities as well as their transition from colonial subject to US national to second-class citizen. Ratification of the 1898 Treaty of Paris, which brought about an end to the six-month war between Spain and United States, had placed the natives of Puerto Rico, the Philippines, and Guam under US sovereignty as colonial subjects.[10] Would these "tropical people" be empowered fully with the rights and privileges of US citizenship? And, in due course, granted statehood? The Filipinos engaged in a violent uprising against US dominion. Puerto Rico did not. In 1900 the Foraker Act established a policy for Puerto Rico and the others as "unincorporated territory"—neither self-governing and autonomous nor a state. One US official called Puerto Rico, as a naval outpost for the United States in the hemisphere, "our national laboratory," wherein "if we pursue a generous policy, we will win the hearts of the people of South America."[11] In 1901, in the most significant of the Insular Cases, a deeply divided Supreme Court decided, in *Downes v. Bidwell*, that the US Constitution did not pertain to Puerto Rico, "a territory appurtenant and belonging to the United States, but not a part of the United States.'"[12] The "citizens of Porto [*sic*] Rico," owed allegiance to the US nation-state, but were not citizens of it. Rather the "Foraker Act granted inhabitants of Puerto Rico the status of United States nationals."[13] The US president would appoint the island's governor and an executive council. There would be a House of Representatives of thirty-five elected members, with a nonvoting resident commissioner in Congress and a judicial system with a Supreme Court—no US senator, no elected representative in Congress, and no vote for president.

On March 2, 1917 President Woodrow Wilson signed the Jones Act, conferring US citizenship on Puerto Ricans, a collective naturalization that was not a full citizenship, but a new status, one of a "second-class citizenship." Puerto Ricans were free to travel to and from the United States without migration visas or other documents, and free to relocate permanently to the continental United States. A week earlier, Wilson had "announced his desire for immediate action on the bill giving self-government to Porto [sic] Ricans as a war measure," a means to "insure [islanders'] loyalty."[14] "Never before," according to Political Scientist Pedro Cabán, had Congress "granted citizenship to the inhabitants of a territory without the explicit condition of eventual statehood."[15] In the mid-1930s, support for Puerto Rican independence and sympathy for the Nationalist Party, its agenda independence, were on the rise in the island. In the decades after World War I, with an era of decolonization beginning and with empires on the verge of collapse, the United States needed anticolonial credentials without abandoning all guise of empire. It recognized Philippine independence in 1946 on the symbolic date of July 4.

In Puerto Rico, in 1948, Luis Muñoz Marín became the first popularly elected governor of the island. On July 3, 1950, President Truman authorized Puerto Rico to draft a constitution of its own. Autonomy went no farther. By October 30, 1950, in a coordinated series of armed revolts, members of the militant Nationalist Party attacked police stations in a number of Puerto Rican towns as well as the governor's mansion in San Juan. Then, two days later on November 1, two Nationalists, Griselio Torresola and Oscar Collazo, tried to shoot their way into Washington DC's Blair House, where President Truman was staying while a White House renovation was underway.[16] Sociologists Rafael Bernabe and César Ayala contend that "Muñoz Marín's bargaining power was greatly enhanced by the pressure exerted on US policy makers by the rise of anticolonialism internationally and by the militant *independentistas* and Nationalist minority in Puerto Rico."[17] Almost eighteen months later, on July 25, 1952, an *Estado Libre Associado* (Free Associated State) for the Commonwealth of Puerto Rico was proclaimed, thus leading, in 1953, to the UN General Assembly's removal of Puerto Rico from its list of non-self-governing territories.[18]

Following the Jones Act of 1917, after the first half-century of colonial rule, fewer than 2,000 on average per year had migrated to the continental United States.[19] Not until "Operation Bootstrap" of 1948, with its accelerated industrialization plan for Puerto Rico, did significant numbers come, most airborne to New York City. The earlier 1946 labor recruitment of domestic and foundry workers to Chicago had been a foreshadowing of a larger plan to lure industry and investment to Puerto Rico. At the same time, this development plan was meant to ease unemployment on the island by transporting workers unwanted in Puerto Rico to unskilled jobs in US urban areas for which workers *were* needed—away from New York and toward Chicago and Philadelphia, as well as other urban and rural areas.

"Ship Them Back in Plane Lots": The Puerto Rican Repatriation Debate

In the aftermath of a US decline of manufacturing jobs, coinciding with the dense concentration of Puerto Ricans in New York City and resulting efforts by the Puerto Rican government, with the assistance of US industries, to manage migration, the Puerto Rican migrant flow was redirected westward. In 1956 the promotional film "*Un amigo en Chicago*" was circulated by the Migration Division to persuade potential migrants of the relative ease in finding employment, better salaries, and desirable housing options in Chicago.[20] A Puerto Rican government Bureau of Employment and Migration (subsequently the Migration Division of the Department of Labor) created in 1947 was charged with providing migrants with information about job opportunities, training programs, and settlement assistance, facilitating their transition to the continental United States. Four regional offices in New York City (the central office), Chicago, Lake Erie (Cleveland) and Camden, New Jersey, were to supervise field offices to coordinate employment and social service.[21] In 1952 representatives from the Migration Division came to Chicago to investigate work opportunities for Puerto Ricans in New York and in Puerto Rico.[22] Migrant social networks disseminated word of job prospects, with Chicago becoming a destination of choice. By 1957, 70 percent of Puerto Ricans registered with the Midwest regional office had come there straight from the island, without stopping in New York[23]

No official count was kept, but estimates reported a wide range of between 5,000 and 20,000 Puerto Ricans in Chicago in 1954.[24] But with the post–Korean War recession came distressing news. The Midwest Office of the Commonwealth of Puerto Rico Department of Labor Migration Division's February 1954 report announced: "for the first time Chicago public relations got out of hand because of unemployment and necessary emergency financial assistance for non-resident persons."[25] "Non-resident persons," in this case, referred to those not eligible for help from the city because they had not yet met the city's residency requirement for public services—one year in Illinois, including six months in Chicago itself. Needy Puerto Ricans in Chicago were out of luck despite the fact that they were bona fide US citizens. A February 2 headline of the *Chicago Sun-Times* announced: "Welfare Council to Weigh Puerto Ricans' Plight." Alvin E. Rose, commissioner of the Chicago Welfare Department, cabled Puerto Rican authorities in the closing days of January 1954: "Puerto Rican migrants who cannot make it on their own [should] desist from going to Chicago at this time when the winter cold and the shortage of work opportunities makes life difficult for those who arrive from outside with intentions to stay."[26] *El Mundo*, an island-based newspaper, quoted from the cablegram and reported: "In some urgent cases, such as the case of homelessness, it is probably necessary that [the Chicago Welfare Department] provide transportation back (to Puerto Rico) for the non-residents wishing to return, even if we do not receive approval (of the Public Welfare Department of the island) in each particular case."[27]

The Most Reverend Bernard J. Sheil, senior auxiliary bishop of the Roman Catholic archdiocese of Chicago, disputed Alvin Rose's perspective, in part: "The Puerto Ricans in Chicago face a real crisis, to be sure. But the problem should be met right here at home by all welfare organizations which are a part of the city."[28] Mary Young, of the Welfare Council of Metropolitan Chicago, took a position in between: "The Puerto Rican problem is not new to Chicago. . . . About eight years ago [c. 1946], it was brought to the attention of the Council that unscrupulous employment agencies were bringing Puerto Ricans to this country on a contract basis. The people were very much exploited, both in industry and domestic service. . . . At the time the Council organized a committee which was composed of interested agencies offering service, and also the Illinois State Department of Labor."[29] Several months later, Young urged the Cook County Department of Welfare to assist: "Our economy depends upon a mobile labor market but in times of unemployment, individuals are hurt. . . . This affects not only peoples from outside our mainland but also a moving population within the United States proper. Wherever possible we will lend influence in aiding the Island of Puerto Rico itself in developing resources for the people on the Island so that there will be less need for migration because of greater business within the Island itself."[30]

Commissioner Rose had insisted, several months earlier, "that public funds be used to ship home jobless Puerto Ricans rather than allow them to become eligible for relief."[31] "An 'open door' policy for non-residents at this time would place a horrific burden on Chicago taxpayers."[32] The Welfare Council of Metropolitan Chicago viewed Rose's "attitude" "toward the Puerto Ricans" as cause of "consternation," especially his solution for "non-residents who become dependent": "Ship them back in plane lots."[33] Rose had told the

Chicago Tribune, in its story, "Puerto Ricans Pour Into City and Ask Dole," "We have been criticized for considering helping able bodied non-resident Puerto Ricans to return home because of their language handicap. This would be far less expensive than giving them relief and, we believe, in many instances better for them."[34] (Airfare from San Juan to Chicago, said the *Tribune*, was $93.30, plus 15 percent tax.[35]) A number of Puerto Ricans had come to Chicago following seasonal agricultural work in nearby states, Rose said. "There has been a similar migration of Negroes from the south and railroad workers now on skid row."[36] On Chicago's Near West Side, where "skid row" was located, seasonal workers and transient laborers—drifters and grifters—and the jobless had found cheap rooms, social services, and some jobs. "We can profit from the experience of New York City," Rose said. "Welfare officials there granted relief to non-residents and the city now has a Puerto Rican colony of 450,000 persons which is posing a tremendous problem for its welfare department."[37] New York had no residency requirement for relief services, whereas Chicago did. Most Illinois-state and private advocates for the poor had urged Chicago to relax its residence requirement, but Rose would have none of that.[38]

Although, technically, US citizenship granted Puerto Ricans free movement to the United States, and although for contracted labor it had protected workers from deportation after completion of labor contracts, Rose in effect sought to counteract this freedom. "Rose Seeks Migration End in Puerto Rico," read a headline in the *Chicago Sun-Times* of February 4, 1954. "I will talk to newspaper editors and use whatever facilities are available to spread the word that Puerto Ricans should not come [to Chicago]," Rose said.[39] He would coordinate the return migration of Chicago's "stranded and desperately situated Puerto Ricans."[40] In turn, he sought an appointment with Governor Luis Muñoz Marín and other government island officials "to make sure that if Puerto Ricans are returned . . . they will have a means of support and 'not be dumped on the beach.'"[41] Rose failed to meet with the governor, but did meet and discuss with Puerto Rico's secretaries of health and labor why Puerto Ricans were "causing economic-social problems in the city of Chicago,"[42] and what should be done about it. In two days on the island, he arranged the return migration of "30 Puerto Ricans to their homes . . . with the welfare department paying their fares," the *Chicago Tribune* reported.[43] San Juan authorities, for their part, agreed to prevent additional groups from leaving for the continental United States.

El Mundo accused Rose of discriminating against Puerto Ricans, whereupon Rose protested, "We're treating them just as any other group but we must realize that the disadvantage of language and training for agricultural and non-industrial work puts them at an economic disadvantage today in Chicago."[44] It was "not," he said, "a Puerto Rican problem, but simply one in which Puerto Ricans are involved."[45] "I believe many Puerto Ricans, including their government officials," he told the *Chicago Tribune*, "now know our position is not one of hostility to Puerto Ricans but one of trying to avoid migrations which would lead to trouble and misery." "I told the officials there flatly that we had enough relief cases in Chicago and didn't want any more."[46] If his trip to San Juan had "saved only one family, which would be unable to adjust in Chicago, from coming here, then the cost of the trip was worth it to the taxpayers."[47] Rose had simply adopted the Puerto Rican government's own rhetoric and strategy on migration; his intent—as he saw it—was not to discourage migration but rather to encourage migration only of the self-sufficient.

There was precedence for Rose's strategy. In the aftermath of a 1919 six-day "race riot," in Chicago, set off by the stoning and drowning of a black youth by whites for crossing an imaginary color line while swimming,[48] Chicago Mayor "Big Bill" Thompson, a Republican with overwhelming African American support, had explored returning "some of Chicago's surplus of Mississippi migrants back to their home state."[49] Theodore Bilbo, Mississippi's governor, wrote in reply: "I desire to state that we have all the room in the world for what we know as N-I-G-G-E-R-S, but none whatever for 'colored ladies and gentlemen.' If these Negroes have been contaminated with northern social and political dreams of equality, we cannot use them, nor do we want them."[50] Indeed, few African Americans would return to the South until some decades later.[51] Socioeconomic conditions and the racial order of Southern states fueled migration to Chicago. African Americans, realizing that achieving "a degree of autonomy based on land ownership" was not a possibility in the Jim Crow South, traveled North in search of citizenship built on a foundation of industrial work and city residence."[52] By the 1920s and 1930s, the citizenship of African Americans had been established at a metalevel, but at the level of the everyday it was still countermanded. Puerto Ricans, too, had sought to improve their lot with migration to northern cities, but also discovered, in the 1940s and 1950s, as migrant citizens, that Chicago's residency requirement effectively denied them full citizenship rights.

In the first week of February 1954, while Alvin Rose was meeting with government officials on the island, Clarence Senior, national director of the Migration Division of New York, went to Chicago for an emergency meeting at Hull House on Chicago's Near West Side, with Anthony Vega, Reverend

Bernard J. Sheil, auxiliary Bishop of Chicago, and representative heads of the Chicago Commission on Human Relations, the Urban League, and the Welfare Council of Metropolitan Chicago.[53] There, Senior accused Rose, in absentia, "of performing a 'grandstand stunt' to keep Puerto Ricans off Chicago relief rolls," as the *Chicago Sun-Times* put it.[54] Vega attempted to redirect discussion from jobless Puerto Rican migrants to Chicago, to his office's dealings with unemployed persons who had been laid off.[55] Senior, responding accordingly to Rose that New York "had a Puerto Rican colony of 450,000 as a consequence of giving relief to non-residents," presented a telegraph message from Rose's counterpart in New York, the welfare commissioner, that "94 percent of this group of American citizens [Puerto Ricans] are completely self-supporting."[56]

A special committee of representatives of twenty-eight social service agencies, working in conjunction with the Welfare Council of Metropolitan Chicago to "study the problems arising from the migration into the city of jobless Puerto Ricans," concluded that the problem of unemployed Puerto Ricans "*se le ha dado relieve exagerado*," or "has been given exaggerated attention."[57] While Chicago unemployment was a general concern, all ethnoracial minorities had been hit by the crisis. As a CIO representative put it, this was "a national problem. We should hope that community support is available to all in equal proportions."[58] Indeed, *El Mundo* insisted that, "according to information collected by Mr. Senior—Puerto Ricans make up the smallest group among those affected by the problem."[59] Robert MacRae, director of the Welfare Council of Metropolitan Chicago, urged the federal government to help, because workers "are essential to modern industry . . . [W]e are interested that all migrants receive fair and equitable treatment, without discrimination against any ethnic group."[60] To the Migration Division, return migration was a last resort.

University of Chicago Professor Rexford Guy Tugwell (an original member of President Roosevelt's "Brains Trust" and governor of Puerto Rico from 1941 to 1946), told the *Chicago Daily News* sardonically: "It wasn't long ago that Chicago employers were glad to see them here. Now they are persona non grata. That's not quite sporting," and told *El Mundo* that Puerto Ricans, "have as much right to move here as Texans, New Yorkers or people from the hills in Mississippi. . . . I think it's Rose's business to take care of them, not to try to make policy between the United States and Puerto Rico. . . . When Mr. Rose comes home, will he go downstate and discourage migration there, too? Far more laborers and farmers pour into Chicago from Southern Illinois than from Puerto Rico."[61] A February 4, 1954, editorial, "Imported Reliefers," in the *Chicago Daily Tribune* sided with Rose: Relaxing residency rules "would only invite the indigent from all over the country to come here and live at the expense of the taxpayer." "[The Puerto Rican] is an American citizen. Like the southern sharecropper, white or Negro, he has full right to come to Chicago in the effort to better his economic lot. An American citizen has freedom of movement anywhere in this country, but at his own risk. He cannot be deported, but local authorities are under no obligation to feed him if job opportunities diminish."[62] Frances Fox Piven and Richard A. Cloward have contended that restrictive regional relief policies were designed to fortify work norms and ground a discipline of work. Relief was considered a grave threat to private enterprise, potentially compromising a free labor market. According to Piven and Cloward, "When a particular racial group does the most menial work for the lowest wages, the relief system cooperates by reducing the amount of aid to that group or by closing off the possibility of any aid whatsoever," its intent, to preserve social and economic inequities.[63]

An editorial in *El Mundo*, published the same day as the *Tribune*'s "Imported Reliefers," protested: "Clearly, the municipal authorities of the cold metropolis do not have a very friendly attitude towards the possible Puerto Rican migration to that city and want to discourage it, by all means possible, *antes de que cobre auge*" ("before it booms"). Since the "United States has been the land of promise and opportunity for millions and millions of people from all over the world," what was the "harm in it being so for a few thousands of Puerto Ricans"? The island did not intend to "unload its problem cases (the sick and disabled) on other communities of the Nation" and thus compatriots in Chicago in grave need should be returned and would be cared for by "our social welfare agencies." The editorial made the point, however, that Puerto Ricans should be judged no differently than everyone else. "Discriminating against them or treating them with measures of prejudice," the editorial concluded, "is to deny US citizens that which is not denied to foreigners of any race who have migrated to the Nation."[64] A Carlos Renta sent observations from Chicago to *El Mundo*. Puerto Ricans, he wrote, "are the first to be fired when cutbacks are necessary. They introduce many hurdles and obstacles to give us any Public Welfare aid. Nevertheless, they have no qualms about giving it to the Mexicans and other nationalities. . . . The Government of Puerto Rico should order an investigation of these facts. Are we American citizens or are we not?"[65]

At about this same time, others were linking Puerto Ricans and Mexican Americans to the "problem" of unemployment and welfare services. Monsignor Robert E. Lucy, Catholic archbishop of San Antonio, suggested that

Chicago's thousands of Puerto Ricans without jobs might be transferred to the Southwest as agricultural laborers. (He, like the CIO and AFL, had opposed legislation to allow recruitment of Mexican nationals without consent of the Mexican government.)[66] "There are thousands of unemployed Puerto Ricans in Chicago who are US citizens," the archbishop telegraphed. "In South Texas we have tens of thousands of Mexican Americans, who gladly would work in agriculture for decent wages."[67] A *Chicago Daily Tribune* letter to the editor, from the Chicago suburb of Melrose Park proposed: "Recent news stories reported troubles with Puerto Ricans here and Mexicans in California. As I understand it, Puerto Ricans are United States citizens, and many of them were brought here for agricultural work. Now that there isn't any farm work in this vicinity, many are trying to get on relief. At the same time, California needs farm laborers. Why not recruit farm workers from among the Puerto Ricans in Chicago and New York?"[68] Both the archbishop and the Melrose Park resident deployed a nativist rationalization, with Puerto Ricans to be seen not as a "problem" but as a "solution" to labor shortages elsewhere. But Puerto Ricans were still perceived as an expendable, transient labor force rather than as members of the Chicago community.[69]

In a Spanish-language version of a radio address, Rose sought to clarify "all of the facts about the so-called Puerto Rican problem in Chicago." "Able-bodied unattached non-residents," were "causing great pressure upon the private welfare agencies who in turn have been asking the Chicago Department of Welfare to waive its rules to give them help. This, as I explained, we cannot do."[70] A February 10, 1954, news story in *El Mundo*, headed "Boricuas Returned by Chicago are Reluctant to Recount their Experiences," told of thirty Puerto Ricans repatriated, one a paralyzed woman, another an ill veteran, others children. Isaac Vega, a worker from Ponce, had found no work in Chicago and had turned to the public welfare agency: "on one occasion they gave him $5.87 and on another $11.70, until finally they offered to pay the return trip to Puerto Rico."[71]

In Chicago, Puerto Ricans decided to improve their own circumstances. The *New Republic* reported that "Many Puerto Ricans, resentful and bewildered, feel they are being treated like second-class citizens. As they doubled up in tiny apartments to share beds and bread during the crisis, they expressed their views through Vega: 'We want Chicago to see it isn't the Puerto Rican that's suffering. It's the worker. We don't want any special consideration. We just want to be treated like all other Americans, that's all.'"[72] In February 1954 the Midwest Office Migration Division reported: "Spontaneous groups of Puerto Ricans have surged all over Chicago and come to the office for . . . contacts with established agencies in the city."[73] The Migration Division featured the activities of the *Comité pro-emergencia*: "Although the first meeting of this organization was very unsuccessful due to heckling by Nationalists," the group reported to have collected fifty dollars for their emergency fund, which would provide "direct relief for persons who do not otherwise qualify for assistance." The Comité planned to organize a five-dollar-a-plate dinner benefit to continue to raise funds for their relief purse.[74] Subsequent monthly reports by a Migration Division social worker emphasized a need to orient Puerto Ricans to obtain proper documents to verify their status as residents. By April, the same social worker noted a boost in Puerto Rican confidence to "solve their problems here in Chicago." They were "not so anxious to go back to the island as they were previously."[75]

"The Urgent Need to Associate": Puerto Rican Nationalism and Puerto Rican Latinidad

The glimpse of good news and reassurance was blown out a month later, on March 1, 1954, near the anniversary of the signing of the 1917 Jones Act that had granted US citizenship. Four Puerto Rican Nationalists, sitting in the Ladies' Gallery of the House of Representatives, had, in the midst of a floor debate on recruitment of Mexican farm workers, "whipped out pistols and sprayed the assembled house with bullets." Five congressmen were wounded, the *Chicago Daily Tribune* reported. The Nationalists in the balcony had shouted "Free Puerto Rico!" and "Viva Mexico!" A Lolita Lebrón had "pulled out a Puerto Rican flag from under her coat and waved it."[76] The four had purchased one-way train tickets from New York City.[77] Antonio Fernós-Isern, resident commissioner of Puerto Rico, accused the four of "carrying out a communist plot."[78] Governor Luis Muñoz Marín "pledged complete cooperation with the house committee on un-American activities in its investigation of Nationalist party members and activities." His government would provide "all available information on 'Nationalist party members and terrorists' known to be in the United States."[79] Mrs. Muñoz Marín, Inés Mendoza, came to Washington for a luncheon hosted by the wives of the five wounded congressmen, the invitation extended, according to the *Chicago Tribune*, "to show the wives did not hold any resentment against Puerto Rico."[80] Lolita Lebrón, from her cell, said that March 1 had been "chosen for the shooting because it coincided with the opening of the Inter-American conference at Caracas, Venezuela."[81] (At the conference, Secretary of State John Foster

Dulles unveiled Eisenhower's policy toward Latin America, a policy that took the offensive against Jacobo Arbenz Guzman's "communist" government in Guatemala.)[82] Lebrón and her Nationalist *compañeros* tied the Puerto Rican struggle to Latin Americans more broadly, and to Mexicans as well. They were calling for a hemispheric anticolonial latinidad.

The *Chicago Tribune* of March 3, 1954, now linked the shooting to Chicago's Puerto Ricans' struggle for public services: "Bare Puerto Rican Terrorism in Chicago," read the story's headline. A "frightened" Mrs. Alvin D. Rose was quoted as saying that "Puerto Rican terrorists" had threatened her family: "[W]hen the debate over relief for Puerto Ricans was at its height, I got a telephone call from a man with a Spanish accent," who had warned, "If your husband doesn't leave my countrymen alone, we're going to get you—all of you."[83] Commissioner Rose himself had refused police protection in Puerto Rico, "saying he was not afraid"; security precautions had been taken nonetheless.[84] (Since he had proposed return migration, "about 83 Puerto Ricans have been sent back to the island at the expense of the welfare department.")[85] Guards were also placed at the Chicago home of Anthony Vega and at the Midwest Office of the Migration Bureau. Five Chicago Puerto Ricans had been arrested in their homes and held for questioning by the FBI.[86] The Chicago police were in pursuit of others, including Gonzalo Lebrón Sotomayor—brother of "the Puerto Rican girl terrorist"—said to be a self-proclaimed leader of the local Nationalist Party, and part owner of a grocery store on Harrison Street on the Near West Side, the commercial and residential strip most identified with the city's Puerto Ricans. The *Tribune* reported that Lolita Lebrón had visited her brother on Chicago's Near West Side several times.[87]

Lebrón Sotomayor, in an exclusive interview with the *Chicago Sun-Times* the day after the attack on Congress, said he had not seen his sister in a year. (He had lived in the United States for ten years.) "We (Nationalists)," he said, "are all ready to lay down our lives at any moment for Puerto Rican freedom. We want to be free citizens. Just like Patrick Henry, Nathan Hale and George Washington. I have read a lot of American history."[88] Chicago's police commissioner "ordered a roundup of all fanatical Puerto Rico [sic] Nationalist Party members . . . for questioning."[89] Thirteen Puerto Ricans, most of them from the Near West Side and West Side of Chicago, had been brought in for questioning "about terrorist activities," but were later released.[90] A few weeks after that, the FBI arrested eleven Nationalist Party members, of whom six were from Chicago.[91]

Spanish-speaking Chicagoans were now heard from. The Woodlawn Latin American Committee organized a blood drive "as a 'gesture of sympathy' for the five US congressmen wounded by Puerto Rican terrorists"[92] and "to partially offset the public relations effect of the shooting."[93] One of the thirty Puerto Rican blood donors had said, "We want to show the people of Chicago most Puerto Ricans are not like the terrorists. . . . We want to let the people know we too were horrified at what happened in Congress."[94] The Mexican American Council of Chicago, represented by Director Martin Ortiz at a meeting at Hull House, adopted a resolution that the shooting "should not be interpreted or construed as the general thinking or actions of Spanish-speaking people everywhere and, in particular, in the Chicago area."[95] Ortiz and Anthony Vega, Midwest director of the Migration Bureau, met with the police commissioner to protest "the mass arrests of Spanish-speaking citizens."[96] The Woodlawn Latin American Committee followed its blood drive with "a program of seeking out resources for Puerto Rican people,"[97] aiming to disentangle the struggle for access to relief from Nationalist radicalism, and, perhaps, from Migration Division politics.[98]

Chicago Puerto Ricans, troubled, even fearful, began to modify the meaning and limits of community in their lives and in the framing of their collective identities, seeking some sense of autonomy and learning the importance of being a "documented" Chicagoan. A Migration Division social worker reported in April that Puerto Ricans were gathering documentation of their status as Illinois and Chicago residents, holding on to "paystubs and rent receipts and . . . getting their birth certificates from" the island.[99] A number applied for public housing. Weeks later, however, this feeling of stability was compromised when Puerto Ricans became the targets of racial violence. Yet Vega attested that the May 1954 "arrest of seven Nationalists in Chicago has made not a ripple on public opinion, Puerto Ricans or otherwise." The office received not even a single phone call from the press for comment on the arrests. It seemed that where the general public and press were concerned, there was little reason to interpret two incidents of robbery and assault of Puerto Ricans by a teenage gang in the area of the Jane Addams Housing Project in the same month as a mark of "general community hostility toward Puerto Ricans," according to Vega.[100]

The Migration Division, for its part, was working publicly with other institutions to improve ethnoracial relations in the city, especially on the Near West Side. It sought to manage quietly, incidents of potential negativity, as when a June 1954 report portrayed the dire straits of two families in public housing of two of the Nationalists arrested in Chicago after the DC shooting. The families, legal residents of the city, had been left "penniless," the women under strict orders from their husbands "not to seek help from the government agencies." Despite the orders, the women had petitioned the Chicago Welfare Department for aid and the Puerto Rican social worker assigned to the case at Hull House referred it to the Migration Division, after which assistance was arranged. Plans were then made to relocate the families in order to avoid further trouble, such as in the South Side of Chicago the year before, after mobs of white residents protested the integration of the Trumbull Park Homes, threatening new black neighbors in the almost exclusively white community of South Deering.[101]

In July came reports of racial attacks on Puerto Rican families in the Jane Addams Project, with one of the two families then being relocated. In response to issues like this one, the secretary of labor of the Commonwealth came from Puerto Rico to consider ways to address the needs of Chicago's Puerto Ricans.[102] Hull House offered English language classes, training in other skills, and citizenship education. Settlement houses, like Hull House, intentionally and unintentionally were schooling Puerto Ricans on how to handle questions of race and space.[103] Anthony Vega warned that "Special care ought to be taken by such agencies to retard the indoctrination of our people with the racial prejudices of the continental United States. Such attitudes are virtually non-existent in Puerto Rico and their acquisition by migrants represents a potentially serious long run liability to the community."[104]

The standing of Puerto Ricans in Chicago was further complicated in July by "Operation Wetback," a paramilitary dragnet with deportation of their Mexican (and, likely also, Mexican American) neighbors. William Rios, at that time living on the Near West Side, told of being stopped on his daily walk to work and being asked for "papers." Organizations serving a specific "Latino" population debated the advantages and disadvantages of aggregation, questioning the notion of an all-encompassing identification for populations with a common language but with no common origin or history. Vega cautioned that bringing together of diverse populations under the rubric of "Spanish-speaking people" must serve only "as an expedient to achieving the general welfare of all citizens."[105]

More than a year before, an editorial appeared in *Vida Latina*, a Chicago monthly bilingual magazine, on "The Urgent Need to Associate," addressing the prospect of latinidad: "[A]t this time in Chicago or any other city of the United States there should exist at least one group representing Latin American countries that have resident citizens in the United States. This grouping should promote all kinds of projects, companies and movements directed to a better cultural, social and moral understanding amongst Latinos themselves."[106]

In fact, efforts to establish associations for people of "Spanish-speaking" origin had risen in Chicago decades before, with the founding at Hull House in 1925 of *La sociedad hispanoamericana*, the Hispanic American Society. Its original ten Puerto Rican families had soon grown to more than 200, representing a number of Latin American countries, coming together to make friends, to network, and to strengthen business connections.[107] With the Depression, the effort had diminished. The Mexican population, too, declined after repatriation campaigns in the 1930s against Mexican nationals.[108] La sociedad hispanoamericana ceased. Identities blurred. The designations of "Hispanos" or "Latinos," used for years to refer to a small group of intellectuals and middle-class professionals from Latin America, the Spanish-speaking Caribbean, and Spain in New York, Chicago, and other US urban centers, gradually came to mean anyone of Spanish-speaking descent, irrespective of class standing.[109] By the 1950s, in some major cities, "Hispano" or "Latino" was considered preferable to "Puerto Rican" because of the stigma attached to this population in New York, and, later, in Chicago.[110] Socially mobile Puerto Ricans who sought to distance themselves from more recent migrants were now referring to themselves as "Hispanos." Both Hispano and Latino identity formations were efforts to create a cohesive representative voice, to underscore distinctions, and, at the same time, to homogenize populations, enabling individuals to cloak themselves in diverse contexts and situations. Yet, the descriptors, simultaneously, enabled outsiders to substitute stereotypes for the living people.

In 1953 Martin Ortiz, director of the Mexican American Council, had initiated a semi-public discussion on the "Spanish-speaking population": "Mr. Vega and I were in full agreement on the fact that its [*sic*] not merely a problem of Mexicans or Puerto Ricans but rather, a problem facing persons of Spanish-speaking background. . . . Of course, Puerto Ricans have one advantage, basically, over persons of Mexican descent in that they are U.S. citizens."[111] Ortiz's memo to Hollis Vick of the Welfare Council was conveying a latinidad that acknowledged variances—the "Spanish-speaking population" clearly shared concerns and circumstances, but as on matters of citizenship, it was critical to recognize intergroup differences. Puerto Ricans were US citizens; Mexicans included citizens but noncitizens as well. The caveats, the ambiguity, and the commonalities were to resonate with later debates on the importance of a unified base without neutralization of distinctions that mark an individual group's experience as unique.[112]

But had Puerto Ricans ever been the "problem" Chicago said they were? The fact was, the 20,000+ Puerto Ricans of Chicago in 1954 represented less than 1 percent of the population on relief in that city. Even more notable, throughout 1954, Puerto Ricans never reached 1 percent of the city's population.[113] Despite this, the city's welfare commissioner had proclaimed them a problem and this had described for many a fact and for others an issue for debate. The residual effect of the Puerto Rican repatriation debate and the roundups of Nationalists would persist over decades to come for a people marginalized by two seemingly contrary tendencies—welfare dependency on the one hand, and radical terrorism on the other—a near fatal coupling of images, both essentially false, but nevertheless effective in shaping Chicagoans' sense of who their Puerto Rican neighbors were. Thus, early Puerto Rican community formation in Chicago was built on misinformation and silences, on episodes incredibly public at one historical moment, and today almost unremembered or never known, but present all the same in consequence.

The events of 1954 suggest how a Puerto Rican identity, latinidad, and claims to the city of Chicago were constructed by, and about, this population, revealing Puerto Ricans' second-class citizenship in practice but also demonstrating how Puerto Ricans made themselves "residents" of the state and the city, gaining a citizenship other citizens did not have to struggle for. Pioneering Puerto Ricans of the first decade, arriving from 1946 to the mid-1950s, troubled themselves to learn how to maneuver through city neighborhoods, how to obtain social services, and, most important, how to lobby for access to public resources and social entitlements. They were navigating the obstacles set in their way over the terrain of residency and citizenry. There was indeed a "problem," but it was predominantly one of US racial prejudice and how it came to modify, but then to strengthen, the sense Puerto Ricans had of themselves, as well as how it came to form a collective consciousness.

3 NEIGHBORHOOD OBITUARIES, RESILIENT COMMUNITIES

Between 1977 and 1979, thirty-two young men and women, all under the age of twenty-one, were murdered in Chicago's Logan Square.[1] In 1978 my cousin Danny was one of those, gunned down by a rival gang at nineteen in an alley near my family home on Armitage Avenue, the tragic circumstances concealed from my sisters and me. My most vivid memory from that time is of walking with my parents and sisters along Palmer Square from St. Sylvester Church with others of the congregation, to join our Near Northwest Side neighbors on our way to demonstrate against gang violence. We headed up Kedzie Boulevard to "The Eagle," a seventy-foot Doric column (about as high as a seven-story building) with an eagle at its top. Designed by the architect of the Lincoln Memorial in Washington, DC, to mark the centennial of Illinois's entry into the Union, it was the heart of Logan Square and we were community citizens.[2]

Twenty-seven years later, in July 2001, more than 300 Logan Square residents followed the exact same route in another procession to The Eagle. The deaths mourned were not those of young male victims of gang violence but deaths of houses. Housing that neighborhood people could afford had died or, rather, had been killed in the wake of gentrification. On the steps of St. Sylvester Church, Father Michael Herman, the quirkily charismatic pastor, proclaimed, "Our funeral procession begins at St. Sylvester because our congregation is being pushed out of the neighborhood, and forced to move away from the community that they built. . . . Many of our people can no longer afford to rent apartments, pay their real estate taxes, or buy homes in this community. Something must be done to make balanced development a reality in Logan Square!"[3] Adult pallbearers carried a coffin filled with tiny replicas of houses, and following them came young and old, each holding a cardboard house like a miniature casket in their hands. The miniature houses represented rental units lost to demolition or to upscale condominium conversions that had evicted neighborhood Latinos. Soon after, *The Eagle News*, official newsletter of the Logan Square Neighborhood Association, published "obituaries" of some of the dead houses and documented the number of families lost to the community.[4] Ana La Luz, a pint-sized, tough-love grandmother, told me, a few months later: *"Ese era el momento de dar a conocer nuestro sentir de lo que esta pasando en la vecindad"* ("That was the moment to make our feelings known about what is happening in the neighborhood"). In my mind, and not in mine alone, memories have survived of these two processions protesting violence and death a quarter of a century apart but intertwined, each a public witness to the long struggle of a people to ground themselves, to build community in a safe neighborhood without threat of death or displacement. Both testified to the death of neighborhood identity but also to the resiliency of community.

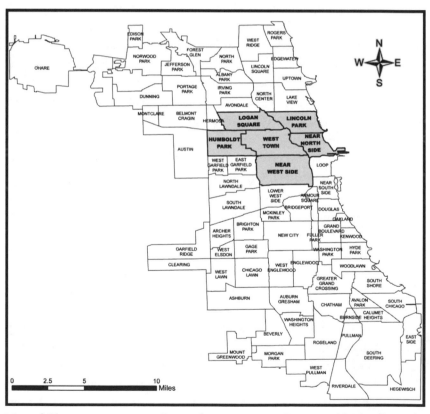

Map of Chicago communities. Past and present Puerto Rican neighborhoods on the North Side of the city are highlighted. *Map by Sharron Macklin, Williams College; data courtesy of City of Chicago and ESRI, Inc., July 2011*

Gentrified Memories: "Seems Just Like Yesterday on Armitage Street"

In narratives of place and community, people who inhabit place evoke their sense of past belonging or of loss of belonging in order to make sense of the present. In the prime of urban renewal, from 1954 to the 1970s, Puerto Ricans were, in effect, expelled from Lincoln Park—which once had a prominent Puerto Rican presence prior to becoming one of Chicago's hottest real estate markets—three miles north of the central business district and near the lakefront. The social and spatial mapping of Chicago has centered on its two most valuable assets, the Lake and the Loop.

The city's location on the edge of Lake Michigan provided a spectacular view and leisure site; the lake was also a principal source of water (and a channel for waste). The Loop, Chicago's central business district, was second only to the lakefront as the city's prime location, the lake to the east, the Loop at the city's core, with the North and the South branches of the Chicago River and the system of railways completing Chicago's semicircular spatial layout. The lakefront properties south of the Loop were favored by the wealthy and, by 1900—once the flow of the North Branch of the Chicago River, in a notable civil engineering feat for its time, was reversed from Lake Michigan, a clean water source, toward the Mississippi River—so were those north of the Loop.[5] In 1917, to make the riverfront more charming while also directing commercial traffic around the Loop, plans were underway to build a double-decker, bascule bridge (a moveable bridge that opens at the center, the first of its kind) connecting north and south Michigan Avenue across the river. Completed in 1920, the bridge was considered an engineering marvel of its time and came to represent the "Chicago style bascule." It made possible a new upscale retail district north of the river, the Magnificent Mile.[6] Chicago's working class settled in the space that remained amid the immigrant enclaves of large industry.

In the 1920s social scientists of the University of Chicago formed a Local Community Research Committee, an interdisciplinary research group committed to theoretical and applied research, and took on the task of ordering the city. The group included faculty members from the departments of sociology, political science, and economics, its goal scientific observation and historical study. The product of the endeavor was a famed "community area" map, which coordinated with the model metropolis (concentric circles' model) proposed by Chicago School sociologist Ernest Burgess. Based on the city's semicircular arrangement, the model identified mutually exclusive geographic areas of settlement. Many decades later, it remains an important tool for tracking the city's demographic changes; the community area configuration in expanded form is still used by students, business and civic leaders, planners, developers and real estate brokers, and even by ordinary Chicagoans, to describe and characterize the city and its people.[7] Burgess's centrifugal model charted the core business district and four other sectors: a zone in transition, a zone of working peoples' homes, a residential zone, and a commuter zone. Movement in the direction of the outer rings signified socioeconomic mobility upward and assimilation of those on the economic fringe into more reputable zones.[8] "Residential zone," apparently, referred discreetly to middle- and upper-class homes. But the model, and the configuration of communities, was more graphic and more conjectural than human in its evidence. While racialized immigrant populations were a central focus of community studies in general, race was not explicit in the model, and consideration of the growing African American community was conspicuously absent. The 1945 publication of St. Clair Drake and Horace Cayton's *Black Metropolis: A Study of Negro Life in a Northern City* changed that.[9] Also adding a ripple, with consideration of populations that did not fall neatly within the sharply bipolar racial imagination of the city, was a 1947 master's thesis in anthropology, "Puerto Rican Immigrants in New York and Chicago: A Study in Comparative Assimilation," by Elena Padilla, the young student-migrant from Puerto Rico to the University of Chicago.[10]

Puerto Ricans in Chicago managed, over the next half century, to live a neighborhood existence within a rigid racially organized black/white Chicago. Though race was not broached in the scholars' model, and played no significant role in the scholarship of the decades between the two World Wars, Chicago still had come to be considered in common discourse a city polarized between white descendants of earlier migrant waves and blacks who had migrated North in search of jobs and a better life. Puerto Ricans were absent from popular accounts, the role they played of intervening between white and black overlooked. Yet, Puerto Ricans had become a buffer of a sort that, together with the earlier migration and immigration of Mexicans, contradicted the political and social sense of the city as dualistic. Urban scholars, especially those of the noted Chicago School, had not fully understood the complex dimensions of identity, race, and space that, in real life, troubled a black and white divide. The Chicago School's ordering of the city meant, further, that class and racialized notions of spaces and their inhabitants came to seem appropriate in describing the making of a Latino Chicago in debates on housing. The people of Puerto Rican descent and identity whom I interviewed consistently turned to the concept of the "community area," as designed by the Chicago School, in explications of themselves and of their neighborhoods and communities within the landscape of the city as a whole. Nonetheless, neither architectural layout of zones nor scholarly model truly reflect the complex realities and life experiences of those who actually live in Chicago and those who have been displaced and pushed out.

A prime example of such a neighborhood is the Puerto Rican community in Lincoln Park, centered on Armitage and Halsted, obliterated by urban renewal.[11] A substantial sum in urban renewal funds was allocated, in 1954, for "redevelopment" in Lincoln Park. The resultant high-end housing priced many low-income, especially Puerto Rican, residents out of their community despite efforts to stave off displacement and despite protests by the Young Lords. The Young Lords, once a street gang of mainly second-generation Puerto Rican youth, by the late-1960s, led by José "Cha-Cha" Jimenez, had become a grassroots political organization of socially conscious young men and women; they took collective action against displacement, organized a much needed, though short-lived, day care program, and demanded a percentage of subsidized low-income housing set-asides.[12] In Lincoln Park, in devalued and segregated spaces, the Young Lords and their collaborators had organized, created, and defended Puerto Rican barrios and Puerto Rican interests but could not prevent the loss of neighborhood.[13]

David Hernández, Chicago's unofficial poet laureate, wrote a poem, "Armitage Street," that was a eulogy to Lincoln Park, the once vibrant working-class community razed by urban renewal, a neighborhood a few miles east of my own Armitage Avenue home in Logan Square. In the poem, he marvels at the neighborhood-scape, contrasting its now polished buildings, upscale specialty stores, and trendy souls with neighborhoods of his memory:

> It seems just like yesterday on Armitage Street
> that Alfredo and Cha-Cha played hide and seek
> with Quinto the cop while Cosmo and Aidita
> made love in the gangway.
>   When radios blared out open windows
>   dressed in five and dime lace curtains.
> when staccato Spanish bounced between
> buildings high above the rolling traffic
> because telephones were insultingly impersonal
> and it was no secret that eyes expressed the heart.
>   When rice and bean smells
>   roamed the hallways covering up

the tracks of other ethnics who had
since faded into the American Dream.
. . ..
When the last summer days were spent
under street rainbow firehydrant showers
and that night you overheard your parents whisper
about moving out because the rent was going up.[14]

In the two decades from the 1970s to the 1990s many Puerto Ricans and other Latino residents moved out of Lincoln Park, especially westward, each time with painful labor and personal risks, converting decaying neighborhoods into spaces of pride and sense of place—a new home space. As the interwoven stories about collective memory, racialization, and belonging reveal, Puerto Ricans who were, in effect, pushed out of Lincoln Park sought to create and sustain affordable and safe neighborhoods elsewhere where youth and families would be neither expendable nor disposable. The history of Puerto Ricans in Chicago has proved to be an episodic pattern of constant movement: of loss and finding and more loss.

The onset of World War II sparked several distinct waves of migration into Chicago, internal and across borders, especially among African Americans, Puerto Ricans, and Mexicans; all three groups had trekked to Chicago in search of jobs and better opportunities, more than 600,000 settling in the city between 1940 and 1960. The rapid influx saturated the existing housing stock, particularly in working-class and poor neighborhoods, spaces sociologist Ernest Burgess named "zones in transition" but commonly known as "slums." The newcomers inherited these spaces. In the postwar era, federal programs hastened growth of the suburbs and decline of the central city, as thousands of white middle class and affluent escaped the urban neighborhoods, accelerated by a federal interstate highway program and a mortgage subsidy for returning veterans. The "inner city" areas (i.e., black communities or what largely became black communities) were ineligible for government mortgage funding because the housing stock there did not meet Federal Housing Authority's criteria, or its minimum standard for lot size and detachment from existing structures. Property owners discovered ways to profit from "racial succession," charging higher rents to African Americans and other incoming residents of color. African Americans paid a hefty price as they sought refuge from the density of their old neighborhoods, and as realtors perpetuated white fears of housing devaluation that might follow black settlement in or near an area. "White flight" unlocked a number of neighborhoods for black residential living in areas adjoining existing black belts, thus enhancing and reinforcing racial concentration.[15]

The Housing Act of 1954 provided federal funds to local governments to acquire and clear land that "targeted not only slums, but also blighted, and even potentially blighted areas," but the commitment to low-income housing development was later waived to make hospitals and universities the key beneficiaries, a program that came to be known as "urban renewal," dubbed "Negro removal" by African Americans, and "Puerto Rican removal" in cities like Chicago with significant Puerto Rican populations.[16] Through displacement of residents, urban renewal, ostensibly intended to improve housing of the poor, intensified the concentration of poverty even more, and the new highway systems served as physical barriers between sections of the city where the poor lived. In Chicago, as elsewhere, it was a dynamic that invariably came to devastate central business districts and to isolate the poor even further.[17]

Puerto Rican migration to Chicago, which had begun modestly in the mid-1940s, reached its highest point in the 1960s, but, between the 1950s and the 1970s, as the Puerto Rican population of the city rose from 2,555 to 79,582, employment opportunities dwindled.[18] A quarter of a million jobs disappeared between 1967 and 1982, 46 percent of them in manufacturing. With the consequent eroded status of labor unions, workers' wages and benefits headed south, as did employment opportunities. Latinos, largely in menial positions in the labor market, found their wages further downgraded.[19] Stable working-class communities, especially those in the direct path of new development projects, were disregarded and disrupted. Between 1960 and 1980, with the movement of white middle-class residents to the suburbs, Chicago lost more than 30 percent of its middle-class families. Declining economic trends and the white flight of the 1960s and 1970s created urban centers with a "majority-minority"—chiefly African American and Latino—encircled by white suburbs.

With the white middle-class out-migration, retail establishments, industry, politicians, and the business and civic elite realized that disinvestment left the central city in a state of economic crisis. City leaders developed a growth plan centered on economic resuscitation of the downtown area, an increasingly popular ideology of growth said to benefit all urban residents. As the city's overall economy stabilized, the argument went, generating profit with the revival of commerce and of the tax-base of a returning middle class, jobs and housing would trickle down to the poor. The federal government, too, experimented with efforts to revitalize the central city.[20] Efforts centered on a rebirth of the Loop as a tourist and convention center; growth of a high-tech, high-paid information economy with a low-skilled, low-wage service labor counterpart; and redevelopment of former mixed-use and industrial neighborhoods and lakefront properties for upscale living—in other words, on the revival of commerce and a tax-base of middle-class residents.[21]

In a 1971 interview in the *Chicago Sun-Times* for a special series on "The Latins," Jesus Zerefino Ochoa, associate director of the Chicago Archdiocesan Latin American Committee, voiced poor folks' understanding of urban renewal: "The city needs revenue to function, and most revenue is going to the suburbs, so the city loses potential revenue. Urban renewal is a try to attract middle class people for revenue purposes. But, poor people say, 'We don't mind renewal, but we ask a place to live, because we're part of society too.' We understand the game. It's revenue . . . we also recognize that poor people represent a problem. We want to be included in solving it."[22] Despite recognizing that urban renewal would provide little room for their own housing and daily living needs, the poor and working class sought to work with city officials and more affluent residents to develop a process that would avoid their own continual displacement from the communities they had labored to build and transform.

The Continuing Trek of the La Luz Family: "Little by Little, We Worked Hard to Raise the Neighborhood"

"Oh my child, here is where the history is." Ana La Luz, a tiny grandmother with a measured voice that conveys a giant presence, was telling stories of Puerto Rican struggles for place in Chicago. I sat at her dining room table on a chilly March afternoon in 2002 captivated by her tale of a pioneering generation that laid a groundwork for future generations in the United States: "Those of us who came first, like we say over there in Puerto Rico, '*molimo vidrio.*' And do you know what *moler vidrio* is?" she asked. Then, before I could offer a response, she replied, "To break glass and mangle your hands. We're always pushed and marginalized but those of us who came— *molimo vidrio.*"

Moler vidrio literally means to grind glass; or, in Ana's words, "to break glass and mangle your hands." It is a saying deployed in accounts of how one (or a collective) confronts difficult circumstances. It implies a willingness to suffer the injuries of breaking down barriers. As a practical consciousness, moler vidrio constitutes the grueling, sometimes impairing, and often undetected daily labor that goes into nurturing hope: the resilient conviction that everyday life should, and can, be better and more meaningful, even as lived experiences demonstrate otherwise. With this phrase, Ana mobilized memories of a working-class politics in which the past is retrieved and revised to make sense of conditions in the present as well as to cultivate the formation of collective identities born out of both affirmative and disparaging circumstances.

Ana La Luz had migrated from Puerto Rico to Chicago on September 19, 1952. Her sister in Chicago had just become engaged and Ana had come to help out. The sister had a "huge apartment" on the Near North Side facing Holy Name Cathedral, the base of the Roman Catholic Archdiocese of Chicago. "It was spacious but, for me, it was like a jail cell because in Puerto Rico we lived in open air." Two years later Ana married and with her husband Jacobo, a worker at Inland Steel, relocated to East Chicago, Indiana, just outside Chicago. In more than three decades together, the La Luz family had lived in numerous neighborhoods, calling each one, in turn, "home," from the Near North Side, East Chicago, and the Loop, to the Gold Coast, and Old Town. As Ana mentioned each locale to me she blurted out, "¡*Olvídate*!" (Forget about it!). "We Latinos can't go over there," she hissed. "Who can live there? Who can buy there?" By exclaiming "¡*Olvídate*!" rather than the familiar "¡*presente*!" that usually accompanies place affirmations, Ana sustained the memory of what had been Latino neighborhoods before latinidad was evicted.

The pattern was evident: as soon as a Latino neighborhood gained some stability it was designated a "conservation" project, an area slated for urban renewal, and thus for removal of the poor, mainly African Americans and Puerto Ricans. Ramon Campos, a former member of the Lincoln Park Association, told a *Chicago Daily News* reporter, "We have the unique distinction of living in the fanciest neighborhoods, but before they become fancy."[23] My own father, Luis Rúa, an astute observer of the changing value of Chicago neighborhoods, told me many times, "if you want to know where to buy property in the next up-and-coming neighborhood look to where the Puerto Ricans are living." Given the historical record, Ana's words "We're always pushed and marginalized but those of us who came [to Chicago] . . . *molimo vidrio*," poignantly convey the daunting task faced by the pioneering generation of Chicago Puerto Ricans who sought to produce locality in inhospitable places.[24]

In the Old Town neighborhood of Lincoln Park, Ana and her brother had purchased the family's first Chicago home in the early 1960s, a three-flat building. "*Trabajamos noche y dia para levantar comunidad*" ("we worked night and day to uplift community") "*antes de subir la vecindad*" ("before the

Aerial view of Logan Square. The map shows the central portion of the community area and highlights points of interest. *Map by Sharron Macklin, Williams College; data courtesy of City of Chicago and ESRI, Inc., July 2011*

I-90/94 E

Logan
Blvd.

W Logan Blvd ☆

N Sacramento Ave

N Milwaukee Ave

N California Ave

St.
Sylvester
Church ☆

N Humboldt Blvd

N
W ✦ E
S

Map Key
☆ Points of Interest
——— Roads

neighborhood went up"). There was a critical distinction between "*levantar comunidad*" and "*subir la vecindad,*" with "*levantar comunidad*" suggesting a communal uplift of people and place, and "*subir la vecindad*" signifying a market-driven elevation of land and property to put it out of reach for the great majority of residents.[25] In the process of "subir la vecindad," scores of Latinos were uprooted by the process of renewal from their apartments and houses in Lincoln Park, the Near North Side, and the Near West Side, "crowding them further into remaining Latin barrios and sending them westward in expanding waves to create new Spanish ghettos."[26] Merging with compatriots from the Near West Side (also undergoing massive urban renewal), a new distinct geographic Puerto Rican community took shape on the Near North West Side (West Town, Humboldt Park, and Logan Square) with Humboldt Park widely proclaimed as the nucleus of Puerto Rican Chicago. In the summer of 1966 Humboldt Park was the site of an early Puerto Rican urban rebellion in response to the shooting of Aracelis Cruz, twenty years old, by a white police officer during the Puerto Rican Day Parade festivities in the park.[27] The rebellion was a public response to a long history of abuse at the hands of police and to the daily experiences of economic and political marginalization in the city.[28] The collective memory of "localization," understanding the role of institutional power arrangements in the regulation and segregation of everyday life, was vital in the history people told of this spatial community.[29]

In the 1960s, as the city implemented the renewal plan, Old Town and Lincoln Park were transformed from "poor peoples'" places into elite neighborhoods. Puerto Ricans and African Americans were displaced by the loss of affordable rental units or priced out of the housing market altogether.[30] The La Luz family, unable to meet the high-end property demands or to fit in with the changing racial character of the area, sold their three-flat apartment building in Old Town. "We sold the building without having a place to live," Ana told me. "We would knock on . . . apartments 'for rent' and when I would tell them—not that we were seven, when I would tell them four or five, the women would faint. And [say] no. And the banks, in everything they rejected us." So the La Luzes bought a small single-family house in the Palmer Square section of Logan Square in the Near Northwest Side. By the 1970s and 1980s, Logan Square, settled by more upwardly mobile Latinos like the La Luz family, was considered a "classic step-up" community.[31] "[T]he fact that more and more Latins are buying houses even if they get cheated by unscrupulous real estate salesmen and even if it means other ethnic groups are fleeing the city, is, to some observers, an encouraging sign of upward mobility," observed a *Sun-Times* reporter in 1971.[32] But, for the La Luz family, Logan Square was hardly a "step up" from where they had moved in the beginning of 1960s—Old Town/Lincoln Park, in the Near North Side was, at the close of the decade, under state-sponsored "revitalization." Logan Square was a "step down" from there.

In the early twentieth century, Logan Square had been a flourishing commercial and residential center, home to Germans, Norwegians, Poles, and Russian Jews. Families had doubled up and subdivided capacious apartments in an effort to survive the Depression. In the thirty years between 1930 and 1960 housing construction was meager and there was a gradual loss in the local industrial sector. A slow but steady population decline began. Construction of the Kennedy Expressway, which bisected the eastern edge of the community, exacerbated the decline and speeded a mass departure. More than 22,000 whites left Logan Square between 1950 and 1960. Along the commercial corridors, businesses closed up shop and some empty storefronts appeared. Even the new construction and refurbishing of aged commercial and residential properties and new retail franchises that prompted revival in the early half of the 1960s failed to stymie the loss of population. In 1930 there were 114,000 inhabitants, in the 1970 census fewer than 85,000.[33] Disinvestment and white flight left the least desirable sections of Logan Square, and other neighborhoods on the Near Northwest Side, to blacks and Latinos, the La Luz family among them.

A reporter contributing to the *Sun-Times'* special series on "The Latins," in September 1971, told the story of Rudolph Melchiore, a real estate agent who had swindled a number of Latinos into buying substandard properties riddled with housing code violations. Mrs. Angela Rivera, "a grandmother with a shock of silver hair framing her handsome bronze face," had had enough. She "poked her finger into [Melchiore's] burly chest" and boomed: "You stop selling the buildings with violations or you don't sell no more buildings in the whole city of Chicago—not to Spanish people or American people." More than 100 Latinos attended a community protest meeting in the gym of St. Sylvester School in Palmer Square organized by an "anti-panic peddling group," the West Side Coalition. The same *Sun-Times* reporter wrote, "Chicago's Latins are pushed into buying homes hurriedly, without careful planning, by a series of circumstances that conspire to make them, along with blacks, the city's poorest-housed minority."[34]

The dire need for accommodations and the difficulties faced in renting apartments had driven Latinos like the La Luzes to buy instead. The house they bought in Palmer Square needed much repair, as did the neighborhood.

"The neighborhood was really bad, full of gangs," Ana told me. The La Luz family, and the other Latinas/os who would arrive in Logan Square a few years later, had inherited a neighborhood in decline. The *Sun-Times* story described in great detail "rotting stairwells, crumbling plaster, and peeling and worn out plumbing." Still, residents feared losing even this housing to "the urban renewal bulldozer."[35] When Ana told me how she and her family *sufrieron* (suffered) in Palmer Square, she did not describe a bleak or irredeemable community, but told a story of community activism: "Little by little, we worked hard to raise the neighborhood." Successive small acts set in motion a transformation of this neighborhood of urban decay into one of pride with a sense of place. A "home" emerged. It took backbreaking manual labor and a great deal of pain of the spirit to transform and create such a landscape anew and to make hope real, while, at the same time reinforcing historical memory of working-class politics in the production of locality—in short, molieron vidrio.[36]

Residents had worked on two fronts to claim each successive neighborhood—one front against the intimidation tactics of young gang members, and the other front, against the excessive actions or inactions of law enforcement. Ana told me of almost daily gang harassment of her youngest son Santiago, in the early 1980s. By then a widow, she kept an even more watchful eye on her son and sent him less frequently to run errands; avoidance was a strategy of protection from gang violence. But, when Santiago, at about sixteen, witnessed a car accident involving a gang member and gave a statement to the police, avoidance as a tactic was no longer possible. Apart from its use of harassment as a recruitment strategy, the gang deployed harassment to protect their prized economic venture—the distribution and sale of drugs— and that evening after the car accident someone phoned Ana's house to threaten Santiago.[37] Panic-stricken, Ana packed bags for Santiago and for Lucia, her youngest daughter, and, early the following morning, her two youngest children were on a plane headed out of state to stay with an older sister in Virginia.

Though a deeply religious person, Ana did not resign herself to fate or "God's will." She went to a neighbor, a police officer, for help. "You alone can't do anything. Me alone—even being a police officer, can't do anything," he had said. Ana told me, "The kids left Wednesday in the morning and Wednesday at 4:00, when I came home from work, I went door-to-door knocking on all the doors. . . . I exposed myself to anything but . . . my kids came first. . . . And I talked to the block." A community meeting was held at the police officer's house to try to stop gang dominance of the neighborhood. Ana was operating from intertwined commitments: mothering, labor, and politics, a set of intersections sociologist Nancy Naples refers to as "activist mothering." In effect, Ana and her neighbors had elected to try "cooperative self-help."[38]

"The whole neighborhood came outside," Ana said of a later occasion, to support a neighbor who had been beaten by gang members after he told a group of young men in the street early one morning to quiet down. "In pajamas, in house dresses, or whatever . . . we came out and the police realized that we were united." A group from the block attended the court session where the judge reprimanded the young man (a friend of Ana's son) who had assaulted the neighbor: "You see all these people here are united so do me a favor and leave these people alone." The neighborhood "didn't change . . . totally, but it did change a lot," Ana told me. "Little by little the block was picking up and cleaning up." But improvement came at a potential cost. "I exposed myself two times" [to possible retribution and] "the man next door also did," she confided. The gang had "threatened to burn down three houses—mine, the man next door['s], [and another] one." Yet Ana continued to believe in, to borrow from historians Robin Kelley and Earl Lewis, the power "to make our world anew."[39]

A constellation of actions had set in motion the transformation of the community—neighbors confronting gang members, residents coming out of their homes to bear witness to altercations of law enforcement's responses, and a critical mass attending the trial as a community. In consequence, law enforcement and the legal system had taken notice of the residents' sense of themselves as a valued and viable community—a space worthy of defense.[40] More broadly, the residents had taken a defensive stance against the stereotype of their community as a "culture of poverty," one of potential crime that continually questions their respectability and national belonging. They acted in what anthropologist Ana Yolanda Ramos-Zayas describes as a "politics of worthiness."[41]

Ana took care not to alienate wayward youth in her neighborhood by stigmatizing them as "bad" or "worthless." She recognized some of the young men as friends of her own son, "good kids" heading down a wrong path. She understood that the failure of the school system and the criminal justice system to serve the needs of youth, among others in the community, contributed to their recalcitrant behavior. Sociologist and Chicago native Marixsa Alicea, drawing on her own family's intracity migration patterns tells a story of racial domination and exclusion, a grounding that provided "a quiet, tacit understanding and knowledge of the larger processes at work that led our

youth to join gangs, . . . [we] knew that not all young people in our community were in gangs."[42] A similar comprehension of larger processes at work was
evident in 1984 when Latina/o parents demonstrated against the dropout
rate of Latina/o students and against gang violence in the schools and in communities of Chicago, understanding that the two were causally related.[43]

The Changing Value of Place

Since the 1980s, Chicago, like other parts of the country, experienced a
marked shift in government policy from public efforts to reintegrate youth
into educational programs and labor markets, to punitive strategies: mass arrests of youth for petty crimes (like loitering and graffiti), harsher penalties
for certain types of drug trafficking (disproportionately singling out youth
from low-income urban neighborhoods), and the imposition of trial and sentencing of juvenile offenders as adults.[44] The State of Illinois's seeming lack of
concern for the future of its Latina/o youths presented an overwhelming
challenge to another longstanding member of the Near Northwest Side community, Otilia Irizarry, a shapely woman of generous spirit who often confronted gang activity while trying to protect the rights of youth in the
neighborhood. Deeply involved in community affairs, especially issues with
law enforcement, during a May 2002 conversation with me, Otilia puzzled
over the difficulties of building decent neighborhoods:

> So it's been very difficult because you have a meeting and the police
> come . . . and you invite a person to attend the meeting, but . . . the
> mother that goes there, [is] the mother of the very kid that's in the
> gang. So how do you talk, how are you going to tell the police that,
> "Look the gang is eating us up." . . . Look at how difficult, if . . . there
> is a kid that has problems with the police, and then you speak out,
> you call the police with that problem and then what happens is that
> the police, when they come, they take that one and all that are with
> him even though they are not at fault. Or else . . . the police take him
> and . . . drop him off in rival gang territory. [Members of the rival
> gang] are going to give him a beating . . . It is very conflicting for a
> person with heart. . . . If you don't have a heart, if you don't care, you
> say, "look, put them in jail, all of them." But I am a mother and I have
> nephews, and furthermore . . . I love the people, I don't want . . . any-
> one to have something bad happen that they didn't deserve. . . . For
> that reason, sometimes . . . if I can't give complete information . . . I've

opted to shut my mouth . . . And it's not that I say, "Oh well, since they don't bother me . . ." Because, yes, it does bother me that the other kids are losing themselves to the drugs they sell.

Such compassion for youth is not purely altruistic. Women like Ana La Luz and Otilia Irizarry imagine an alternative way of life for themselves, their families, and their community, and to realize such a vision they take part in community affairs. Because they want to feel safe where they live, they, in turn, seek to help others feel safe. The question for them becomes, how do we create safe spaces? And, much more difficult, how do we do so inclusively? Otilia, addressing issues of police involvement in neighborhood affairs, considered both the position of a gang member's mother and of the members of the gang. She pondered the possible repercussions before expressing her apprehensions in a public forum, prudently taking into account the role her public statements play in outside judgments of her community, the geographic area and the people. She tried to ensure a sympathetic space where even the most disruptive "insiders" feel they can contribute in some fashion. Dismayed by the many "lost" youth, Otilia still desperately searches for ways to improve the quality of life in the community, in the hope of assisting youth without exiling them, without locking them up, or without sentencing them to death.[45] She has spoken out against mass incarceration used as a remedy for unsafe neighborhoods precisely because the suspension of justice for underserved and systematically targeted youth in the name of the public good further exacerbates economic, social, racial, and educational disparities. Her broader sense of fairness stems from an ability to theorize from the personal.[46]

Yet the daunting realities of these communities can provoke, even in the most dedicated, a degree of indifference. Former Chicago Mayor Richard M. Daley once accused Puerto Rican parents of protecting the criminal actions of Puerto Rican gangs. What some interpret as protection or indifference or abetting criminal activity, others interpret as a means of maintaining some sense of fairness for a population often routinely perceived as criminal. In Chicago, unfortunately, "being Puerto Rican and young has been made synonymous with being criminal," in the words of urban studies scholar John Betancur.[47] Refusing to take part in an injustice in the name of justice, Otilia sometimes opts for silence on matters where she feels that cooperating with police will produce no beneficial outcomes for the community, in particular for systematically targeted members.

Otilia Irizarry, like Ana La Luz, is living evidence of responsibility for enlisting the police in community affairs. "We call police" read flyers in the windows of homes in the community, but policing, for these women, and in this context, requires much thought, tact, and negotiation. For Otilia, to call police is almost a last resort.[48] Akin to Patricia Hill Collins's notion of "Black feminist thought," Otilia and Ana's grounded Latina standpoint visualizes the world in which they live not as a place of mere survival, but a place they feel they possess and are accountable to.[49]

Celebrated Broadcast Journalist Ray Suarez, refugee from the now polished neighborhoods of Lincoln Park, bought his own first home in Logan Square "after a lifetime in apartments." In his book, *The Old Neighborhood: What We Lost in the Great Suburban Migration, 1966–1999*, Suarez writes of the real risks residents faced in efforts to create a safe and attractive neighborhood.[50] People exposed themselves to the potential of fatal retaliation, as when Ana's home was targeted for arson. For Suarez, an indication of the effectiveness of the courage of such individuals had been the entry of "young white buyers, who wouldn't even have driven down this street a few years before." The residents I spoke with myself, however, were less sanguine about the movement of "young white buyers" into the neighborhood as a gauge of success. "I think that we've done a grand 'improvement' as white people say," Ana boasted cautiously. "Even though we are much happier in one sense . . . in another we're not . . . They are pushing us, once again, west." Residents spoke of "young white buyers" coming into the neighborhood as a gauge of regress, and also as an indication of something else: a loss on their own profit. The idea of risk for long-term residents is qualitatively different from the investment risk faced by potential homebuyers and private developers. The investment of long-term residents, which had led to community stability, is now experienced as loss. Potential buyers benefit, although they may not acknowledge it, from the gains (labor) of those who came earlier with limited residential options and who upgraded the property and the security of the community.

Some Latinos did not credit the marked improvements in the community to the labor and risks of their Latino neighbors. Luis, a Palmer Square resident interviewed by Suarez who came to Chicago from Puerto Rico in 1953, lived on the corner of Palmer Square and Kedzie Boulevard for seventeen years. He had dreadful memories of his first days in the neighborhood with his three young sons; his eldest had been stabbed in the head three times by gang members, though he survived. For Luis, Palmer Square was "now getting real nice." He did not see "the 'whitening' of Palmer Square as any kind of threat, or part of some wider conspiracy to relocate Puerto Ricans from an established barrio." The white people moving into the neighborhood, his "new, unknown neighbors—naturally brought better police protection, garbage pick-up, and the power to get the city to fix up the park with them." Implied in Luis's remarks was the idea that the city government and other social institutions would do little to improve neighborhood life for people like him.[51]

Palmer Square had been designed and developed, at the beginning of the twentieth century, "along the lines of an old carriage-racing oval," as Suarez described it, with a row of old homes and apartment buildings, "with ornamental stone and terra-cotta facades."[52] In the center of the square was a seven-acre green space, Palmer Park. I myself was a student at St. Sylvester grammar school in the 1980s and Palmer Park served as our playground and, sometimes, our gym. My classmates and I would see Ray Suarez walk to the train station on his way to work downtown at WMAQ (Channel 5, an NBC affiliate), and yell, "Hey, Ray!" He always waved back at the young Latinas and Latinos in their brown and yellow uniforms playing in the park. We watched him faithfully on the evening news. The park was the dividing marker between rival gangs, after dark their gathering place for drinking, joyrides, and fighting. Later, the park itself was contested between old and new residents, the old to preserve it from danger, the new to preserve it from the damage of leisurely use by those who did not live on the square.

Those with homes on the square formed the Homeowners Association of Palmer Square. They had restored their homes to their original glamour and wanted now to restore the park as a pedestrian place. Police thinned out the shrubs and plants to simplify maintenance and to provide a clearer view for policing. "NO BALLPLAYING" signs erupted from the lampposts. But, for neighbors from the crowded side streets and apartment buildings "short on safe parks . . . and open space," Palmer Park was "a place for cookouts, bicycle riding, and ball games."[53] "The homeowners also bought trees," Suarez said, "and planted them throughout the park" to make playing ball difficult.[54] Carlos, a community activist and neighbor of Suarez's, said: "Look, yuppies who live on Palmer don't want young guys to have a place to play. They want someplace to walk their dogs." (Carlos, ironically, walked his own dog there.) "For many Latinos in the neighborhood," Suarez explained, "even those climbing the ladders of American status and economic clout, it is easy to see that change in Palmer Square—from a disputed gang turf to a 'quiet' urban park—meant keeping young Hispanics out."[55]

During my own research in Chicago in the millennium, the threat of losing the barrio came up multiple times in the front office of Caribe Funeral Home on Armitage Avenue, a few blocks west of my childhood home, the dividing line between Humboldt Park and Logan Square. In the plant-filled office one late morning were Gina, her two adult children, Becky and Julio, Nilsa, the office assistant and wife of one of Gina's nephews, and my younger sister, Lissette. Some of us sat on the office bench, the others gathered in a semicircle around the bench. As so many times before, our casual conversation turned into a discussion about changes in the neighborhoods. "People are mad about losing Humboldt Park," Gina said. The park was popularly considered the heart and soul of the Puerto Rican community in Chicago, and, for Gina, the prospect of losing place brought to mind past losses, especially of Lincoln Park. "There are no more Puerto Ricans there," she said. "If tomorrow they changed the name of the street [Armitage Avenue] to Mrs. Bishop, when the neighborhood changes they change the name as if it never existed. Puerto Ricans are always pushed out." In the early days of Puerto Rican Humboldt Park, Gina reminded us, landlords had hired arsonists to torch their own buildings, "to get rid of Puerto Ricans and to collect insurance." "When they wanted that area they tried to force people to sell, [and] if that didn't work they burned them out."[56] There were wakes in Caribe Funeral Home for people whose buildings were set on fire, with local hospitals, being a principal beneficiary of the destruction. Some of the land was then cleared for parking lots: "How do you think it got there?!" Gina asked, adding, "For now, they haven't tried to get rid of us yet." That morning, she pointed out the wrongs of urban renewal and the resultant disinvestment in certain people and places that later came to benefit particular institutions.

A 1993 feature story on Logan Square in the "Apartment and Homes" section of a local paper indicated that some brokers believed "prices will continue to appreciate rapidly in Logan Square, and that it will eventually look more like Lincoln Park than Humboldt Park."[57] Ana's brooding on Latinos' diminishing prospects of living or even walking in Logan Square reflected the fact that balanced development and affordable housing had become urgent community concerns, replacing in priority issues of safety. Residents question whether average families can afford to live there still; they have toiled tirelessly over many years to build a community, only to become strangers in their own place. As landlords themselves, women like Ana La Luz, Otilia Irizarry, and Gina Bishop counter by charging affordable rent for their properties as a means of stabilizing the area in their own way. I myself was able to conduct field research in the rapidly gentrifying neighborhood of my youth only because Gina, who rented me an apartment above the family's funeral parlor, lived her beliefs. This new effort to keep the neighborhood affordable makes evident a community's restorative ability, as well as the new challenges that past achievements (large and small) generate.

The Structure of Feeling of the Barrio

On a Sunday afternoon in April 2001, I walked in on a conversation about crime in the community as I came down the stairs from my apartment above the front office of Caribe Funeral Home. Gina Bishop, my landlady, had asked Ana La Luz, her longtime friend, if she had found tenants for the basement apartment in her building in Palmer Square. "No, not yet," Ana said. The unfurnished $500-a-month, three-bedroom apartment included the cost of heat and had been recently painted. Ana could have rented the apartment at a much higher price but resisted charging the market-rate because she is not a greedy person and is more concerned with finding tenants who neither smoke nor make a lot of noise, and who will maintain the social harmony she has tried to preserve in her building and in her community. The neighborhood borders the communities of Humboldt Park and Logan Square, an area now coveted by real estate in part because it is in Chicago's historic boulevard system, where, in the early part of the twentieth century, wealthy Chicago merchants—the immigrant families of Schwinn, Goldblatt, and Weiboldt (then shunned by Chicago high society)—had built stately homes of their own.[58]

The Shakespeare, a handsome, half-block-long building complex next to Saint Sylvester Church memorialized in *The Eagle News* "housing obituaries" of 2001, during the 1990s had housed thirty-five low-income families—the majority of them Latina/o, and some of them African Americans—under Section 8, a rent subsidy voucher program. The families were notified by the new property owner that they had a year to find other housing—the Shakespeare was to be renovated.[59] Gina and Ana mourn these changes in their community. The losses have been personal, the only Latinos left on Gina's street being her own family and two other families she knew. Thus, Ana spoke of Carmen, a former member of the St. Sylvester Church choir who was paying approximately $1,000 dollars a month for an apartment, "*¡frío!*" (unheated), and desperately sought a more affordable place. The apartment building across from Gina's house, where "all the Latinos were," had been vacated, and she supposed it would now be converted into market-rate condominiums. "*¡Es un crimen!*" ("It's a crime!"). For Gina and Ana, and others like them, this crime meant displacement, the perpetrators outside private developers and the state, all of whom stood to benefit at the expense of the community itself. Once gutted and remodeled, the apartments neighboring St. Sylvester Church itself were not converted into condominiums but advertised as affordable rental units, ranging in price from approximately $1,100 to $1,800 a month.

Many tenants forced to leave were either Section 8 tenants or tenants who had been paying approximately half the current rental rate. Valeria Girón and her husband, Miguel, who had lived in The Shakespeare for more than two decades, now unable to find a comparably sized and priced rental unit or a property to purchase on their factory workers' income, bought a bungalow away from Logan Square in a far Northwest neighborhood following a Latino trend westward, renting out the basement to help pay the mortgage.[60] As I sat across their dining room table in February 2002, Valeria explained, "The poor can no longer live there [Logan Square] because of the prices they are putting on housing." She confided, "For real, Mérida, if they hadn't sold the building I'd still be there today." But, a return to The Shakespeare was out of the question, with the renovated apartments advertised as "affordable" priced from $1,100 to $1,800 a month, even the lowest 80 percent higher than what Valeria had been paying. "What poor person is going to be able to pay that?" She answered her own query: "Only a government employee, or a police officer, or a teacher, or a lawyer, and that's if they don't have a family, because, if they have a family, it will be difficult for them to maintain a family and pay that kind of money. . . . Too much, too much."

Valeria noted the role of race and racism in these power plays over real estate. "They're putting many whites [in Logan Square]. . . . They don't want the Hispanics and, much less, the blacks. They are paying whatever for a piece of land . . . And I don't know if it's because they want to get Hispanics out or because they want the barrio." At $1,000 in rent, it made more sense to Valeria to put that money toward purchasing a home elsewhere, so she did.[61] Araceli, a young, bright Mexican student from the University of Illinois, Chicago, told me, "Hispanics are moving to the suburbs because it's cheaper." Her friend Frida, raising a point that arose in one of her classes at DePaul University, commented that, before, those who had the money moved to the suburbs and the poor stayed in the city. "Now, it's switched." Suburbs, for long considered the epitome of economic success and material consumption, no longer represented that. The city-suburb binary of traditional interpretations of urban decline has taken on lesser value; today, fewer view the city as a place for poor and working-class Latinos and other people of color—especially families.[62]

Private development, concerned principally with financial profit and not with neighborhood dynamics, controlled most of Chicago's new housing construction. Valeria Giron, sensitive about her own displacement from Logan Square, took issue with the extensive construction of condominiums; she believes it has compromised barrio aesthetics not only by marring the character of the built environment (the facades of older structures not maintained in the design of new condominiums), but also, more pressingly, by limiting access to affordable units, thus transforming the ethnoracial, class, and familial composition of the area. Condos, Valeria maintained, do not belong in the barrio; they belong "over there, in Lake Shore Drive, where all those big buildings are because they are taking away a lot of the *barrio's structure*, changing too many things." As a consequence, lakefront development has become housing for upper- and middle-class residents, and is now expanding farther into working-class and poor neighborhoods. Valeria has posed a penetrating critique against the destruction of the physical structures of the neighborhood and the structures of feeling of the barrio.[63] Her defense of the "barrio's structure" echoes the contention of sociologists John Logan and Harvey Molotch that "'sentiment' is indeed at work in structuring the city. . . . but these feelings are bound up with forces originating outside residents' immediate milieus, far beyond the social and geographical boundaries of their routines." Moreover, they remind us: "The city is the setting for the achievements of both exchange values and use values; and the neighborhood is the meeting place of the two forces, where each resident faces the challenge of making a life on a real estate commodity."[64]

Roberto Escalas, in his early thirties, a quintessential Chicago Latino — that is, half-Puerto Rican and half-Mexican — told me:

> We're losing, what *I* saw as a . . . Latino, basically, Puerto Rican community . . . I mentioned before, man, I never *ever* in my life saw people running the dogs in Humboldt Park. . . . It seems like somethin' small, but to me that was . . . big.
>
> I remember walking from [my grammar school] to my grandmother's house [in Wicker Park] and *all* along the way there was . . . *nothing* but kids around . . . I mean there was kids *everywhere*. Every block you went to. I go over there now, you do not see kids out there. I mean, wow . . . that's strange to me.

The unsettling of Roberto's "neighborhood sensibility" helps frame a story about race, place, and power in the urban sphere. His comments reflect a sentiment repeatedly expressed in my interviews with Latinas and Latinos in Chicago's rapidly gentrifying Near Northwest Side and echoed also by the mother of one of my colleagues: "*Ya no hay niños aquí, solamente perros*" ("There are no more children here, only dogs").[65] The child-to-dog allusion marks the structure of feeling and of the felt intensity (and, for some, the absurdity) of gentrification. On many neighborhood sidewalks and parks formerly populated by young people, walking, running, jumping, bicycling, or just hanging out, pedigree dogs are now promenaded by well-to-do owners or hired dog walkers. The number of rental apartments dwindles as pricey, renovated or new, dwellings proliferate. Fashionable shops, eateries, and other businesses appear, some catering to dogs, or advertised as "dog friendly."

A 2007 study that analyzed the remarkable changes in Chicago's housing stock over the last decade and a half identified Logan Square, along with West Town and the Near West Side, as the community areas that have experienced some of the most striking condominium growth and simultaneous apartment decline.[66] The developer of one controversial condominium project insisted that a local first-time buyer could afford the $159,000 selling price of a one-bedroom condo.[67] His logic gave credence to Valeria Girón's conclusion that new developments are not devised for a moderate-income, working-class family, let alone a poor family with children.[68] The decline in state and federal housing assistance, too, has left working-class and poor families vulnerable, especially families of color. Thus, housing advocates, like the Logan Square Neighborhood Association, support an inclusionary zoning policy, with developers required to set aside a certain percentage of new, rehabilitated, or condo conversion units as affordable housing (reiterating the Young Lords' demands of decades earlier).[69]

Isaías Abreu, a young police officer and childhood friend of Ana La Luz's son Santiago, who had left town in a hurry, has noted the decline in families and in the diversity of people in Logan Square: "When I first moved here [in 1994], [the neighborhood was] Latino, black, . . . families, a lot of the young kids." "Now," he told me, in May 2002, "you see a lot more white-collar people . . . no families, just young people . . . quite a drastic change actually." Isaías purchased his house when he was single, as did many of the young professionals who now live in the neighborhood. But, "I see change, unfortunately. . . . A little change is fine," he said, "but . . . I don't want to see it . . . White American." "Improvement" ("going up" and "gotten better") is broadly understood to have racialized meaning. Ana's earlier comment about "grand improvement" in Palmer Square/Logan Square underscored this racialization by speaking the word "improvement" in English. Aware that the private gains of neoliberal redevelopment that contributed to a rise in property values have been to her advantage, she spoke in the voice of a collective *identidad* in referring to the social cost of "improvement" by drawing on a collective past: "Where are Latinos to go? They're pushing us

out once again." Locality is precarious. Ana once again bemoaned the drain-
ing of a community's latinidad. Latinos are not part of a white definition of
"improvement."

A few weeks after our conversation, Isaías asked me to help him write a
letter to try to block a zoning variation applied for to build six condominiums
by the purchaser of a narrow lot adjacent to his home. By law, the new owner
had to inform his abutting neighbors of his intentions. Since Isaías's own property is within 100 feet of the proposed construction site, he attended the public
hearing of the Zoning Board of Appeals, where neighboring property owners
can oppose or support a proposed project, and spoke up about his list of objections. His most pressing concern was safety: a multicondominium building on
the narrow lot would compromise his own entranceway and create a tight
gangway between the two structures. Yet, despite Isaías's objections, within the
year the prefabricated multicondominium building was standing. Ana La Luz,
too, profoundly resented the "three ugly condos" across from her own home in
2002, replacing a livable family home. "When the machine came to knock
down the little house, it knocked it down in less than ten minutes. *I cried.*"

The demolition of the "little house" meant that another family, a Puerto
Rican family, no longer lived on the block. True, there hadn't been "much
neighborliness," but Ana had "counted on them as Puerto Ricans," and when
they left there was "one less family that we now have." The identity of the
family as Puerto Ricans had less to do with actual relationships than with the
ability of Puerto Ricans to hang on to a sense of place. The departure came as
a stark reminder to Ana of her own family's dispossession from Old Town
almost three decades earlier. "I suffered this *'en mi propia carne'*" ("in my own
flesh"). The gang members' threat to burn down her house, just like the bull-
dozing of the "little house" by developers, had been a show of force intended
to render people who are the community insignificant and powerless. The
"little house," like the miniature houses in the casket carried in the funeral
procession to "The Eagle," was a metaphor for a lost sense of belonging to
Chicago. The layers of pain, both embodied and signified from that aged scar
of moliendo vidrio, remain fresh in Ana's memory and bitter in her voice.

Ana draws on her personal experience of displacement from Old Town in
the Near North Side to identify with the current debates about housing and
development in Logan Square in the Near Northwest Side. She is in a better
position than most in the area (her mortgage is paid and her taxes are frozen
because she is over sixty-five years old), yet she has refused to disentangle herself from this issue because, "they did the same thing to us in Old Town, they
pushed us out." "So how am I going to . . . because I now have my house that

is worth a lot, turn my back on the poor. No way!" Ana's, Otilia's, and Gina's lives exemplify how individuals who have attained higher socioeconomic class status and more stable financial resources can maintain connections to, or still see themselves in, working-class ways. Such residents are now caught in a new crossfire, now not with gangs but with real estate speculators who barrage residents with unsolicited telephone calls and junk mail encouraging them to sell for a profit and move on.

Some Latinas and Latinos who can remain in Logan Square have been benefiting from the rising property costs, among them the Quiñones Delgado family. In January 2002 I interviewed Cándido Quiñones, a state trooper, and his wife, Damaris Delgado, a public school teacher, who bought their modest single-family house in Logan Square as an investment. "I knew that it would be a good way to make money," Cándido said. About seven miles from downtown and with easy access to the Kennedy Expressway and public transportation, their acquisition had been a sound investment with a good profit potential that could further secure the family's prospects of social mobility.[70] The young couple, with a preschool age daughter, Mireya, considers the area "reasonably safe," stressing the absence of "gangbangers," the fading of graffiti, and "the fact that there's not a lot of public housing around here." (The lack of gangs in the neighborhood is likely not an indication of their altogether disappearance, but rather their relocation to another neighborhood, or possibly to prison or six feet under.)[71]

Damaris and Cándido have observed an in-migration of young non-Latino families. "I would love if [Mireya] grew up around Puerto Rican kids, and black kids . . . and white kids, and all kind of kids," Damaris said. "*And still know what she is.*" They had noted a "modest counterprocess," identified as "family gentrification," with an influx of young, white middle-class professionals now considering the city a place to raise a family.[72] Yet, many newcomers, in deciding to move into an early-to-mid-stage gentrifying neighborhood, avoid living fully in that neighborhood. Damaris told me that not one of the children of her more recent neighbors on the block attends the local public school. Her new white neighbors have approached Damaris with questions like "'What's going on at Brentano [the public school]? Why is that such a bad [school]? Why does no one here wanna send their kid?'" As a public school teacher, a Latina, and a resident with tenure, Damaris is consulted as an "ultimate insider," and as one of the neighborhood's upwardly mobile families. She does not say that racial ideologies drive the questions she receives but the school's nearly 900 students are overwhelmingly low-income (95 percent) and Latina/o (89 percent).[73] Taken with comments about public housing, the lack of racial diversity may seem to these residents not question of race but largely one of class, one that obscures the mounting disparity of the community's everyday life, such as educational inequalities.[74]

The changing demographics of Logan Square in the twenty-first century as well as the perceptions of the neighborhood reflect another chapter in Chicago Puerto Ricans' ongoing struggle to claim city space and community. A February 2004 story in the *Chicago Tribune* about "thriving" Logan Square reported: "Some people believe the gang problem in Logan Square is slowly waning because there are fewer children. There was a 12 percent drop in the number of people under age 17 between 1990 and 2000, census data show."[75] This shift in demography was part of the area's gentrification, as well-educated, often childless, professionals moved into Logan Square, attracted by the neighborhood's proximity to downtown Chicago with its financial center and high tech employment. Even newer professional residents with children are unlikely to choose local public schools, or to have extended family in the neighborhood, let alone cherish memories of Logan Square as space created and nurtured by Puerto Rican culture.

Although challenges to Puerto Ricans' ability to form community in Chicago characterized the era of urban renewal and the more recent context of gentrification, none significantly diminished Puerto Ricans' aspirations to create a sense of place. Individually and collectively, as allies and as rivals, Puerto Rican and other Latino residents fought for better housing, for safer neighborhoods, and for their rights as community citizens. Puerto Ricans, for their part, were not ignorant of the marginalized status of their citizenship, both at national or at state and local levels; they drew on histories of displacement to imbue citizenship with broader meanings and actions that shape new kinds of commitments to community even in the face of losing battles. Taking part in public demonstrations, writing letters to zoning boards, or as owners themselves charging affordable rents and calling the police for assistance, then standing outside their homes as witnesses are only a few of the many ways in which Chicago's Puerto Ricans and other Latinos have made evident that community—the people and the place—matters and is deserving of continued struggle. They carry on in their belief that everyday life, city life, can, and should be, different from what they have experienced; they persist in the confidence that in the urban sphere there is still room for youth and families. Their story is, primarily, one of the loss of neighborhoods, in the Near North Side, in Old Town, in Lincoln Park, and, perhaps even in Logan Square, but not at all a story of a community's loss of spirit and intent.

4 TANGLED RELATIONS OF *IDENTIDAD*

It was the spring of 1954 in Patillas, Puerto Rico, when Petronila Delgado, then in her later forties, made a bold decision to break all ties with her abusive common-law husband, Francisco Rúa, whose house she still tended to though they no longer shared a home. "*Yo tenia capacidad pa' poder cocinar y eso,*" she said later of the union, "*pero el amor no lo tenia.*" ("I could cook, and stuff, but love I did not have"). "*Ese era un miserable*" ("That one was a miserable one"). Of her ten children, seven had died in infancy or early childhood. The ninth was my father Luis. Over the years in Chicago, time and again, my *abuela* (grandmother) would retell the story of her efforts to rid herself of Francisco. After one awful beating, she waited, with a machete under her pillow, for him to drift off to sleep. She had planned to hack off his head, but he lay awake and kept his head. The next morning, with their son and daughter and nothing else, she went to her parents' home in Patillas. When I spoke with her, almost a half-century later, about that nightmare and its aftermath, she was as agitated as if it had all been yesterday. She had been foolish (*zángana*), she said, to endure such pain for so many years. She was still angry: "*¡me da un coraje!*"

Her daughter Carmen, in 1954 already an adult at twenty-one, wanted to move to the United States to find work and join her older brother, Inocencio, in Defiance, Ohio. Because abuela did not want Carmen to migrate unescorted, nor did she herself want to stay behind, on April 19 she abandoned the small coastal town of Patillas and came with her two younger children, Carmen and my father-to-be, a month shy of fourteen, to join her older son in Ohio. Within six months, my abuela had made her way, with my father, up to Chicago's Near North Side. As with many new arrivals, she found a place to live by word-of-mouth. A Cuban man she met at Spanish American Foods, a grocery store in the neighborhood known as *La Clark*, told her of an apartment on North Dearborn Street, near West Superior on the Near North Side, today an upscale neighborhood a stone's throw away from downtown Chicago. Petronila applied for, and received, a monthly welfare check and supplemented it by caring for neighbors' children in her apartment, up to ten at a time, and by working as the custodian of her building. She and the landlord, a Japanese American, negotiated—she in Spanish and he in English—a five-dollar reduction in her rent for keeping the halls clean. She told me this story, too, over and over. But not until my abuela's death in 2006 did I consider the significance of the partnership of these two overlapping diasporas of Puerto Ricans and Japanese, or what could be called, in the scholarship, parallel "relocation" histories.

With the propensity of Chicago and its leaders, political and academic, to imagine and study the city in a polarized black and white, encounters like that of my abuela and her Japanese American landlord/employer have been overlooked by policy makers and scholars alike. One wonders what would happen if other past histories of similar everyday collaborations or tensions were permitted to enrich the standard narrative of US race relations. When observed on a multiracial canvas, experiences such as the ones considered here would point to connective histories among communities of color within and beyond a black-and-white-only schema. A connective history approach would uncover important episodes that heretofore have been rendered imperceptible because studied independently. American Studies scholar Gaye T. Johnson encourages us to seek out junctures in which individuals and groups inserted themselves into what she calls the same "constellation of struggle."[1] More recently, scholars of urban community formation have begun to acknowledge the difficulty of understanding urban processes, particularly black urban life, without taking Latinos and latinidad into account in the forging of new forms of collective identity and strategies of collaboration.[2]

Anthropologists Paulla Ebron and Anna Lowenhaupt Tsing contend, "[W]e build alliances with a rhetoric of solidarity, but we have few tools with which to create critical and reflexive conversations that recognize our differences as well as our common stakes."[3] Such observations, in line with those of scholars ranging from critical geographer Ruth Wilson Gilmore and historian Lorrin Thomas, to sociologist Moon-Kie Jung, suggest that *recognition* is an integral component in the messy shifts from a "rhetoric of solidarity" to collective work, to coalition politics, a complex process produced from a combination of skepticism and self-reflection.[4] If building identities and coalitions from the inside out seems impossible, or even contradictory, what we *are* able to see are Puerto Ricans negotiating relations among themselves and with other Latinos, with African Americans, and even with Asian Americans: associations of tangled relations.In this process, differences are not transcended or negated but, rather, intermingled, and, indeed, are seen as in conflict.[5] Attending to particularities of race, class, gender, and of citizenship, and their necessary connections, can be a powerful resource in efforts to nourish social and political engagement. Consideration of the tangled relations of identidad offers a more grounded way of thought about the bonds among multiracial constituencies and about potential future forms of collaboration.

Connective Histories of Identity and Community from the Inside Out

The Japanese presence in Chicago was a consequence of vastly different circumstances from that of the arrival of Puerto Ricans or of Mexicans. Postwar unease in some policy circles about the dense Puerto Rican concentration in New York, now identified as a "problem," had in the 1950s resulted in their dispersal to the Midwest, particularly to Chicago and even further within the city itself.[6] The Japanese migration, on the other hand, was the result of the US government's wartime internment of West Coast Japanese Americans as potential spies. Yet, both Japanese and Puerto Ricans shared an experience, if almost a decade apart, of social service agencies advising them against living near neighbors of a shared ethnoracial background, and encouraging them instead to scatter throughout the city. Puerto Ricans, however, unlike their Japanese counterparts, did not remain dispersed, but drew together to form a distinct community, one marked by tangled relations primarily with Mexicans and African Americans. As for Japanese Americans, as historian Henry Yu writes, "a limited number of Japanese Americans were gradually resettled after 1943 into supposedly safe locations such as Chicago and Minneapolis."[7] Anthropologist Jacalyn Harden points out that "for about twenty years after World War II, Chicago had the largest concentration of Japanese Americans in the country."[8] In this resettlement, Japanese Americans had found accommodations and employment with the assistance of the War Relocation Authority (WRA).[9]

The owner of the building where my abuela lived after 1954 had, very likely, been one of the Japanese Americans interned on the West Coast in wartime and relocated after the war in the Midwest, making a return home difficult. A member of the generation of relocates in Chicago had told Harden, "'See, the WRA ... told us don't clump together, keep a low profile. They didn't encourage people to stick together ... establish a colony. You know, the Chinese established Chinatown. But not the Japanese. They told us not to. . . . We never had a neighborhood of our own because the WRA wanted us spread out.'"[10] In Chicago, perceived as nonblack, the Nisei (second-generation Japanese Americans) had not been subject to the most pernicious forms of the city's racism. They did, nonetheless, gain an intimate experience of the city's prevailing racial order.[11] A Japanese American landlord became my own abuela's effective accomplice, despite the language barrier, in learning how to navigate Chicago's racial landscape.

The flow of Puerto Rican labor migrants to the United States had, essentially, been redirected from New York City by the Migration Division and local social service agencies to prevent concentration and, hence, to ease the process of assimilation. Thus, by the mid-1950s, pocket communities of Puerto Rican migrants had been established throughout the Midwest as a destination alternative to New York. The first group in Chicago, the fewer than 1,000 contract laborers of domestics and foundry workers who had arrived in 1946, by the 1960 census had grown by a multiple of more than thirty-two.[12] At first the city's social agencies had recommended placement in Mexican neighborhoods, but, by 1951, efforts were made to discourage intermingling.[13] Anthony Vega, director of the Midwest Office of the Migration Division, had a "policy," as stated in a letter from the Chicago Council Against Racial and Religious Discrimination to an individual at Maryville College in Tennessee, of "urging the Puerto Ricans not to settle down with any Spanish-speaking people, but to distribute themselves all over the city in Polish, Italian, Czechoslovak and other areas. . . . stressing Puerto Rican's [sic] scattering all over the city and warning against the formation of colonies or residence with Mexicans."[14] In the process of directing the distribution and concentration of Puerto Ricans in Chicago, government and private groups alike may have taken account of, among other factors, regional labor necessities like the shortage in domestic and foundry labor.

When I began archival research on Chicago's Puerto Rican community, I found documents in the records of the Welfare Council of Metropolitan Chicago in the Chicago Historical Society (now the Chicago History Museum) correlating Japanese resettlement to Chicago with Puerto Rican settlement. In the year my abuela migrated from Puerto Rico to Ohio and from there to Chicago, Mary Young, executive secretary of the division on family and child welfare of the Welfare Council of Metropolitan Chicago, in a memo on "Puerto Ricans, for discussion in Cabinet," proposed that the Council assemble a committee to deal with the "Puerto Rican problem," principally with their "nonresident" citizenship status and the potential "development of ghetto communities." The pattern the committee should follow, Young said, "would be similar to that which we had previously used in dealing with the Japanese resettler problem."[15] The Council appeared concerned, according to its April 9, 1954, minutes, over "the tendency for colonies of Puerto Ricans to grow within the city," stating that "unless efforts are made to integrate these groups into the community as a whole, there will be a tendency for them to remain in these groups."[16] At the time I found this memo, I was unprepared to pay critical attention to this evidence "hidden in plain sight," to borrow from anthropologist Micaela di Leonardo.[17] I have, however, thought much about it since. Had my abuela's personal introduction to the politics of housing in Chicago offered her a more nuanced insight into the racial landscape of the city and multiracial collaborations than was held even by policy makers and scholars? Was her personal experience a disruption of the seemingly fixed racial covenant of persons the larger society considered nonwhite and non-black? Or could it be understood as a deliberate arrangement to preserve the racial system, to keep African Americans out of the area, thus not undermining white supremacy?[18] A comparative and connective history of Japanese and Puerto Ricans in Chicago remains to be written.

Puerto Ricans' affiliation with Mexicans and African Americans in Chicago became a dominant feature of their experience. By the 2000 US census, Chicago would house the third largest Latino population in the United States, with its Puerto Rican and Mexican communities each the second largest in the nation. So, too, Chicago, by 2000, had the second largest black urban population in the United States. Latinos constituted 26 percent of Chicago's total population, with Mexicans and Puerto Ricans together making up approximately 85 percent of all Chicago Latinos (Mexicans 70 percent, Puerto Ricans 15 percent).[19] Only New York City had more Puerto Ricans and more African Americans and only Los Angeles had more Mexicans. Almost half a century before that 2000 census, Elena Padilla, in her 1947 University of Chicago master's thesis, had already documented the experiences of the first Puerto Rican migrant workers to postwar Chicago, and had already identified their relationships with Mexican coworkers and neighbors, and, to a lesser extent, with the city's black residents.

The Mexican community of North Chicago, among them *braceros*— recruits for World War II's farm labor program and industrial workers— were employed by the same Chicago Hardware and Foundry Company that, in September 1946, recruited Puerto Rican migrants through the Chicago employment agency of Castle, Barton and Associates. The foundry workers, Mexicans and Puerto Ricans, would gather on Thursdays and Sundays with Puerto Rican female domestic workers in the suburbs of the North Shore district for Puerto Rican meals prepared by Puerto Rican cooks in a recon-verted railroad car. The workers would then proceed to Happy Hour, a local nightclub, and "in the Happy Hour as well as in the foundry," Padilla wrote, "the Puerto Ricans contacted many Mexican *braceros* with whom they devel-oped certain kinds of social relationships that in some occasions manifest themselves as conflictual whereas on other occasions they were cliquish in nature. Some of the foundry workers established consensual relations of marriage with Puerto Rican household workers and moved out of the rail-road cars, and rented rooms in Mexican homes in town."[20] Thus, pockets of communities of Puerto Ricans and Mexicans in North Chicago had origi-nated in common employment and in common social activities. So, too, Puerto Rican domestic workers housed on the North Side of Chicago fre-quented the Rancho Grande, a Mexican nightclub near the YWCA, where they learned of a large Mexican community. After tea socials arranged for them in the YWCA, Puerto Rican women would often get together at Ran-cho Grande, Padilla wrote, "to chat, to eat Mexican food, and to dance, to Latin American music."[21]

Social service agencies directed early Puerto Rican workers dissatisfied with their jobs to Mexican neighborhoods to find new jobs and housing because the two groups shared a common language. The Mexican Civic Com-mittee helped some Puerto Rican migrants find shelter in Mexican homes. But Padilla had recognized also that, while some Puerto Ricans developed great appreciation for the Mexican community, others "dislike[d] being iden-tified as Mexican." Although group conflicts were rare, individual disputes "along nationality lines" were frequent.[22] One cause of such friction was the consensual relationships between Puerto Rican women and Mexican men cultivated at the Rancho Grande and the Happy Hour. Padilla observed that "the non-permanent and illegal marital relations that have followed these contacts have resulted in situations not approved by Puerto Rican standards of social behavior."[23] Although unions of unmarried Puerto Rican couples, or "illegal marital relations," were accepted by most Puerto Ricans as stable and permanent, transitory affairs between Mexican men and Puerto Rican women were not, and also were seen as leading to a "disorganizing effect" of animosity in both populations.

Beyond concerns of the acceptability of inter-Latino romances, however, some "Spanish-speaking" professionals had maintained that the advancement of broad Latino interests in the "enormous city" of Chicago hinged on an ability to convince recent arrivals from Mexico, the Southwest, Puerto Rico, and New York City that they were "now part of a new community." An appeal in the June 1957 editorial of *Vida Latina*, "the only Spanish and English magazine in the Midwest," was a prime example of that effort. The editorial urged Spanish-speaking readers to welcome new Puerto Rican and Mexican American migrants as well as Mexican immigrants to Chicago:

> We've [that is, Latinos in Chicago] already taken this trip to the enormous city. Here the huge shapes of the skyscrapers and the roar of the public streets frighten us. Nobody here seems to be friendly, nobody here cares whether we're dead or alive, or are victims of hunger pangs. But somehow we live our lives.... Here the newcomers find themselves lonely, alienated and depressed.... We should smile and say '*halo*', we could tell them where the Church is located and what time Mass is held, we could indicate to them where to learn English, tell them where there's work and warn them of the trader, the dealer, the salesman or the lawyer that we know to be racketeers. But most important of all would be to make them understand that they are now part of a new community, just as they were before in their communities.[24]

Whereas Mexican and Puerto Rican men were not directly competing for jobs or for neighborhood space, in the courtship of Puerto Rican women they *were* adversaries, partly because few Mexican women had migrated across the border.[25] Anthropologist Nicholas De Genova writes, "Due specifically, then, to struggles over access to Puerto Rican women's bodies—or more precisely, their sexuality—Puerto Rican and Mexican men apparently encountered one another as rivals."[26] In any event, in Chicago, inter-Latino romances were commonly considered suspect because of the impression that many non-Puerto Rican suitors might be more interested in courting US citizenship than in courting Puerto Rican women whose US citizenship they might, by marriage, acquire.[27] In a November 1958 report documenting "examples of incidental service" under the category "*PROBLEM*:—'Other,'" Hull House, the famed Jane Addams settlement house on Chicago's Near West Side, referred to a *panameño* whose visa had expired: "Mr. B in office from Panama, age 30, visiting time in U.S. is up, no extension time granted. Wants to stay here. Asked us to find him a Puerto Rican woman whom he could marry and thus remain in U.S. Unable to help him."[28]

Gina Bishop, the wise and equally opinionated landlady of my Chicago research years, shared with me some stories of Mexican and Puerto Rican relations during the early period of Puerto Rican migration. Puerto Rican women, she said, apparently sometimes deliberately played off sexual rivalry to their own advantage with potential suitors. One day, in the Caribe Funeral Home, Gina, her niece, and Antonio, a mortician of Mexican descent, were talking with me about the expectations men (and society, in general) held for women. Gina mentioned a young man who had once invited her out dancing to a Mexican nightclub, leaving her seated alone at a table while he chatted with men at the bar. "*Los mexicanos no esperaban*" ("the Mexicans didn't wait"), Gina said; "they liked Puerto Rican girls and jumped when they saw one alone." Gina was not fond of dancing, but accepted a Mexican's invitation rather than wait for her date to return from the bar. Her new partner did not go unnoticed. For the remainder of the evening, her date did not leave her side. The story was all the more intriguing to me because that inattentive date, as it happened, was her future husband, Julius Bishop, himself African American. In some ways, her tale showed that Puerto Ricans viewed Mexicans *and* African Americans as rivals in the personal arena, even while viewing them as collaborators in other matters.

Padilla had, in the 1940s, observed among Puerto Ricans "an attitude of dislike" of African Americans. African Americans, one migrant had told her, "were not equal to white people." Padilla believed this negative posture "toward the American Negro" was a consequence of the conditions under which the Puerto Rican government and Chicago business selected Puerto Ricans to hire. In theory, in response to the public advertisement for Puerto Rican workers, migrants recruited "only included white workers," but "many of them would be considered Negroes in the United States" because of the color of their skin.[29] Becky Bishop, the third of Gina and Julius Bishop's five children, understood that her parents, as an interracial couple, were, in US racial terms—particularly in 1950s' Chicago—a matter of "black or white": "He being African American and my mom, depending on who's categorizing her, 'cause at the time you're either colored or white, [and] here she is Puerto Rican, they can either place her as black or white. I would tend to think most people would categorize her as white. So, yes, there were issues." Unlike her brother William Rios, who never said he was taken for white, and who at times used being mistaken as African American to his advantage, Gina benefited from a situational whiteness. After a stint as a nanny, she had found a job in a factory on Chicago's West Side. While there, she was allowed to use the "white" facilities, a fact that upset some of her black female coworkers. "I don't know about these racial things," Gina told me. "I learned my job. I didn't care where I washed my hands, used the bathroom." But she *did* use the white bathroom. Some time later, once Gina was promoted to supervisor, racial tension in the factory increased.

"Knowing about these racial things" would matter, especially in the wake of the West Side riots in Chicago following the April 1968 assassination of the Reverend Martin Luther King, Jr. The night of the assassination, two of Gina's male coworkers—one white, one Puerto Rican—offered to escort her home due to rioting on the West Side. Police had closed off the principle thoroughfares. Gina told the white male coworker, "I don't think they're going to let *you* through. For *me*, they don't know what I am." The three were, nonetheless, permitted to pass the police barricade. Through incidents like this one, Gina realized that she had troubled the racial line between a polarized black and white Chicago. Soon after that, the Bishop family moved out of the West Side, Gina attributing her departure to the family's purchase of a building on Armitage Avenue on the Near Northwest Side. With business at the funeral home picking up, the family had decided, she said, to live in an apartment above their funeral parlor (the same apartment I would rent more than thirty years later to work on my research for this book).

But Gini, the second eldest Bishop child, told me she believed her family had really moved because they were considered an interracial family, and it was a dangerous time. "We left suddenly because when they started rioting . . . a lot of the anger was turned against anybody who they perceived to be white . . . and then they firebombed the house next to us. Considering the similarity between their house and our house was the fact that . . . whites and blacks [were] living in both, my parents decided to get the hell out." Logan Square and Humboldt Park, to which they moved, was at the time predominantly Polish and German; there were few Latinos, with most of them Cubans. "So almost all my friends were Cuban, I had one Dominican friend, I didn't have *any* Puerto Rican friends when I went there, and the rest were Caucasian," Gini told me. "We were [also], technically speaking, the only African American family at St. Sylvester [School]."

Stresses over the family's interracial status were not limited to school and neighborhood, however. Gini confided to me that neither her mother's nor father's families were happy about their union. Gina's older brother, Oscar, for instance, had been none too pleased with his friend Julius's interest in his sister. As for Julius's family, once he had decided to marry Gina Rios, an island woman with limited formal education, they opposed it on class *and* ethnoracial grounds. "I know my grandmother was very much against it," Gini told me; her father's family had "teachers and social workers," so "he was sort of in the middle class." Ethnicity and color were part of the dynamic of the interracial marriage that took place despite opposition, as became apparent when the part-Puerto Rican and part-African American Bishop clan attended an

African American Bishop family reunion in Alabama. "[M]y brother and sisters and I, and my father, were probably the darkest ones there," Gini said. "My father had never, *never*, never prepared [us], we were shocked. He was always 'black' this, 'black' this, 'black' this and we go down there and we see these blue, green-eyed people [with] long hair. . . . We were like, damn, maybe they didn't want him to marry *mami* 'cause she was darker." The social acceptability and underlying intent of such inter-Latino and multiracial romantic relations thus set the stage for animosity as well as for love.

Such love affairs would shape the contours of future identity and community formations. Elena Padilla herself did not believe that Chicago's Puerto Ricans would form a *colonia* of their own as they had in New York City. Chicago Puerto Ricans, she predicted, would, instead, become "Mexicanized" because of the comparatively small numbers of Puerto Ricans and their scattering across the city, especially in majority Mexican neighborhoods, but, most significant, because of "mixed" Puerto Rican-Mexican offspring.[30] In her final assessment of the future of Chicago's Puerto Ricans, she did not consider African Americans at all. Drawing, with some modification, on the tradition of the Chicago School of sociology, Padilla recognized that Mexicans, with or without US citizenship, had a more extensive history of community formation than did the Puerto Ricans of Chicago, and subsequently, had a greater comprehension of the politics of race and space. Further, even though Puerto Ricans, by legislative decree, possessed US citizenship, Chicago did not consider them fully "American," nor did they themselves develop distinct geographic communities in their early process of "assimilation and acculturation."[31] The distinction between citizenship and Americanness reveals one of the great paradoxes of the Puerto Rican diaspora's experience in the United States. Padilla, working within the confines of immigrant community formation (i.e., Chicago School assimilation cycle theory) as an initial step toward assimilation, had charted the "Mexicanization" of Puerto Ricans in Chicago as the likely route toward a racialized "Americanization."[32] Her theory of probable "Mexicanization" provided an early insight into latinidad: a situational identity and practice, simultaneously consisting of cooperation and competition, antagonism and friendship[33]—put differently, the tangled relations of a grounded identity.

When I conducted my own research in Chicago almost half a century after Padilla's study, I took seriously her speculation about the "Mexicanization" of Puerto Ricans. In 1999 I heard from Olivia Velasco, whose parents, a Puerto Rican mother and a Mexican father, met at a Latin American Task Force meeting that sought to recruit Latino electricians in Chicago: "Yeah, all the time I'm asked. I say I'm Puerto Rican and Mexican, but . . . when anybody hears me speak . . . or the way I act, it's like, 'Eh? Hey, you look Mexican but you act Puerto Rican, what are you?' I'm a PortoMex." Olivia's own Puerto Ricanized Mexicanness was a promising vantage point from which I sought to examine the multifaceted but uneven ways latinidad takes shape and is deployed.[34] My own understanding of *colaos* (mixed Latinos or inter-Latino subjectivities), is not Padilla's assumption of a route to assimilation from Puerto Rican to Mexican, but one that has been shaped by Frances Aparicio and Susana Chavez-Silverman's framing of *tropicalizations*—the bidirectional, if unequal, influence of cultures on each other.[35]

"Especially in Chicago," Raquel Sierra, another mixed Latina told me, "Mexicans hate Puerto Ricans and Puerto Ricans hate Mexicans. There's always prejudice . . . there's the tension. . . . [G]rowing up . . . I'd be around a lot of Mexicans and somebody would ask somebody else if they were Puerto Rican and then that person would get insulted, 'I'm not no Puerto Rican' . . . and then, there I am, being half-Puerto Rican wondering why is that an insult?!" Time and again, I found stories about inter-Latino encounters in Chicago reduced to an idea of "absolute antagonism" such as "Mexicans hate Puerto Ricans and Puerto Ricans hate Mexicans," a simplification uncritically counted as an essential truth.[36] But Raquel, half-Mexican and half-Puerto Rican, complicates glib interpretations of inter-Latino dynamics by her very existence."[37]

In her adolescence, Raquel had relocated in and out of predominantly Puerto Rican and Mexican communities: Humboldt Park to Hermosa (an area directly north of Humboldt Park and west of Logan Square), to the state of Texas, then returning to Chicago's Brighton Park neighborhood, a predominantly Mexican community on the South Side. At one point, she and her family lived near her father's relatives, leading to more frequent encounters with Puerto Ricans; later, when her mother's family had a greater presence in her life, the Mexican side influenced her primary sense of identity. Still, Raquel's Puerto Rican father remained present even after her parents divorced. At times, Raquel identified herself as only Puerto Rican or only Mexican because it was easier than explaining, "my father's Puerto Rican and my mother's Mexican." Experience had also taught her that, in a Mexican setting, her Puerto Rican identity was usually ignored, while in Puerto Rican circles there was an inverse erasure. Raquel is included while simultaneously excluded from certain social spheres. Individuals like Raquel redefine, for themselves, what identity means, linking it not only to family but also to neighborhoods, to educational experiences, and to circles of friends and acquaintances.

For Miguel Ayala, proud of his roots in Humboldt Park, space and place also matter: "I always identify . . . more strongly with being Puerto Rican because . . . of the fact that I grew up . . . in a predominantly Puerto Rican neighborhood, went to a predominantly Puerto Rican high school, grew up with my uncles and . . . my mother's side of the family more than my father's side of the family. But, you know, I embrace both." As an adolescent, besides living in and around Humboldt Park, Miguel spent a few years in California, getting the opportunity to visit paternal relatives in Tijuana and to visit Jalisco, México, his father's hometown. He had traveled to Mexico repeatedly but, as of November 1999, when I spoke with him, he had never been to Puerto Rico. His comment about purposefully recognizing his Puerto Rican side could lead one to presume that he had little or no contact with his Mexican family or Mexican culture. His Mexican identity is expressed from a pronounced Puerto Rican standpoint, a position informed by his day-to-day existence.

Olivia, the self-proclaimed "PortoMex," found, as both Puerto Rican and Mexican, that hurtful wisecracks were made at her expense. "I'll have Mexicans telling me . . . shame on me that I don't know, that I could've . . . gone to Mexico already. That . . . I had chosen not to. That's not really the case. . . . And all the time I go to Puerto Rico, it's like *mojá* [wetback]. I'm the *mojá*, I'm the *prieta* [black] . . . 'cause my family is light skinned," she said, expressing both difficulty and discomfort in having to justify these sentiments. Her racialization as "Mexican" by her Puerto Rican family is packed within a discourse of citizenship and "illegality."[38] By describing her as the *mojá* and the *prieta*, Olivia's family delegitimizes her as Puerto Rican through problematic associations of Mexicanness with an undocumented immigrant status in the United States. In Puerto Rico, Olivia's "blackness" is identified as a non-Puerto Rican trait, a sign of her Mexicanness since her Puerto Rican family on the island consider themselves "light skinned."

The parents of Bobby Escalas, a talented local musician, had the reverse experience. Bobby's Puerto Rican father and *Tejana* Mexican mother had grown up around Chicago's Western and Harrison area, known as the Near West Side, and attended Precious Blood Grammar School with many Mexican and Puerto Rican neighbors, resulting in some amorous relationships.[39] Bobby has cousins and a few friends of both Puerto Rican and Mexican parentage. Members of this inter-Latino generation are principally products of neighborhoods consisting of both Puerto Ricans and Mexicans. Despite this, his mother had a falling out with the aunt who raised her because the aunt considered as transgression a romance with a "nigger"—that is to say, a Puerto

Rican. (Ironically, Bobby's father would be identified as "light skinned" by many, even "white" by some.) In both cases, blackness and ideas about blackness were deployed as weapons, as a means of claiming distinction, difference, and superiority, but, above all else, as what in the academy is referred to as a privileging of and an "investment in whiteness."[40]

In 1986 the Latino Institute of Chicago, in a report titled, "*Al Filo/*The Cutting Edge: The Empowerment of the Latino Electorate," called for the study of "Mixed Latinos" and political processes as "innovative and particularly worthy of discussion in further detail."[41] The report suggests to me the significance of the growing number of mixed Latinos in the political empowerment of Chicago's Latinos. In the study of latinidad, observers tend to neglect the everyday relations among Latinos of distinct ethnoracial national backgrounds who take part in these movements. Manifestations of latinidad, both official and unofficial, I suggest, begin with ordinary, tangled exchanges of fellowship and friction.

Diasporic *Puertorriqueñidad*: Stretching the Borders of Community

Even as Chicago Puerto Ricans defined and refined their own identities and social relations with others within the city's neighborhoods, they continued to negotiate a complicated diasporic *puertorriqueñidad*. Thus, notions of locality for Puerto Ricans stretch beyond the intimate borders of the neighborhood to other neighborhoods, other cities, and even back to the island of Puerto Rico, while still remaining in place. For Chicago Puerto Ricans, in the new millennium, the politics of a grounded identity (puertorriqueñidad, latinidad, and citizenship) intersected in new ways. In 2001 Puerto Ricans, on the island and of the diaspora, put aside deep divisions to come together in a dramatic campaign to save *la isla nena* (the little island), the island-municipality of Vieques, off the eastern coast of Puerto Rico, which, since World War II, the US Navy had used as a bombing playground.[42] Anywhere and everywhere I set foot in Chicago in 2001, "*¡Paz para Vieques!*" was declaimed, in prayer petitions in Sunday mass at St. Sylvester Church, in daily gossip in Caribe Funeral Home, and in discussions in households in Chicago's Near Northwest Side.

The military presence in Puerto Rico's small island of Vieques brought together variegated objectors in Puerto Rico and the United States just as it also revived discussions of the vexed relationship between the island and the diaspora. Six miles off the southeast corner of Puerto Rico, and a mere four miles wide and approximately twenty-one miles long, Vieques has a population of around 9,400. Between 1941 and the mid-1950s, through eminent domain, the US Navy expropriated 26,000 of its 33,000 acres as annex to its Roosevelt Roads Naval Station in the Puerto Rican coastal town of Ceiba. Sugar companies were compensated for their loss of land; the thousands of displaced families were not. With military training exercises, weapons tests and ammunition, napalm and Agent Orange (of Vietnam notoriety), the Navy advertised Vieques to NATO allies as a practice site. Between 1978 and 1983, Vieques fishermen demonstrated against military maneuvers. Anthropologist Katherine McCaffrey attributes the strength of the protest movement of the late-1970s and early-1980s to a disciplined and committed local network supported by groups—both statehood supporters and *independentistas*—in Puerto Rico and in the United States, across divergent ideologies and political affiliations.[43] Beginning in April 1999—after a navy jet on a practice run misfired, its missiles destroying a Vieques military observation post and killing a civilian employee—and until May 2000, thousands engaged in nonviolent civil disobedience, using their bodies as human shields. With civilians in the firing range, exercises were suspended, but, in January 2000, Pedro Rosselló, governor of Puerto Rico, accepted a presidential directive for the navy to continue in Vieques, reversing an official policy of "not one more bullet, not one more shot." The so-called Rosselló-Clinton agreement of 2000 committed the Puerto Rican police to support US marshals in removing civil disobedient protestors from target zones.[44] In return, a referendum was scheduled at a date set by the navy for citizens of Vieques to choose one of two options for the future of training operations: a halt by May 1, 2003, or a continuation with live ammunition.

On May 4, 2000, in a dawn offensive, US marshals and FBI agents in riot gear evicted more than 200 demonstrators from a bombing range, among them Illinois Congressman Luis Gutíerrez and Lolita Lebrón, who had served a twenty-five year sentence for leading the 1954 shooting attack from a US Capitol balcony against Puerto Rico's colonial status. The removal of human shields became a galvanizing event for Puerto Ricans at the same moment that another federal offensive was inciting Cuban Americans. Almost two weeks earlier, a young Cuban castaway named Elián González was at the center of a ten-month battle in the courts, the media, and among a Cuban American, Cuban, and US public on granting him asylum in the United States or returning him to Cuba with his father. Ultimately, in a predawn raid by the US Immigration and Naturalization Service (INS), Elián was removed from his uncle's Miami home and placed in his father's custody.[45] "Many Puerto Rican people feel the same way about Vieques as the Cubans did about Elián," said a Humboldt Park resident interviewed by a *Chicago Tribune* reporter.[46] But, as there had been among the Cuban community with the Elián saga, Puerto Ricans expressed divergent feelings and perspectives about Vieques, and its relevance to the question of Puerto Rico's status. Ana La Luz, puertorriqueña and energetic member of the St. Sylvester community in Palmer Square/ Logan Square, told me, "I've always thought Puerto Ricans on the island should resolve the problems over there." Cándido Quiñones, an Illinois state trooper living in Logan Square, commented, "From what I understand . . . the US's position is that 'hey, this is a strategic location . . . there's no other location like this in the world.' We need to keep doing this for US defense. [F]rom what I heard from [Congressman Gutíerrez] and from the other . . . people active in it . . . that's nonsense . . . they could do this anywhere else . . . but the reason why they do . . . is because [of] the . . . status of Puerto Rico." When, after almost a year of moratorium, the navy resumed training exercises during the last weekend of April 2001, Congressman Gutierrez once again joined protestors, crossing into a restricted area to force the navy to halt fire.[47]

Political Scientist Amílcar Barreto submits that for island-based Puerto Ricans, Vieques symbolized a colonial condition and for diasporic Puerto Ricans "internal colonialism," an echo of struggles for social justice in US barrios made almost three decades earlier by the Young Lords.[48] Yet, it was precisely a discussion of colonialism that was absent from the contemporary debates about Vieques. Perhaps the issue served as an effective rallying call because it became disentangled from the politics of US colonialism. Instead, it was interpreted as a Puerto Rican movement that, as Political Scientist Pedro Cabán contends, "successfully avoided being drawn into the interminable and ruinous politics of territorial status," framed rather as a struggle for "resources and environmental protection, social justice and human rights, public health and safety, sustainable development, demilitarization, autonomy and government accountability."[49] Dissent was in the spirit of democratic ideals, in evocation of "American" principles of fairness and social justice. Like Vieques, the issue of voting underscored the contradiction rooted in Puerto Rico's political status and the strategic positioning of the diaspora in island politics. Sila Calderón, the commonwealth governor in 2001, said: "We are Puerto Ricans who are US citizens, we are not US citizens who happen to be Puerto Ricans. We are Puerto Ricans first."[50] Testing this hypothesis, Calderon's administration initiated a voter registration drive for the pending 2002 mid-term US election season: *Boricua, ¡Inscríbete Y*

Vota! Que Nada Nos Detenga! (Boricua, Register and Vote! Let Nothing Stop Us!). The objective was for Puerto Ricans in the continental United States to vote in the best interest of the wider Puerto Rican public and of the island itself. The campaign deployed the Spanish words *orgullo* (pride), *unidad* (unity), and *fuerza* (strength) to punctuate what it meant to *feel* and *be* Puerto Rican. It resembled the 1950s' speeches of Luis Muñoz Marín, the island's first popularly elected governor, who had advised Puerto Ricans in the diaspora to adapt to US life by registering to vote while also asserting their pride in being "Puerto Rican."[51]

In the 1990s US Puerto Ricans, for the first time, were permitted to take part in congressional hearings on who should be allowed to vote in the referendum on the island's political status. A debate ensued when a report commissioned by the US Senate (June 1989), examining the citizenship of island Puerto Ricans, considered "legislative" versus "constitutional" citizenship, and maintained that Puerto Ricans' citizenship is not protected under the Fourteenth Amendment because the Jones Act of 1917 had conferred citizenship legislatively. The commission and its findings had thus made even more apparent the second-class citizenship Puerto Ricans hold, simultaneously insisting on a critical distinction between continental US-born Puerto Ricans as constitutionally protected, and island-born Puerto Ricans as relegated to "legislative citizenship."[52] In the interface between *puertorriqueñidad* and US citizenship, diasporic Puerto Ricans used their citizenship status as an expression of *puertorriqueñidad,* their vote serving as an invaluable political remittance. Although those on the island are ineligible to vote for US president or to elect a voting member to the US Congress, Sila Calderón, as governor, flew to Chicago to campaign for Gutierrez in his bitter battle with a Mexican American lawyer to retain his congressional seat.[53] Even those Puerto Ricans in Chicago who had identified themselves as "radical," which, in the past, included abstaining from electoral politics, now participated in voter registration drives.[54] Expressions of puertorriqueñidad among Chicago's Puerto Ricans, according to anthropologist and Latina/o studies scholar Ana Yolanda Ramos-Zayas, entail both a popular nationalism with nationalist sentiments for the island as ancestral and symbolic homeland, and with political resistance to US colonial practices. Thus, Puerto Ricans' status as US citizens is strategically deployed—what Ramos-Zayas terms "citizenship identity"—to reveal a thorny set of political arrangements and commitments in the formation of Puerto Rican identities outside of, and yet deeply connected to, the island, a practice that anthropologist Michel Laguerre has theorized more broadly as "diasporic citizenship."[55]

Human Chain, Human Shields, and Rainbow Coalitions

The issue of Vieques had broad support among Puerto Ricans and, although amnesty for undocumented immigrants did not directly affect Puerto Ricans, their participation in amnesty efforts made visible the potential of challenging collaborations in which diasporic puertorriqueñidad and latinidad were not mutually exclusive, as neither were efforts to pursue multiracial coalitions. In the early evening of May 1, 2001, a collective, mainly of Puerto Ricans, gathered on the contested crossroads of Chicago's Division Street and Western Avenue, the border in race, class, and culture between a rapidly gentrifying West Town and Humboldt Park. They were preparing for a May Day human chain. The corner of Division and Western, in front of Roberto Clemente Community Academy, since the mid-1960s, a site of confrontations for Puerto Ricans. Almost any neighborhood resident and barrio historian can recount at least one such struggle there: a conflict over the building of Roberto Clemente Community Academy, a heated bilingual education debate, a student walk-out.[56] Hosts of young and old have been subjected to police surveillance there. The corner serves also as the starting place of *el desfile del pueblo* (the peoples' parade), the annual Puerto Rican Day Parade of the barrio.[57]

On the evening of May 1, 2001, the Juan Antonio Corretjer Puerto Rican Cultural Center was in charge of organizing the people at the corner of Western and Division. An older woman stood at the protest junction in blue jeans and a red t-shirt, with buttons across her chest, one a photograph of Pedro Albizu Campos, a Puerto Rican nationalist hero. She held a *pandereta* (a tambourine-like instrument) with a Puerto Rican flag and a wooden spoon. I walked with that gathered group, with its posters and banners, eastward to Ashland Avenue en route to the human chain for unconditional amnesty of undocumented immigrants and for peace in Vieques. Our route was through a gentrified terrain of once predominantly Puerto Rican (also Mexican) communities of East Humboldt Park and West Town, now a "hot" real estate market where most Latinos are priced out. "*¡Que se vaya, que se vaya! ¡La marina que se vaya!*" ("Go, go! The Navy should go!"), we chanted to the beating of panderetas and conga drums, in the tradition of the Puerto Rican *plena*, Afro-Puerto Rican music of the working class.[58]

Heading one group was an old timer with long silver hair, a stylish black beret, and a trimmed white mustache; not far behind a child was being pushed along in a blue stroller. High school and college students and some teachers

from a local alternative high school carried handmade posters and large pho-
tocopies of a *New York Times'* full-page open letter asking President Bush to
"stop the bombing of Vieques now." Evelyn De Jesus, a Puerto Rican city
worker in her mid-forties, would later tell me she decided to join the human
chain after a forum on Puerto Rican issues at the University of Illinois at Chicago.[59] "It's not that I hate America 'cause I don't," she said. "I love America ...
I wouldn't be wearing little flags and stuff ... I just have a different point of
view when it comes to Vieques." Not opposed to the navy stationed there but
against the bombardment and tactical maneuvers' disruption of daily life,
Evelyn accepted a handmade poster that proclaimed, "I want the Navy out."
"I really didn't care either way," she said. "But, it was the only one that was left
and I thought what the hell. You know, it's for the cause."

Evelyn's insistence that she was not "anti-American" can be understood in
terms of the history of the Puerto Rican Nationalist Party from Chicago's Near
West Side in the 1950s, as well as of the Young Lords in Lincoln Park in the
1960s and 1970s, and of the FALN (*Fuerzas Armadas de Liberación National*,
the Armed Forces of National Liberation) in the 1970s and 1980s.[60] In the
wake of 9/11, ideas about Americanness had become even narrower, and defense
of one's Americanness more insistent. In an unpublished letter to the *Chicago
Defender*, Evelyn De Jesus had written, "days after the attacks, my sister was told
by a white woman to go back to her country. Imagine that! The nationality of
my family is Puerto Rican. The Puerto Rican island is a commonwealth island
of the United States, and *all* Puerto Ricans are American Citizens by virtue [of]
reward for fighting past United States wars, reaching back to the Civil War."[61]

In articulations of puertorriqueñidad to mark the distinction between
Mexicans, regardless of actual status, and themselves, Puerto Ricans do concede a difference between their citizenship and the citizenship of "real Americans," an identity they see as linked to notions of whiteness, and encapsulated
in the concept of "legislative citizenship." That activist grandmother, Ana La
Luz, told me she had taken part in an amnesty march in downtown Chicago
"to help the illegals," her aim to support the undocumented, but she does so by
employing a vocabulary that criminalizes their existence and, in the process,
"legalizes" her own. William Rios, Gina Bishop's older brother, had told
of proving he was "not Mexican" but a "citizen" and a veteran during early
"Operation Wetback" deportation sweeps on the Near West Side. Political
Scientist Pedro Cabán attributes Puerto Ricans' conflation with more recent
immigrants or with temporary workers without US citizenship, in part, to
their belonging to what is seen as a monolithic Latino population.[62] If President George W. Bush's statement about why the US Navy should depart from

Vieques—"these are our friends and neighbors and they don't want us there"—sounded calculating, Puerto Ricans heard it as undermining their actual US citizenship status.[63]

A June 2001 *Newsweek* article, "On Vieques, No Hispanic Is an Island," expressed wonder that Vieques, an "insular" issue, had transcended ethnic divisions among Latinos more broadly. Yet, the article was also dubious of the formidability of this Latino solidarity.[64] Vieques, the article said, had been the first issue raised by the eighteen-member elected Congressional Hispanic Caucus of Puerto Ricans, Mexican-Americans, and Cuban-Americans in a March 2001 meeting with newly elected President Bush. A pamphlet issued by the Puerto Rican Federal Affairs Administration reported that Puerto Ricans comprised between 2 and 5 percent of the electorate in seven states; it magnified the significance of a Latino voting bloc and an impending swing vote in presidential elections. The Latino vote had already been cited as critical in some key elections, particularly in New York and Florida.[65] "But can Latinos pull off a second act?" *Newsweek* wondered. Could this political latinidad champion "thornier" issues like the question of Puerto Rico's political status, US foreign policy toward Cuba, or the issue of immigration, most identified with Mexicans? The article concluded, "other Latinos won't necessarily take to the streets for an amnesty bill for undocumented workers."[66]

But, in Chicago, Puerto Ricans, non-Mexican Latinos, and others *did*. In the march through the streets of Chicago on May 1, 2001, the first chants had been about Vieques, a reflection of the "Puerto Rican neighborhoods" through which the Humboldt Park collective, of which I was a part, walked. But historically, Mexicans lived side by side with Puerto Ricans here, and, as we approached Ashland Avenue, the rallying calls diversified, in recognition of that greater Mexican presence.[67] "*¡Amnistía, Si se puede!*" and "*¡Raza si, Migra no!*" along with "*¡Boricua, mexicano, luchando mano a mano!*" ("Boricua, Mexicano, struggling hand in hand!"). The human chain stretched across Chicago city limits for approximately 20 miles, from North to South. The communities represented had consisted not only of Puerto Ricans and Mexicans, but also Argentines, Colombians, Salvadorans, Guatemalans, Koreans, and Poles.

About three months later, I had breakfast at a neighborhood diner with Enrique Obregón, director of a Latino social service agency on the North Side with roots in the Chicago settlement house tradition. "I was there," he said of the human chain, "because I'm an immigrant." Born in Mexico, Enrique had come to the United States as an undocumented youth, and amnesty was deeply personal to him and his family. His mother had joined the demonstration with a group from Our Lady of Tepeyac Parish, on the predominantly Mexican South Side community of Little Village, accompanied by Father Jim Miller, who had been pastor of St. Sylvester Church during my childhood. Of his support for the Vieques cause, Enrique said, "It's a health issue" and, besides, "the Navy shouldn't be there if they don't want them there.... It's the right of people to determine what goes on." Enrique remembered his own range of emotions as part of the human chain: "uncomfortable, embarrassed and even happy." When demonstrators linked hands to stop traffic for eleven minutes as a symbolic gesture for eleven million undocumented immigrants, some passengers on a city bus, its black bus driver, and people on the street shouted at the demonstrators to get out of the way. When others screamed, "Go back to your country!" Enrique cried out, "Rosa Parks!" and the bus driver stopped arguing. Soon after, the son of a slain local Mexican political activist boarded the bus to explain the purpose of the demonstration. The power of a historical referent had created possibilities for understandings across groups, and maybe even for concerted actions. Enrique had linked the human chain to the beginning of the Montgomery bus boycott, assuming it would stir a sense of solidarity based on a shared understanding of history to make sense of the present. (Despite the driver's dark skin color, conceivably he shared little history with African Americans.) Black civil rights history was repeatedly evoked during the Puerto Rican campaign for peace in Vieques, and, for many, for amnesty for undocumented immigrants.[68]

On August 29, 2001, Congressman Gutierrez was sentenced to three hours in the custody of a federal marshal and to six months of unsupervised probation on misdemeanor charges of trespassing in entering a Vieques bombing range in April. At his sentencing in Puerto Rico three months after the May 1st human chain, he borrowed from Dr. Martin Luther King, Jr.'s "I have a dream" speech: "We refuse to believe that the bank of justice is bankrupt. We refuse to believe that there are insufficient funds in the great vaults of opportunity of this nation. So we have come to cash this check—a check that will give us upon demand the riches of freedom and the security of justice." Congressman Gutiérrez added, "Judge, I believe it is time for the people of Vieques, of Puerto Rico, to cash this check. It is payable immediately—not two years from today—it is payable immediately."[69] Gutiérrez was relying on the power of history and on historical figures to frame the significance of Vieques and the actions of dissenters on the island.[70]

With the direct involvement and arrests of high-profile African Americans in 2001, among them Al Sharpton and, later, Jacqueline Jackson, in

Vieques, there was talk of a new black and Latino coalition. Jesse Jackson spoke, from Puerto Rico, of an African American and Latino alliance forged through struggles for civil rights and economic, social, and political equality.[71] Census data for 2000 had indicated that Latinos were on track to surpass African Americans as the largest "minority" group in the nation by 2003. Of the implications, an African American journalist based in Chicago wrote, "The Latino population will soon exceed the African American population. This demographic reality will add yet another dimension to the architecture of power relations in the nation. Black leaders should follow the example of Sharpton and Jackson and make bold gestures that outline common interest. If we're lucky, we may get a coalition that can nudge the United States toward greater democracy."[72]

It was not the first time Chicagoans had tried to put together a multiracial political alliance. Richard J. Daley, mayor since 1955, had controlled Chicago through a well-oiled political machine that was supported by working-class white ethnic communities and downtown business interests but that shut out both black and Latino communities. In a 1970 interview, José "Cha Cha" Jimenez, leader of the Young Lords, explained, "When you live in a big city like Chicago[,] it's kind of hard to live by yourself . . . because the loners usually get beat up or shot down and they don't live too long. So you have to belong to some kind of a group. . . . This is how I got involved in the Young Lords, for protection."[73] Yet, he recognized "that we need to form coalitions outside of the Puerto Rican community. That's why we formed the coalition with the Black Panther Party."[74] A November 9, 1969, *New York Times* story from Chicago announced "Black Panthers Join Coalition With Puerto Rican and Appalachian Groups," "with a unifying rallying cry of 'Black Power, Brown Power and White Power.'"[75] A flyer of the Young Patriots, a predominantly Appalachian poor white group, asserted: "Black, brown, and white groups working in a coalition to educate the people in their respective communities . . . educate them to fight racism in the system and in themselves. *The Rainbow Coalition of Chicago is the first multi-racial coalition in America which represents oppressed working class people.*"[76]

With few exceptions, most accounts of this era simplify the complex, and undoubtedly difficult, process and negotiations that made possible the formation of a radical multiracial coalition to aggrieved communities that were simply modeling and subsuming themselves and their politics under the banner of Black Power.[77] "The Panthers' Rainbow Coalition was a defining event in the history of black Chicago," in the opinion of historian Jon Rice, "a political coalition that respected ethnic communities of all kinds led by poor, black youth."[78] But the Black Panthers, although central, were neither the sole archi-tects of coalitional politics nor the only source of political inspiration for other marginalized groups in the city. And, in fact, African American strug-gles for equality and rights had used experiences and efforts of other oppressed communities as a critical resource to make sense of and to address their own circumstances. Historian Lorrin Thomas reminds us that, "the long history of radical nationalism and anti-imperialism in twentieth-century Latin Amer-ica, which formed the ideological roots of both Puerto Rican and Chicano nationalists, was also essential in shaping black nationalists' ideas by the mid-sixties. A more specific borrowing from the Latin American left was the theory of 'internal colonialism.'"[79] Even earlier—in the 1940s, according to sociolo-gist and Puerto Rican studies scholar Carlos Alamo —the black press, *Chicago Defender*, in particular, had turned to "the American outpost in the Carib-bean" whose "racial composition, monocultural economy, and colonial status" were deemed "useful points of comparison for African Americans seeking redress from the US state."[80] The turn to Puerto Rico in this era was grounded in Pan-Africanist internationalism but was also a means to examine compara-tively patterns of inequality and resistance *within* the contours of US Empire.

As arduous as it may be, the pursuit of multiracial collaboration has endured, as has the trope of "Rainbow Coalition." The alliance of the Young Lords, Young Patriots, and Black Panthers was the foundation on which Har-old Washington, an African American lawyer and politician, organized the retooled Rainbow Coalition that in 1983 put him in City Hall.[81] The road to his victory had been paved in events like the chilling reception Washington received on Palm Sunday outside a Northwest Side Catholic church, St. Pascal, where a throng denied him entrance to the church and "DIE NIGGER DIE" was spray-painted across the face of the church.[82] Lissette Rúa, my younger sister and one of the few students of color then at St. Pascal, remem-bered: "None of the teachers at the school EVER addressed what had hap-pened the following day at school but I do remember students using the word 'nigger' in the classroom that day and they were speaking about the inci-dent.... I guess they thought if they don't address it, it never happened. What they did do was a few months, or weeks later, they had us (8th graders) visit an all-black school and interact with the students (interesting why they didn't invite them to our school) but they never made a correlation between what happened that Sunday and the reason for the 'field trip' to the 'ghetto.' St. Pascal had no black students enrolled in the school at that time."

Activists in both the Near West Side and the Near Northwest Side regis-tered Latinos to vote, with 80 percent of the city's Latino population voting for Harold Washington. Latinos ran candidates in aldermanic and committee person races.[83] The coalition that mobilized in his favor had shaken the Chicago political machine, and greater hopes were expressed for the political futures of African Americans. Jesse Jackson, especially, hoped to derive benefit from Washington's triumph in launching his own campaign for US president, in 1984, with a call for a new Rainbow Coalition.[84] In his 1984 and 1988 presidential campaigns, Jackson addressed the issue of demilitarizing Vieques, and, more than a decade later, Jacqueline Jackson championed the cause of Vieques. On June 18, 2001, Mrs. Jackson, one reporter wrote, "dressed as if she were going shopping, pushing through the thick underbrush of Vieques, on her way to being arrested."[85] On June 27 I accompanied a group of around twenty from the Juan Antonio Corretjer Puerto Rican Cultural Center and *Centro Sin Fronteras* (Center Without Borders) to O'Hare Airport to welcome Jackie Jackson home from Puerto Rico. With news reporters and the general public milling around Terminal 3, Gate L8, surrounded by microphone stands and camera pods, Jackie Jackson told the crowd, "I dressed in my suit because I wanted to be treated like a lady should I be arrested, although I was advised to wear blue jeans and gym shoes. . . . And should have . . . but I wanted the military, when upon my arrest, to understand they had a special lady [applause and whistles]." "Mr. Luis Gutierrez, has supported us," she said, "and I wanted to support him. Human rights are indivisible. . . . [W]hen we fought segregation we didn't ask those who came to help us if they were Puerto Rican[s], if they were whites, if they were Germans, if they were Jewish, we just said thank you . . . we lived in a very small world and we need each other." She was enlisting historical memory on behalf of the present.

When Jackie Jackson addressed the court itself, she told us, she had informed the judge, "that he was responsible for helping me to assume my dignity and I want it back ["yeah, mhm," from the audience]. And I wanted to be released on my own recognizance. He . . . gave me a bail of $3,000. The fishermen in this town, on this island of Vieques, earn about $3,000 a year and I said that was excessive. . . . A young lady was coming into the prison as I was leaving because she trespassed. A misdemeanor, mind you . . . She trespassed. And she's 80 years old and she was given $30,000 bail [audience: "Oh, oh"]." Puerto Ricans recognized the unnamed "young lady" Jackson referred to but seemed not to show an awareness of, their nationalist icon who had continued to oppose US control over Puerto Rico. (I heard Puerto Ricans in the gathering make the connection—"that's Lolita," "she's talking about Lolita.")

"Long live a free Puerto Rico!" Lolita Lebrón, then eighty-two, had shouted as her group of six cut through the fence to the bombing range.[86]

Arrested in June 2000 and released on her own recognizance, she had returned to the bombing range a year later to protest once again; this time she was not released until she served a sixty-day sentence.[87] Her tactics against US colonialism had changed since 1954 when, from a balcony in the US House of Representatives, "I lifted the gun and shouted 'Free Puerto Rico Now!'"[88] Now, more than fifty years later, she was protesting US military presence using nonviolent civil disobedience.

A July 15, 2001, *Chicago Sun-Times* op-ed column by Juan Andrade, head of the United States Hispanic Leadership Institute (USHLI) questioned the Jacksons' proclamation of a "new black and brown coalition." Why had there been no talk of a Latino-white coalition when Robert Kennedy Jr. was detained in Vieques for using his body as a human shield? Like the writers of the *Newsweek* story, Andrade took issue with the "rhetoric of solidarity" circulating in the media, pointing instead to issues in which there seemed to be a failure of recognition between African Americans and Latinos. Andrade was especially critical of Jesse Jackson's absence and silence during a hunger strike by Mexican women demanding a high school in Chicago's underserved Little Village community.[89] At his PUSH headquarters in June, when Jackson had asked the audience to applaud a "first-class superintendent," Paul Vallas, former CEO of the Chicago Public Schools, the Latinos had shaken their heads in disbelief and refused. Weeks earlier, Vallas had called the Little Village hunger strike a publicity stunt and accused the fasting women of "blackmail."[90] "When Harold Washington was first elected mayor of Chicago," Andrade wrote, "he won by roughly 50,000 votes. In November 1983, Washington addressed a gathering of Hispanic leaders, and I heard him say it was the Latino vote that put him over the top. . . . No[,] it is fair to say there is no emerging black-Latino political coalition, and there won't be until blacks do for a Latino candidate what Latinos did for Washington."[91] Both the Jacksons and Andrade were framing the struggle for rights within a black and white paradigm, at the same time complicated and fixed, with Latinos an addition or a buffer simply reinforcing polarized racial dynamics in explanations of social struggles.

In Chicago, each of the principle ethnoracial minorities, Puerto Ricans, Mexicans, and African Americans, sought to incorporate its special concerns with broader issues, negotiating participation and working toward collaboration, as allies, often under tentative and fragile circumstances. In attempts to enter into meaningful alliances, both individuals and communities recognized and *misrecognized* themselves and one another.[92] The interracial marriage of my landlady Gina Rios and Julius Bishop was one such collaboration, which, on a daily basis, withstood their tangled connective histories. A constant debate in the Bishop household had been Julius's contention that Puerto Ricans do not think enough about race, with Gina countering that African Americans think of nothing else. Yet these two raised a family, at once "very Puerto Rican" and with a black diasporic racial consciousness. It made for interesting Sunday afternoon conversations in the Bishop household. So, too, the 1950s association between my own Puerto Rican abuela and her Japanese American landlord offered a varying yet connective history, embodying a range of the power of social relationships, and the potential for complex collaborations in grounded identidades.

"NOBODY DIES ON THE EVE OF THEIR LAST DAY"

RITES OF PASSAGE AND PERSONHOOD

A wedding announcement in *Vida Latina*, a Chicago bilingual monthly magazine of October 1955, read: "The honorable Miss Georgina Rios joined her destiny in a touching and gracious ceremony to that of the gentleman groom Julio Bishop." As a photograph showed, "the newlywed bride shone her enchantments decorated in nuptial finery," capturing Gina's striking beauty and her eighteen-inch waist.[1] It was a find I prized because it was Gina and Julius Bishop who later established Caribe Funeral Home on the border of Logan Square and Humboldt Park, my most important field site and my "office" and home for more than two years of research. From February 2001 to August 2003 I had rented an apartment upstairs from the Bishops' plant-filled office, their embalming room, the casket storage area, and the two viewing rooms, but had not foreseen that the world of the Caribe Funeral Home would become an integral part of the research itself. I had moved, unaware, into a central site of my study, a vital place, one to which many of the Puerto Rican community came daily to gossip, to reminisce, to enjoy each other's company—to renew ties. It was, in a multiplicity of ways, a center of life, not only a center of death. I learned there how sacred and secular rites of passage are tied to notions of personhood.

The story of a community is a narrative of persons who come together through a series of passages—commemorative acts that mark stages over a lifetime, from childhood to adolescence to adulthood, from one social position to another, from birth to death.[2] Commemorations of both life and death are central to community in Puerto Rican Chicago, where family histories are passed on through the arts of storytelling and singing, a call-and-response that foster a collective consciousness. Through daily and seasonal cultural rituals and practices, as mundane as learning how to make *café con leche*, elders pass down ways of being Puerto Rican in Chicago. Contours of that complex cultural identity have taken shape through many weddings, baptisms, yearly masses in honor of patron saints, birthday parties, and wakes. At wakes, along with much Puerto Rican food, family and friends engage in lively debates about whether a life has been one of success or of failure, hence reflecting the values and experience of the community itself.

The sites and practices of memory—the cherished, the tucked away, and the traumatic—are intimately entangled, both for individuals and for collectives. "Secondary mortuary" rites (activities and observances long after the death) enable the living to commemorate a loved one who has been transformed into an ancestor.[3] Younger members learn to remember what they did not experience firsthand and the new knowledge helps craft identity.[4] As anthropologist Steven Gregory suggests, "not only are social identities transformed over time, but they are also grounded in social relations, experiences, and commitments that endure through time. People recollect and rework the past through social practices of memory that bring the meaning of the past to bear on conditions in the present."[5] My own examination of memories focused not on whether they were apt and "true" but on their context, the meanings that emanate and circulate from them, and their influences on the social dimensions of identity. Contests over identity, power, and recognition mobilize memory, over and over again, of place and of practice, to establish legitimacy and to affirm claims to belonging.[6]

The Departed as Symbols of Collective Identity

Julius Bishop was not a fountain of information on his own life, that of an African American with deep roots in the South, but he did know some "stuff," so he admitted, about Puerto Ricans in Chicago. "Thursday night was the maids' night off to have coffee and tea," he told me in November 2002. "There were dances on Saturday night," and at one of these he met Medelicia Rios and "his boy" Oscar Rios, his future sister-in-law and brother-in-law. As it happened, Julius liked keeping company with Puerto Ricans, since he could practice his Spanish and perfect his dance moves at their weekend soirées. This was how Julius became Julio. He had learned Spanish years before in Tampa, where "quite a few people spoke Spanish—broken Spanish," and he read *La Prensa*, from New York, and *El Diario de la Marina*, Cuba's oldest newspaper, purchased at a downtown Chicago "out-of-town newspaper stand" that carried the Spanish-language papers. Of his own arrival from Florida, he said, growing up you "moved where you could find accommodations." He came of age in the 1940s in the Bronzeville community on the South Side, two blocks from the home of Harold Washington, Chicago's future mayor, and made friends among a small group of Afro-Cubans. (In later years he would travel to Cuba, as well as to Puerto Rico and the Dominican Republic.) In 1955, married only a few weeks, Julius was drafted in the Korean War and left for Germany, where he served for two years and developed a taste for sweet German wine. Upon discharge he found work with the US Postal Service but also enrolled in the Worsham College of Mortuary Science. In 1966 Julius purchased a wide, brown brick building near the corner of Armitage Avenue and Kimball, in Chicago's Logan Square/Humboldt Park community, which became the Caribe Funeral Home. In 1992 Julius told me of his experiences as a black entrepreneur when I interviewed him for an undergraduate research paper for my University of Illinois course on "Black Business History in America." "See, there was a lot of prejudice back there in those days," he told me. "I lost business, me being black." Yet and still, his funeral home had provided invaluable services to socially neglected populations. "Many people have patronized Caribe because the business caters to Spanish speakers and will serve the poor."

In *Passed On: African American Mourning Stories*, literary and cultural studies scholar Karla F. C. Holloway illustrates the unique role of black morticians in the black community that emerged after the exclusion of black bodies and black cultural practices from proper burials by white undertakers. Black morticians served their communities in diverse ways beyond embalming, from providing hearses as ambulances for the sick to lending folding chairs for neighborhood affairs.[7] Of black-owned funeral homes, St. Clair Drake and Horace Cayton's classic study of black life in the urban north, *Black Metropolis*, observed: "Since an undertaker's success is based upon popularity as well as upon service and efficiency, 'morticians' are very careful to maintain wide connections with lodges, churches, and civic and social clubs."[8] Julius himself was African American but the identity of his business was based on its clientele and legitimated by the cultural identity of his wife, Gina Bishop, who was Puerto Rican. Caribe was the first Puerto Rican funeral home in the city; it was "thought of as Latino owned," Julius said. Both Julius and Gina had served as loyal members of St. Sylvester's Church, the Lions Club, the *Congreso Puertorriqueño de Ayuda Mutua* (Puerto Rican Congress of Mutual Aid), and the Puerto Rican Chamber of Commerce. They donated time, money, and materials for community events, and were equally generous with friends. In 1988 they opened a second and fancier funeral home, on Damen

Avenue in the Ravenswood neighborhood. With Julius's retirement, however, it became more difficult to maintain two locations, and with the gentrification of the Ravenswood area, they could profit by selling. As a result, Caribe Funeral Home II closed in 2004. Today condominiums stand where it once stood.

For more than two years, I lived in my comfortable six-room apartment above the funeral parlor that had once been home to the Bishops, their five children, and the occasional long-term visitor. But I had known the Bishops long before I arrived to do research. I had grown up attending wakes at Caribe, stopping in with the Bishop daughters after school to say hello or to run errands with the girls, and, later, I worked part-time in the front office, in both Caribe I and II. I made the coffee during wakes, displayed the memorial cards, and closed up the premises afterward. At the time, Julius Bishop was semi-retired and, in 2001, when I began my fieldwork, fully retired, but Becky, the third Bishop child, had earned her own funeral director-and-embalmer license from Worsham in 1995. I visited with "Mr. Bishop"—I never called him Julius or Julio—some weekday afternoons or on any given Sunday when dinner was a guarantee in the Bishop home. At family gatherings, he would sit at a corner of the dining room table, a pile of books from his personal library on one side, a stash of sweet imported German wine on the other. If he found someone's company agreeable, he would offer a sip and talk about one of the books, such as *They Came Before Columbus: The African Presence in Ancient America*; *Castro, the Blacks, and Africa*; or *Black Athena: The Afroasiatic Roots of Classical Civilization*. I began to accompany him to cultural events or to his favorite restaurants, hole-in-the-wall joints, each a gastronomic gem.

One of the first times I picked him up for an outing, I made the mistake of asking if he should let someone know he was leaving the house. (He had diabetes, high blood pressure, and heart disease.) "I'm grown," he growled. "I don't need to ask for permission." He then announced a taste for steamed fish from Chinatown, which required taking the Kennedy and Dan Ryan Expressways amid horrendous traffic. It took us more than an hour to get to the Near South Side and almost two hours to get back in the dark, when we found the second eldest daughter, Gini, making phone calls. "I was about to call the police," she said. Later that evening I received two phone calls, one from Gina, the other from Elsa, the youngest daughter, letting me know how worried they had been. I was always to let someone know if I took Mr. Bishop out of the house, whether he knew it or not. I continued to pick Mr. Bishop up for what became our special outings, but surreptitiously informed his family of our whereabouts. He would tell me (and sometimes

guide me) about Chicago, its sites, sounds, tastes, and people. On rare occasions, he shared stories about himself and about Puerto Rican life in that
multiracial and deeply segregated city.

After her husband's retirement, Gina Bishop worked in the front office
most evenings. A gambler at heart, she played the slot machines and the
lotería (numbers), but her biggest gambles were on youth and the down-
trodden. She rented to young people starting out and to those who had fallen
on hard times. It was the beginning of my lessons in "reciprocity in the field."
Incredibly opinionated and critical of her tenants' lifestyles, she nonetheless
consciously charged, and charges today, below-market rental rates in a rapidly
gentrifying neighborhood. For me the affordability of my living quarters
came at a price I was happy to pay. On a weeknight, whenever my phone rang
at around 8:30 p.m., I knew Gina was calling: "Girl, can you give me ride
home." It was never posed as a question. Out of sheer politeness she would
inquire about my day and I shared my research with her, in part, as proof that
I actually did *work* but, more so, because she was my ideal interlocutor, my
sounding board, an expert on Puerto Rican Chicago, whether she acknowledged it or not. One evening she called me to come downstairs for the wake
for a *pionero*. There would, she said, be people I might want to speak with for
my "project," and plenty of good food in case I was hungry. Some weekends,
when she had a family obligation, which meant that none of her children,
nieces, or nephews could tend to the funeral home, Gina would ask me to
open up and tend the front office until she could get there. She repaid me
with food, her own home cooking or a plate brought from a function she had
attended. For me, helping out was a blending of what a neighbor and friend
would do and of my own need to reciprocate.

In the Caribe Funeral Home memories of the past permeated everyday
conversation. The bodies waked there told a larger story of Puerto Rican
urban life, of hardships with housing, gang violence, or the police, and also of
evidence of a community's resilience. In an arson wave that hit Humboldt
Park—from 1970 to 1978, 29 percent of the housing stock in a thirty-two-
block tract east of the park was lost to flames[9]—and in an accompanying tide
of gang warfare and police brutality, families and communities came together, mourned, and fought back. Hundreds from the Puerto Rican community attended a wake at Caribe Funeral Home for six persons killed in a
1977 New Year's Day fire on the Near Northwest Side (two other bodies were
flown to Puerto Rico for burial). According to the *Chicago Tribune*, "At
the funeral home service, the crowd of more than 200 overflowed into the
street. . . . When the five hearses had departed for the cemetery . . . it was

announced that more than $2,000 had been raised for the families' survivors."[10] A photo-essay by Carlos Flores, "Capturing the Images of Chicago's Puerto Rican Community," included a picture of a 1973 wake in Caribe for a community activist, Orlando Quintana, who had been shot and killed by an off-duty police officer.[11] Quintana, a college graduate and a supervisor of youth programs at Association House, a settlement house on the Near Northwest Side, had been working with gangs. The official police report of his death differed from the community version; the police officer claimed Quintana had shot at him first. Association House partially funded the defense to clear his name.[12] When I showed Gina the picture in the photo-essay she told me of that evening: "Police closed off Armitage Avenue because so many people came to pay their respects, the street was filled with people." The police formed parallel lines with their bodies, from the funeral home entrance through the office into the first chapel, leading people to view the casket and then out. "There were police in the alley, too, in case if anything happened," since they wanted "to get people in and out as quickly as possible." Celebrations of the lives of those who died of natural causes also were testimony of the juncture of memory, identity, and place. A Maria De Jesus, born in Puerto Rico in 1899, 107 years old at her passing in 2006, and one of the oldest persons to die in Chicago in recent times, was commemorated at Caribe Funeral Home.[13]

Caribe, the subject of scandal and hearsay, urban legend and local lore, in some circles is referred to disparagingly as the "gangbanger" funeral home. Reymundo Sanchez (pseudonym), in his memoir, *My Bloody Life: The Making of a Latin King*, claims that, in the "gang wars" of the late 1970s to early 1980s, "hundreds of Latin Kings" surrounded Caribe Funeral Home determined not to let a rival gang member "rest in peace." "We blocked off the road to both people and cars. Many King brothers had guns pulled out. They were watching rooftops and guarding gangways against Gangsters [the rival gang]. Several King brothers went inside the funeral home and carried the dead body out with them. . . . The body was thrown in the middle of the street and repeatedly shot." The Latin Kings scattered; no one was arrested.[14] Growing up I had heard a version of this story, but, in fact, it was another funeral home, *not* Caribe, that was the site of the desecration. With the publication of Sanchez's memoir many accept that Caribe Funeral Home was the place where it all happened, though the Bishops denied it and I have found no record of it. Still the tale persists. Violence of other kinds, however, did affect services there sometimes. Thus, I wrote in my field notes of October 2001:

I knew right away what the popping sound was. I didn't get scared; I just walked over to the front of my apartment and looked out the window. I then realized that the shooting was a lot closer than I thought. It began around the corner from the funeral home where a group of young men attending a wake stood in front of a store. They ran for cover into the funeral home; the person with the gun followed, continuing to shoot. I had gone downstairs to check on Gina and saw people coming out of their apartments and onto the street to figure out what had happened. Four people were injured, mainly grazes. The front entrance of the funeral home had two bullet holes: one near the bottom of the wooden door and the other in the canopy. The police surrounded the area and put the yellow "police area" ribbons up around the funeral home. One officer reprimanded Gina: "I don't know why you cater to gangbangers." She corrected him, "it wasn't a gangbanger funeral; the man weighed 400 pounds." The people in the funeral home were crying. Women were trying to calm down the little kids who had witnessed the attack. As I sat around with Gina a woman asked, "does this happen a lot here?" I said "no" even though I've heard gunshots in the area recently, but not aimed at the funeral home. More than anything, those in attendance couldn't believe the disrespect to the dead and those in mourning. Gina remorsefully admitted, "I hate the fact that rents are going up but maybe that will get rid of the gangs."

I know why I moved back into this neighborhood, but, realistically, I don't always feel safe. Yet I do feel comfortable in this space. . . . This is not the ethnography I want to write, but I can't deny that [violence] has been part of my experience "in the field."

Gina Bishop, like her neighborhood friends Ana La Luz and Otilia Irizarry, does not conceal violence in her account of her community. When the deceased is young and male, Caribe inquires if the death was gang-related and arranges for a police patrol during the wake. Violence, in various forms, in some measure, has shaped the diverse experiences of Puerto Ricans in the working-class neighborhoods of Chicago, and cannot, and should not, be edited out of accounts of life there.

Over the years, more socially mobile Puerto Ricans have chosen to mourn their dead in funeral homes that seem to represent their own newly achieved class status. To such, Caribe is a funeral home of last resort, and for those who have no money; I have heard it described as "low-class" and "dirty." Caribe is, indeed, a no-frills establishment in cost, service, and setting, with no fancy rooms, no fancy front columns. A pragmatic space. For many it is a place replete with history and strong social relationships, whether they choose to wake their dead there or elsewhere. Caribe has served principally Latinos (as of 2010 or so, more Mexicans than Puerto Ricans), some, if not many, blacks, and, more recently, a growing Muslim clientele.[15] Caribe Funeral Home's identity, however, remains tied to the Latina/o working-class and poor of the city of Chicago.

Researcher as Eulogist

It was the summer that I was preparing my tenure file for Williams College. I was sitting in the sunroom of a house I had rented in Williamstown, Massachusetts, and writing about the funeral home. My phone rang. Julius Bishop had died. He had survived several heart attacks had lived to see his children have children of their own, and some of these to marry. I thought now about the death of my own father, in November 2006, eight months after the death of his mother, my *abuela* (grandmother). A new death reminds one of other absences. Elsa Bishop had asked if I would deliver the eulogy at the requiem mass at St. Sylvester's. For me, it would be a test of how well I had observed and listened to people's stories. Mindful of my writing woes, Gina reassured me, "Maybe he'll be able to help you more now from the other side." I "had done enough" and she was "not expecting anything else from me." She was letting me off the hook if I wanted to be let off. No, Mr. Bishop had been generous with me; I needed to pay my respects in person.

The death notice in the *Chicago Tribune* of June 15, 2008, read: "Julius Bishop, 79, beloved husband of Georgina, nee Rios; loving father of Rose, Dr. Virginia (Ronald Townsend), Rebeca (Marco) Sabbi, Elsa (Orlando) Rodriguez and Julio; loving grandfather of Rosa, Micaela, Andrea, Isaiah, Angela, Shawn, Ibrahim, Julius, Nicolas, Ethan and Elias; loving uncle of Diane Moxley. Founder and owner of Caribe Funeral Home."[16] Generations of family and friends gathered for the wake the following evening, Caribe Funeral Home overflowing with those who came to pay last respects and offer condolences, some from as far as down South. My mother, two sisters, brother-in-law, and three nephews attended with me. The casket, front and center in the main viewing room, was surrounded by floral arrangements and mounted photographs, including two of the Bishop family with their multiracial kith and kin and the 1959 graduating class photo of the Worsham Mortuary School, along with pictures of birthday parties, wedding anniversaries, holiday gatherings, and a portrait of a dignified, round-faced Julius Bishop wearing wide-frame glasses and a dapper suit, like the prime minister of a Caribbean nation. (Maurice Bishop of Grenada came to mind, perhaps more so because of the name association than because of physical or political resemblance). The thin body in the casket was a fragile semblance of the man in the impressive portrait; the body appeared tired yet rested, both at the same time. I said my farewell as a Cuban *son montuno* played from a boom box beside the casket. On a small table nearby was a display of some of Mr. Bishop's prized possessions, most prominent among them his books on Africa and the African diaspora. Those seated before the coffin were speaking in hushed tones, those at the back more boisterous, while adults with small children as well as a few preteens were in the smaller viewing room enjoying coffee, soft drinks, and snacks. Interlaced in the conversations of what had made the departed unique were words of what bound "us" together and what made this community distinct.

When Rosie, the eldest daughter, turned off the music, it announced that the time had come for the formal reflect on the life of Julius Bishop. An Afro-Cuban from the South Side, Don Julio's *compadre*, spoke of "my good friend," and many others told their versions of how Julius became Julio—because he spoke Spanish, read Spanish, taught his daughters to dance a mean *son montuno*. Becky Bishop had told me earlier, "A lot of family friends always thought my father was either Cuban or Dominican and they're shocked when I have to argue with them that 'no my father is not from Latin America, my father is black.' And they still don't believe it." Her younger sister Elsa was, in fact, difficult to convince that her father was African American. "We were raised with more Puerto Rican culture . . . food and music," Elsa said, but "also raised with Cubans—major. And for a long period of time I thought I was Cuban 'cause all of my father's friends were Cuban." Carlos Flores, who is known for his wondrously mundane photographs of past and present Puerto Rican Chicago, spoke of Julio as an intellectual committed to the study of people of African descent who had inspired Puerto Ricans, especially Afro-Puerto Ricans, to become students of the black diaspora and Afro-Puerto Rican history, citing relevant parallels to African American struggles. I was reminded of Gini Bishop's description of her father: "He made sure that we knew about his history, about our history, about the similarities between both of our cultures." He had pushed his daughter to become a critical observer of her own social world: "When you went to Puerto Rico and you were [watching] TV did you see anybody your color or darker? Did you notice in the airport who were the people that were cleaning, who were the people that were selling the tickets?" Gina, her mother, was convinced her husband was transferring his own negative experiences with race in the United States to the island and tainting his children's perspective.

Ana La Luz was now speaking of the Bishop-La Luz friendship, of how Julio and Jacobo, her husband, would mercilessly rib one another about who would sire the first son. "Gina and I had three daughters in a row and no sons, and then comes Gina along with the fourth girl, and my fourth one was a boy. Julio and my husband were very good friends; they hassled one another whenever [a girl] was born, but we were all very, very good friends." Ana's family prevailed; it took the Bishops five tries before Julito was born. Now, another woman was speaking of "the lack of role models for Puerto Rican youth" in her day. Julius Bishop was one for them, she said, an African American deeply rooted in Puerto Rican and Cuban culture and community. Because he had affectionately berated the young people to "buy books rather than new cars" and had demonstrated hard work and respectability in his own life, she had attended law school and stood before us today as a judge, "a role model for Puerto Ricans." Some were applauding her remarks with enthusiasm; others were complaining, "This isn't a political event." "Is she running for office?" Politicians, too, had come to pay their last respects, current and former aldermen and appointed city officials. One gentleman spoke of the support Julio had offered to those "willing to work hard and needed a hand up," praising him for having raised "professionals" and pointing out his own children in the assemblage—"*Aquí hay profesionales*" ("Here there are professionals").

Narratives of success and social mobility were told to put to rest negative depictions of the community, though a few mumbled questions about what constitutes a collective sense of success or failure. Elsa Bishop reminded those around her that her son was born out of wedlock before she had finished pharmacy school. The paths some Bishop children took toward professionalization had experienced more detours than the speakers portrayed. But did that mean that Elsa was not respectable? She was recognizing alternative paths to social mobility that deviated from narrow middle-class conventions. In this rite of passage honoring Julius Bishop, stories were told of the ways individuals believe they had partially overcome systemic marginalization, sharing their greatest aspirations and what was possible under certain circumstances. In front of me—all around me—was an internal debate about the meaning of Puerto Rican-ness in the past, in the present, and in the future.

What was left for me to say in my own eulogy for the next day's service, one I had not yet written? Of all those who had spoken at the wake, I was the one who had known Mr. Bishop the least—only about twenty years, the first ten of these spent avoiding the patriarch in my visits to the Bishop home. Mr. Bishop had intimidated me as an adolescent, with his seriousness and reserve, though I had attended St. Sylvester grammar school with the two youngest Bishops (Elsa in my older sister's class, Julio in my younger sister's) and had become close friends with Elsa in high school. So, too, Becky had taken me to visit her classes at Loyola University when I was a high school sophomore and, a few years later, Gini, completing her medical residency in Washington, DC, had opened her home to me when I was considering graduate programs there. Elsa had asked me to be a baptismal godmother for her son Isaíah. The family believed I could convey a different dimension of Don Julio's personality—what was important to him. I decided to focus on what was most beloved to him (besides his family)—books. Although books were part of my own agenda (I was, after all, in the process of writing this one), I questioned whether I could convey a veritable snapshot of who he was. Writing the eulogy became, for me, a demonstration of intellectual and communal reciprocity. Here it is as I delivered it from the lectern before his casket.

Julius Bishop (July 9, 1928–June 11, 2008)

"I have a book I want you to take a look at. It's got some *very* interesting information." These words will forever remind me of Mr. Bishop. While of course he was talking about one of the many books in his personal library, I now think he was also talking about himself.

This book Don Julio spoke of was one I wasn't ready to open when I first made my way into the Bishop house as a teenager. I came to hang out with the girls and eat the food. I steered clear of the serious man with wide-frame glasses who would make his way up from the basement, his sanctuary, where he practiced the violin, listened to old LPs of Cuban music, and studied from his vast collection of books, *National Geographic* magazines, or African American newspapers, amassing a global black perspective. That stuff was boring!

In college, I became curious about this book, but was still not committed to actually reading it. When I needed information for research papers I probed it, and, with encyclopedic knowledge, Mr. Bishop would easily rattle off names, dates, and events in Chicago history, Black history, or anything I needed to know about early Puerto Rican life in the city. Only concerned with the basics, I didn't pay too much attention to his elaborations or interesting asides. At that time, I think he thought I was boring.

Once I became serious about my studies, I was ready to learn something about history and community, so again I turned to this book. It was a book that compiled the achievements and disappointments of people of African descent. It told the story of a local business that has served and supported thousands for more than 40 years. Don Julio told me that he chose the name "Caribe" because of the personal connections he felt to the Caribbean, having roots in Florida and his friendships with Puerto Ricans and Cubans. Those of us in the funeral home last night were witness to the true strength of those relationships.

In time, I was hooked. It was a book I could not put down. It took me places, like the DuSable Museum of African American History to experience *los Muñequitos de Matanzas* or the Newberry Library to explore a family lineage that included Creek and Cherokee nations; it taught me about the hidden culinary treasures of the city—*rabo encendido* [oxtail stew] from *Rinconcito Cubano*, steamed fish from Chinatown, and palm wine from the Ethiopian restaurant that once stood in Wrigleyville.

It was a book that demanded one's attention. It was never an easy read, sometimes it wasn't even enjoyable, but it was always critical, in the best sense of the word. Its purpose was to make the reader think. Julius Bishop, Don Julio, is a classic, a wonderfully complicated book.

The Bonds of Kith, Kin, and Community

Gina Bishop and Ana La Luz, friends for more than fifty years, had called on one another on a variety of occasions—family gatherings, baptisms, birthday parties, graduations, weddings, anniversaries, wakes, and funerals. Sometimes they simply sat together and caught up in the front office of the funeral home. Every December after 1981, Ana has organized a memorial service for her husband Jacobo in their Palmer Square home. I had attended one with Gina (who needed a ride). Gina knew almost everyone there: Ana's children and *their* children, Ana's brother, his family, other nieces, nephews, and a great many friends from over the decades. Gina would introduce me in one of two ways: "She is my friend and Isaíah's godmother," or "She is one of my '*hijas postizas*' (fictive daughters). She grew up with my kids and our families are often together." She had me meet a friend who had the oldest account at the *Los Caballeros de San Juan* (Knights of St. John) Credit Union, a lending institution established by Puerto Rican men from the pioneering genera-tion.[17] (Young bank tellers were often left flummoxed when Gina's friend gave them his account number, 2.)

In the dining room at the memorial service were rows of folding chairs and an "altar" (a folding table covered with a linen tablecloth, a candle, an angel, and garland). Overflow guests sat on the living room sofas or stood as mass was said by Father James Miller, in his nineteenth year of celebrating this sec-ondary mortuary rite with the La Luz family and their friends. After the short mass came requests for prayers for sick family members or for one who had gone astray. Ana's grandson asked us to "pray for the people of Afghanistan because they're getting bombed." With the formal ceremony over, guests helped clear the altar and moved chairs in preparation to break bread. Gossip and *indirectas* (innuendos), usual where family and friends gather, were exchanged as I caught bits of conversations about old family "secrets," inept childrearing, the preservation or lack of preservation of culture, troubled re-lationships, and other challenges to identity. A woman of light hue asked Gina, "Are you Puerto Rican?" "No," she answered with an edge. Gina was not unaccustomed to others questioning her identity, especially compatriots of lighter complexion. She turned to me and spoke of her friendship with Ana: "Every time Julio and I moved, Jacobo either rented or bought near us. When he got upset with Ana, he'd show up at our house." When Jacobo was dying, Gina had devoted her mornings to caring for him so Ana could go to work. "That was the first and last sick person I cared for," she said. It had been hard to see him deteriorate. She was with the family the evening Jacobo took his last breath.

About two months later I saw Ana again, at Gini Bishop's house for her son Nico's first birthday party. Children were playing or watching television in the basement (with some adult supervision), the younger ones dashing up and down the stairs. Adults were scattered throughout, in the living room, the kitchen, sitting around the dining room table, and in the TV room upstairs. As in other Bishop gatherings, food was served buffet style with comfort foods: rice and beans, chicken, salads and other greens, mac-and-cheese, and birthday cake. There was wine and beer for adults, water and juice for the kids. A group of women gathered in the living room while the sun set, the room grew dark, and Gini lit candles: "I'm a bit embarrassed *porque me llevaron la lámpara*" ("because they took my lamp"). Recently divorced, Gini was in the process of dividing up possessions with her ex-husband. "*Gini, no te apures*," Ana interjected, "*menos que limpiar*" ("Gini, don't worry about it, less to clean"), a comment seemingly directed to the women in the room, who broke into sudden laughter. Deeply disheartened by her own daughter's divorce—women of her generation did not give up on marriage or the family, Ana told me once—she nonetheless saved her judgments. I wrote in my field notes, "It's amazing how these friends [Gina and Ana] have stayed in touch over the years and how they have become family." Anthropologist Carol Stack found that "[t]he offering of kin terms to 'those you count on' is a way people expand their personal networks. A friend who is classified a kinsman is simultaneously given respect and responsibility."[18]

Questions about friendships made and friendships transformed into fictive kin were rooted in place and in rites of passage. "Thanks to God I have many friendships, many friends," Ana told me, "but one of the people I most esteem as a friend is Gina Bishop. We met when I came from East Chicago, Indiana, and started working in a factory on Loomis [on the Near West Side]. . . . We discovered I was married on an August 13 [1954] and that the following year on August 13 [1955] she was married. . . . I went to live near her when she was expecting her second child." The friends had celebrated their nuptials in the same church, San Francisco de Asís (Saint Francis of Assisi), where each of their older brothers had also wed. San Francisco "belongs to the Mexicans," William Rios, Gina's brother, told me, but Puerto Ricans went there, too, because "that's the one that there was; . . . it was the most known." Since the mid-1920s, San Francisco, the oldest Spanish-speaking church in Chicago, has served the spiritual and social needs of Mexican communities in the Loop, the West Side, and the North Side of the city, but has also long been the locus of a broad *latinidad.*[19]

The founding in 1952 of the bilingual monthly *Vida Latina*, a publication of and for the Latinos, reflected the coming of age of Chicago's Latinos as a community, another kind of rite of passage. Within its pages one could find local, national, and international news, profiles of community members, editorials, society news, reviews of cultural events, creative writing and poetry from readers, and advertisements for local businesses, along with announcements of marriages, baptisms, and special masses at San Francisco for Mexicans, Puerto Ricans, Dominicans, and other Chicago Latinos.[20] News of Latino organizations, like the Chicago Council of the League of United Latin American Citizens (LULAC), the Mexican American Council, and the *Caballeros de San Juan* (the Knights of St. John) kept the community informed.[21] In its inaugural issues, an editorial explained the magazine's purpose: "The more numerous the fine publications a community can rely on, the greater the cultural prestige it acquires from an educational point of view": "VIDA LATINA, an illustrated monthly magazine. . . . will be like a camera whose pages highlight only that which emphasizes to outsiders more than to our own brethren, the appropriate profile of the great Indo-Hispanic people. Thus, within the domestic US sphere, it will deal with our/their social, athletic, cultural, and artistic life. . . . . . [It would not limit] itself to any specific geographic region, but rather circulating in areas where the great languages of Cervantes and Shakespeare do."[22] A following issue honed the mission further: "All work must have a defined purpose, ours is to collect and consolidate all that is Latino in the environment that surrounds us."[23]

Thus the triumphant performances of ballerina Alicia Alonso (Cuba) and iconic singers Pedro Infante (Mexico) and Ruth Fernandez (Puerto Rico) were reported with a clear designation of national origins, as was the "joy of Latin Americans [in Chicago] when [welterweight champion] Kid Gavilán retained the world title."[24] On a Friday night in November 1953, Gina's brother William Rios was one of more than 19,200 at the Chicago Stadium to witness the Afro-Cuban boxer's "unanimous 15 round decision over Johnny Bratton."[25] A photograph in *Vida Latina* captured Gavilán with "the popular priest Father Tomás [Thomas Matin] of San Francisco de Asís . . . after the unforgettable fight."[26] (Before the bout he had attended mass at San Francisco.)

Other ways in which *Vida Latina* displayed the dynamics of latinidad in the city was its profiles of community members. Thus, the May 1953 issue ran a profile of local radio personality José Noemí Gómez, Sr. with a brief history of his radio show. Latin music lovers could tune in to AM 1450/WHFC to catch the "much loved" radio show "*Hora Hispana*" (Hispanic Hour), hosted by the Dominican-born announcer, *El caballero daper* (the dapper gentleman), as Noemí Gómez was nicknamed. Gomez's show's success was attributed to his unique style and his ability to appeal to the musical tastes of his diverse listeners. The radio broadcast pioneer was honored for his service and achievement by the *colonia mexicana*,[27] and the Puerto Rican community acknowledged him a local dignitary at the coronation dance of Miss Puerto Rico 1954.[28] Honored by other Latino groups, Noemí Gómez was a central player in making certain the *colonia dominicana* was especially recognized as a distinct group in the city and in *Vida Latina*. The cover of the magazine's November 1956 issue was dedicated to "*Generalísmo Doctor* Rafael L. Trujillo," president of the Dominican Republic, on the occasion of his birthday, celebrated by Chicago's Dominican community.[29] Special services for the health of General Trujillo, and for *la virgen de la Altagracia*, the Dominican Republic's virgin patroness, were observed at San Francisco in 1954 and in Holy Name Cathedral in 1957 by the city's Dominican *colonia*, religious acts initiated by Noemí Gómez, as was likely the case with the magazine cover itself.[30]

As a chronicle of community life, *Vida Latina* covered both calamities and conflicts, as well as celebrations. A May 1953 editorial told of "the tragic and unfortunate disaster" at the "Haber Corp." factory on the Near North Side, a fire that killed thirty-four workers, most of them Puerto Ricans. A number of bodies had been sent back "to their native land where they will find eternal rest under the warm sun in the Puerto Rican soil that witnessed their birth."[31] Earlier that year, a Salvador Heredia of 1110 West Harrison Street, in a "letter to the editor" expressed a desire not to rest in peace but to live in peace:

> *No quisiera yo pecar de adulador, pero forzado por las circunstancias y sabiendas de que tengo algunos enemigos espontáneos, le suplico de antemano la publicación de esta carta en su interesante revista VIDA LATINA con el exclusivo interés de felicitar a la . . . persona que me reportó al Servicio de Migración.*
>
> *Lamento demasiado que la visita de los empleados del Servicio de Migración a la humilde casa de su servidor, haya sido para sentarse a tomar café debido a que resido legalmente en este país.*
>
> *Antes de terminar deseo recomendarle a mi admirador que la próxima vez use otro método más eficaz y menos cobarde.*

I do not want to succumb to the sin of flattery, but forced by the circumstances and the knowledge that I have some spontaneous enemies out there, I ask you in advance to print this letter in your interesting magazine VIDA LATINA, with the exclusive aim of congratulating the . . . person who reported me to the Immigration Service.

I regret, too, that the visit of the Immigration Service employees to the modest home of this humble servant had to be merely to sit about and sip coffee due to the fact that I reside legally in this country.

Before concluding, I wish to recommend to my admirer that next time around he use some other more effective and less cowardly method.[32]

With time, *Vida Latina*'s society pages expanded, more and more community members sending photographs of the momentous events in their personal lives.[33] A photograph of "Georgina Rios accompanied by her siblings William, Oscar, Ana Delia and Medelicia of the same name, on her birthday," appeared in *"Tópicos Sociales"* (Social Topics) in August 1954.[34] By

1955, "*Rincon Borincano*" (The Puerto Rican Corner) was *the* forum Chicago's Puerto Ricans chose to announce birthday parties, baptisms, graduations, weddings, and anniversaries. Elena Padilla, in her study of Puerto Ricans' identity and community formation in postwar Chicago, wrote that "*Rites de passage* revolve around the Catholic beliefs."[35] Most of the society pages in *Vida Latina* did, indeed, concern sacred ceremonies, as, for example, baptism. It is the Catholic custom for a child to be baptized in its first year, with sponsors, or godparents (*padrinos* and *madrinas*) promising to provide religious education and guidance.[36] A relationship of *compadrazgo* (coparenthood) develops between parents and godparents. In a formal church ritual, the child is blessed and received into the larger religious community. The parents' selection of godparents from distinct social classes, vertical relations of *compadrazgo*, it has been suggested, indicate the parents' hope for social and material benefit.[37] Godparents are expected throughout their godchild's life to make social visits, and attend birthday parties and other significant life cycle ceremonies.[38] Still and all, bonds between *comprades* can break, families fracture, and friendships come to an end, especially when expectations are not met and individuals become disappointed with one another.

In the announcements and their accompanying photographs in *Vida Latina*, class distinctions became legible, especially through public displays of titles and in the naming of places in the celebration of sacred rites. "With satisfaction reflected on their faces, parents, godparents and children," a *Vida Latina* photographer recorded after Jose Noemí Gomez Jr. received "lustral water from the hands of Fr. Tómas in the baptismal font of San Francisco of Asís," in a three-quarter page announcement, "Enlace Religioso" (Religious Bond). The radio host Jose Noemí Gómez, Sr. and his wife had selected "Mr. Engineer Architect Carlos Magro" and Doña Alicia Magro as their son's baptismal godparents.[39] A handful of photographs documented the socioreligious ceremony, one taken at the baptismal font, another in front of the church, and one at the dinner table with little Jose Noemí Gomez Jr. surrounded by siblings, his mother and godmother dutifully serving them.[40] Francisca Rivera, daughter of Mr. Fernando and Rosa Rivera, was sponsored by "the well-known impresario" Saul Gonzalez and his wife Enriqueta Jimenez with a party afterward at Club El Mirador.[41] Other announcements were more modest: "Little Emma Iris Ortiz recently received baptismal waters at San Francisco, her godparents were Manin and Mariana Ortiz. The parents of the new Christian are Mr. Luis and Ramona Ortiz. . . . The party took place . . . with several friends of both marriages gathered."[42]

Weddings were the most recorded social events in *Vida Latina*'s eleven-year run (it stopped publishing in 1963) with San Francisco the church of preference.[43] Over time, as the Puerto Rican community grew, the places where they worshiped and celebrated rites diversified, as can be traced in *Vida Latina*, with newer Puerto Rican neighborhoods on the Near North Side (Holy Name Cathedral) and in Old Town/Lincoln Park (Saint Michael's Church). When urban renewal bulldozers razed Puerto Rican neighborhoods on the Near West Side, the Near North Side, and Old Town/Lincoln Park, St. Sylvester Church in Logan Square became an important religious and social center for Puerto Ricans and other Latino groups.

Rites of Passage in a Puerto Rican Family

When Mérida Maria Cruz married Luis Rúa in Chicago in 1968, the newly-weds, my future parents, made a promise that the bride's parents in Puerto Rico would know their future grandchildren. (Most of Luis's family had migrated to the United States, mainly to Chicago). It was probably their second compromise as a couple, since Mérida would share her new home with her *suegra* (mother-in-law). Within a year of her birth, Lorraine, their first child, was baptized in St. Vincent de Paul, in the Lincoln Park neighborhood (where the couple had married), her godparents a mixture of family—Luis's sister and Mérida's first cousin—and friends—a Puerto Rican couple they had befriended in Chicago. Yearly trips to the island began either for holidays or in the summer. In 1971 and again in 1974, Hermino and Margarita Cruz awaited their visits with special anticipation to meet newborn granddaughters, Mérida and Lissette. Visits became less frequent after *abuelita* Margo's death in 1975 and even less frequent after *abuelito* Miño's death in 1980. Airplane rides were replaced by road trips to New York to visit my mother's sister and cousins in Brooklyn, Queens, and, later, in Long Island. The rite of visiting allowed a Puerto Rican family to identify with place of origin and places of diaspora, making evident what Paul Gilroy refers to as the "root and routes" of identity formation, social relations constituted by "the flows between locations rather than by some simple combination of the fixed points that they connect."[44] Visiting documented the healthy tension between continuities of identity and the changes and flows, a means of affirming the affective bonds of kith and kin, of selfhood and personhood.[45]

My paternal abuela, Petronila Delgado, was a permanent fixture in our daily lives, a tiny, plump woman who seldom smiled and was as hard as a rock. She, indeed, served as the rock of the family, her nickname, "Petra" (rock), describing her perfectly. (In her nineties she would grow slim, soften a bit, and more freely share her wonderful giggle.) Doña Petra had worn but elegant hands, despite the left's contorted fingers, result of a mishap with a machete digging for *malanga* (cocoyam) roots in the hills of Puerto Rico. She could still make a delectable *arroz blanco y habichuelas guisadas* (white rice and stewed kidney beans), and a sinful *budín* (bread pudding). It was cooking that sustained her reign over the kitchen, and, by extension, over the family in her *nuera's* (daughter-in-law's) house. (There was a tense truce between my abuela and my mother.) Petronila would begin the family's morning ritual of café con leche, "drugging sleep into awake," as Nuyorican poet Tato Laviera described in his ode to "café," linking sound, smell, and taste to a Puerto Rican identity.[46] She would slowly pour the brew into a cloth strainer (it looked like a small butterfly net), filtering it into an aluminum coffee pot, *café colao* (strained coffee). She heated milk, whisked it with a fork, and combined the *café* with the *leche*. It was over café con leche that important conversations took place, as well as family gossip. As a treat, abuela would flavor a grand-daughter's warm milk in her bottle with a few drops of café. We loved it with heaps of sugar, until my mother was diagnosed with diabetes. A blasphemy to some café con leche aficionados, there is now no "*azuquita pa'l café*" (sugar for the coffee), in words of Puerto Rican salsa legends El Gran Combo's hugely popular hit song. To this day, I stay true to the café con leche morning ritual.

Summers in Chicago were filled with music and cultural festivals, one way in which my parents enhanced their daughters' experience of the city within and beyond identifiable Puerto Rican neighborhoods. On the third Sunday in June we attended the Puerto Rican Day Parade, at the time on Dearborn Street in downtown, and my sisters and I marched in a few parades over the years or waved from a float. My younger sister held the title of "juvenile queen" in 1982; my eldest sister was crowned "queen of the parade" in 1985. After the downtown parade, most of us went on to a festival in Humboldt Park with carnival rides, food kiosks, and live music in the Near Northwest Side park. Our mouths watered at the smell of *frituras* (fried fritters)—*alcapurrias* (tuber and plantain dough stuffed with meat or seafood), *rellos de papa* (potato balls with ground beef), and *bacalaitos* (salt cod fritters)—washed down with an icy cold "pop" (soda to non-Midwesterners), or a frosty can of beer for adults. At the festival we reunited with family and old friends, com-munity folks, though there was a latent vigilance among the adults since Humboldt Park twice had been the site of massive unrest during Puerto Rican festivities—a riot in 1966 and another in 1977. Such tumultuous episodes were not the norm (small-scale skirmishes among community members and with police more common), but someone was bound to resurrect memories in conversations about the festivities.

July was occupied with secular rites—backyard barbeques, or family picnics at North Avenue Beach or Montrose Beach along Lake Michigan or Cedar Lake in Indiana. At one such barbeque, when a pig was roasted on a spit in a pit dug and filled with coal, I could smell the *lechón asado* blocks away. In August, for a few years in the 1980s, the Pan-American Festival was held in Olive Park on the lakefront. One rainy August weekend in 1986, crowds cheered as Harold Washington danced a cha-cha with Queen of Salsa Celia Cruz.[47] Later, September became the month of festivals with the 1989 initiation of ¡*Viva*! Chicago Latin Music Festival in Grant Park, and, in 1994, *Fiesta Boricua*, a Puerto Rican block party in Humboldt Park.[48] In September 1997, at one memorable *Fiesta Boricua*, my parents were introduced to Lolita Lebrón by a former coworker of mine from the Pedro Albizu Campos Alternative High School. (As I worked on this chapter, I received an e-mail from my mother: "*Murio hoy Lolita Lebrón,*" "Lolita Lebrón died today," August 1, 2010.) At the summer festivals we met historic figures and we cultivated memories of Latino culture beyond Puerto Rico, the making of a Latina/o identity and of a sense of place in Chicago.

Baseball was another significant summer ritual. A student with perfect attendance at St. Sylvester grammar school won baseball tickets to a White Sox game. Every year the Rúa family went to the old Comiskey Park on the South Side to catch at least one game. (The Cubs may have been, geographically, closer to our home on the Near Northwest Side, but my father had raised his daughters to admire the South Side club.) In the new millennium, six months after the birth of my nephew Clemente, named for the legendary Puerto Rican baseball player and humanitarian, Roberto Clemente, he was baptized at St. Sylvester Church in a custom-made white linen *guayabera* (a classic Caribbean dress shirt) with matching linen shorts.[49] My sister, Lorraine, and my brother-in-law, Richard, chose college friends as his godparents. The priest, also a college friend, polled those in attendance on baseball loyalty: "Who here is a White Sox fan? Who is a Cubs fan?" In true Chicago style, the room was divided. The priest spoke of the strength of family and of baptism as a way to fortify family ties, even among those with longtime rivalries.

In between the seasons were birthday parties, graduations, first communions, births, weddings, and funerals. And, at each, sagas and legends of family and community were told and retold. Latino Studies Scholar Rina Benmayor writes that oral histories chronicle the lives of working-class communities; "in every society the elders tell life stories to the young, to their peers, within the intimacy of the family, or in larger community contexts. . . . Stories are threads to the past, to one's personal history and to a collective identity."[50] I created my own memories out of the memories of others. Yet, I longed for a tender memory of *el viejo* Rúa, my paternal grandfather, and was convinced that, one day, my abuela would concede it. But concession never happened. She had no happy memories of him, "Nothing. Nothing good." When I showed pity for el viejo, she rolled her eyes, made a "tsss" sound with her tongue, and said, "He haunted me when he died."

Two or three days after Francisco Rúa's death, abuela told me, she had tried to sleep but "all of a sudden he was chasing me. . . . And he would go this way (swooshing her stretched arms and torso to the left) and he would go that way (swooshing to right). The last time that he haunted me was when I went to Puerto Rico to Compay Zacarías' [her brother] house [in Patillas]." "What's with all the fuss?" she demanded. "What the heck are you doing going after me?" Abuela, as she spoke to me, began to make haunting sounds, "Whooo whooo," raising her arms as if she were a ghost flying in the air. *"Arrastrado como una yegua* (he was ragged and in despair). He had been haunting me for many weeks until that last day, it seems that God gave him permission to enter." (I have a vague memory of her admitting that she had forgiven el viejo Rúa that dawn in Patillas so he would stop haunting her.) Had she herself any plans to haunt anyone? "No. . . . Let whomever wants to sleep, sleep, but I'm not chasing after anyone. After I die, what I want to do is rest, if rest is what one does when one dies."

Sociologist Avery Gordon contends, "Being haunted draws us affectively, sometimes against our will and always a bit magically, into the structure of feeling of reality we come to experience, not as cold knowledge, but as transformative recognition."[51] The haunting by el viejo Rúa may well have been about abuela's relationship to the island of Puerto Rico. She did not return there until the birth of my older sister. It seems she needed to make peace with the island and the reason for her long-ago migration, for her leaving home. She was making peace with the few choices available as a woman in the rural landscape of a rapidly transforming island, one that sought to rid itself of the poor and uneducated in an effort to become a showcase of modernity in the Caribbean, where women were the casualties of development policies and often blamed for lack of progress. There would be no longing for her for Puerto Rico, or for her husband. She never asked to be buried there, instead saying, "Bury me *here . . . Yo quiero que me visiten* (I want to be visited). " Here was Chicago. Nostalgia and memories are not the same. In some ways, her wish was a reflection of what American Studies scholar Rachel Buff calls "the political economy of home": the belief that a person's sense of belonging is related to one's socioeconomic and political power and rights that can be claimed in a place, even in death.[52] Abuela had had few choices in her own life, only great constraints; until her dying day she regretted accepting el viejo Rúa. In leaving, she was living proof that opportunity can be created out of despair.

Perhaps el viejo Rúa served as the/a symbol of Puerto Rico for me as well, a longing for an island I have never really known, yet an island not wholly unknown—my abuela, who had claimed belonging to the Puerto Rican diaspora, had made sure of that through her stories, her cooking, and her way of being. Later it became apparent that I did not need el viejo, the island, to claim a Puerto Rican identity; I was a granddaughter of the diaspora. Petronila Delgado died on March 5, 2006, about a month-and-a-half shy of her centennial birthday. She was waked in Caribe Funeral Home and buried in a Catholic cemetery facing Lake Michigan on the border between Chicago and Evanston. My family selected Caribe because the Bishop family knew my grandmother in life and would prepare her body to reflect that life. We had witnessed bodies in fancier funeral homes heavily made up with excessive olive-tone coloring representing "Latino-ness," with the departed unrecognizable to family and friends. Abuela was pale in complexion with light rosy cheeks and lips and remained so in our final image. When I go home, I honor her wish and visit her grave.

About two months after abuela's death, my father received a diagnosis of cancer. For years he had spoken of Patillas, Puerto Rico, as his final resting place but as death approached he told me he should be buried in Chicago. But where? I wondered. Suburban cemetery plots were less expensive than their urban equivalents, but my father was never fond of the suburbs in life, in good conscience we could not relocate him there in death. We needed to find a plot within the city limits to honor his life and his love of Chicago. But Catholic cemeteries had no available plots so, to my mother's dismay, we settled on Graceland Cemetery, a nondenominational cemetery, in the Uptown neighborhood. When the family went to preview the plot, my brother-in-law reminded us, "We're near Wrigley Field," home of the Chicago Cubs, "you can probably hear the crowd from here." My six-year-old nephew Clemente, concerned, said, "I don't think abuelo will like that." Clemente had understood the depth of his abuelo's identity as a White Sox fan. "We should put abuelo's White Sox cap in the casket with him," he suggested. When family and friends paid their last respects to Luis Rúa at Caribe Funeral Home, my father's body was dressed in a white long-sleeved guayabera and black slacks, his worn black White Sox cap by his side. A cultural identity and urban identity had been negotiated in death, as it had been in life.

The selection of Graceland Cemetery honored my father in ways we had not imagined. It turned out that some of the city's most influential personalities and history makers have been buried there. Only recently have I taken the time to explore the grounds (after having taught a seminar on Chicago) and have been struck by the famous, and, in some cases, infamous, Chicagoans interred there: railroad tycoon George Pullman (1831–1897), inventor of the Pullman sleeping car, controversial figure at the center of one of the most widely known and widespread labor conflicts at the close of the nineteenth century; Philip D. Armour (1832–1901), titan of the meat-packing industry, instrumental in making Chicago, in the words of Poet Carl Sandburg, "Hog Butcher for the World"[53]; Potter Palmer (1826–1902), department store magnate, later real estate developer, who bought and widened State Street, constructing new buildings and creating a new commercial center. (In 1875 Palmer built the Palmer House where Puerto Rican pioneers, eight decades after its construction, worked as busboys and kitchen help, my godfather Inocencio among them.[54]) The men and women who built Chicago, who profited from the labor of poor and immigrant classes, lie in rest in Graceland. It goes without saying that women were vital to the vision of the city, although not highlighted in the walking tours of burial grounds.

But, in the fieldtrips my father took us on around the city, we had seen the grand works of Chicago architects who call Graceland Cemetery home, among them Louis Sullivan (1856–1924), architect of the Auditorium Building, a masterpiece of Chicago architecture; Henry Bacon (1866–1924), architect of the Lincoln Memorial in the nation's capital and the Centennial monument ("The Eagle") in the heart of Logan Square; and Daniel Burnham (1846–1912), the force behind the 1893 Chicago Columbian Exposition, designer of the "White City" and coauthor of the *Plan of Chicago*, in which he presented his ideas to reconfigure the lakefront, and to maintain it open and free.[55] The one outsider to the group of Chicago notables, Jack Johnson (1878–1946), first black boxer to win the world heavyweight championship, in 1908, and two years later to defeat the "Great White Hope," Jim Jeffries, to retain his title, is around the corner from my father's headstone. The architect of his family's vision of Chicago, my father remains an urbanite. A walking guide of Graceland Cemetery informs readers, "You'll like Graceland. If you're interested in art and architecture, if you're a Chicago history buff, if you like stories about famous people, or if you're only looking for a little peace and quiet in the busy, you'll like Graceland."[56] I believe Luis Rúa likes his final resting place.

Usually a joke about death or cheating another's desire for one's death leads to a solemn reflection of the ways in which one had lived: "Only God knows how long I can live. Sometimes I get so bad that I even sit and wait to see if I die. And I don't die; *vuelvo y prospero*" ("I continue to go on"). When Petronila Delgado, my abuela, made such comments about her own impending death, which was often, my father routinely responded, *"Mami, nadie muere en la víspera"* ("Mom, nobody dies on the eve of their last day"). It was a ritual saying that became enshrined as family wisdom. Since one cannot die on the eve of her last day, what is to be done in the meantime? How does one "continue to go on?" In other words, what does one make of the present circumstances?[57] The varied ways in which Puerto Ricans in Chicago expressed the very meaning of Puerto Rican-ness told a story of who we are, what we had done, and where we believed we were headed. Some expressions were in concert, some were in competition; each reflected a grounded identidad. Commemorations showed that, even in death, there is social life and that, even as identity is a matter of becoming, so is it deeply historical.[58] The memories, for me, are filled with a continuum of rites of passage of a family, what I have been told, what I have experienced, and what I have researched and read about. The life history of a family is part of the story of the Puerto Ricans in Chicago, as perhaps of people everywhere.

A migrant worker carries a heavy load: deductions from his paycheck, racial prejudice, official neglect, and harsh climate—without any help from the Puerto Rican Department of Labor. Recruited contract workers sent complaints of their exploitation to the Puerto Rican Department of Labor but no actions had been taken on their behalf, other than a promise that the department would inform Castle, Barton and Associates of their charges. *El Imparical, December 16, 1946*

Georgina "Gina" Rios with an Asian American co-worker at the Gudeman Company, an electronics manufacturer on the Near North Side, about 1953–1954. Puerto Rican women often left their jobs as maids for factory work, earning more money working fewer hours. In the 1950s, Chicago was home to the largest concentration of Japanese Americans in the United States, resettled from West Coast internment camps after 1943. *Photo courtesy of Gina Bishop*

Gina Rios poses in her wedding gown. *Vida Latina,* a local bilingual monthly magazine, announced the union of Gina Rios and Julius Bishop in its October 1955 issue. Early Puerto Rican arrivals took great pride in building their families and their communities. The couple would later establish the Caribe Funeral Home in the Logan Square/ Humboldt Park community. *Photo courtesy of Gina Bishop*

Oscar and William Rios (right) are dressed to the nines in this 1956 photograph. Puerto Ricans often confounded the rigid black-white-only racial order of the city. Members of the Rios family shared stories of how each negotiated conceptions of race and space, citizenship and belonging. *Photo courtesy of Gina Bishop*

With their Puerto Rican mother, Gina, and African American father, Julius, the Bishop family celebrates Julio's first birthday in 1975: Gini, Julio, Gina, Julius, Rosie, Becky, and Elsa (center front). *Photo courtesy of Gina Bishop*

Mourners spill into Armitage Avenue for community activist Orlando Quintana's wake in Caribe Funeral Home in 1973. The bodies waked there tell a larger story of Puerto Rican urban life, of hardships with housing, gang violence, or the police. The funeral home, a space where individuals come to remember, feel connected, and think collectively, is evidence of a community's resilience. *Photo courtesy of Carlos Flores*

Mayor Harold Washington (center) campaigns in 1987 in Humboldt Park with Alderman, later Congressman, Luis Gutierrez, (right), at his side. With a strategic alliance of multiracial and divergent class communities—African Americans, Mexican Americans, Puerto Ricans, and white lakefront liberals—Washington became the first black mayor of the city in 1983, and won re-election in 1987. In addition to supporting Washington, Latinos ran candidates in aldermanic and committee person races on the Near West Side and the Near Northwest Side. *Author's collection*

Jacqueline Jackson with Illinois Congressman Luis Gutierrez (right) at a press conference at Chicago's O'Hare international airport on June 27, 2001 after Jackson's release from a Puerto Rican jail for protesting the US Navy's use of Vieques as a bombing range. In Chicago, Vieques became a symbol and focus of political *latinidad* and multiracial coalitions. *Author's collection*

A Humboldt Park group spells "Peace for Vieques" on May 1, 2001. A manifestation of political *latinidad,* they were on their way to form a May Day human chain, which also supported immigrants' rights. *Author's collection*

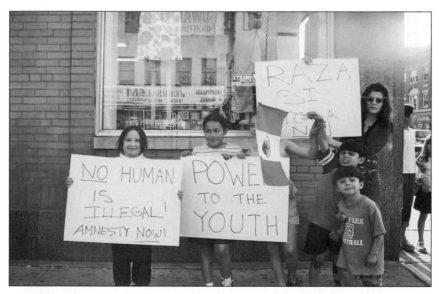

Children hold hand-made signs in support of amnesty for undocumented immigrants while participating in the May Day human chain. The human chain stretched across Chicago city limits—about twenty miles along Ashland Avenue from north to south—taking possession of the streets and obstructing traffic for eleven minutes in a symbolic gesture to demonstrate support for the unconditional amnesty of 11 million undocumented immigrants and for an end to the US military presence in Vieques. *Author's collection*

This list of housing obituaries for low-cost rental units converted into luxury apartments or condominiums ran in *The Eagle News*, official newsletter of the Logan Square Neighborhood Association. Although Logan Square residents organized against their displacement, many low- and moderate-income families have been pushed out of this Near Northwest Side community. *Photo courtesy of the Logan Square Neighborhood Association*

A trio plays at a Near West Side house party in the 1960s. Musicians were often hired or offered their talents as a gift for special occasions—birthdays, weddings, or baptisms. At these festivities, Puerto Ricans danced and sang to music that reminded them of Puerto Rico. *Photo courtesy of Mérida M. Rúa Cruz*

Newlyweds Luis (left) and Mérida Rúa (right) enjoy a weekend basement party in a Lincoln Park neighbor's house in 1968. At the end of a long week of factory work, Puerto Ricans found pleasure in dressing up to socialize with their family and friends. *Photo courtesy of Mérida M. Rúa Cruz*

A third grader from St. Sylvester's grammar school dresses in white from head to toe for her first communion in the late 1970s. The Sacrament of the Eucharist is a core aspect of Roman Catholic families' religious life, as the first reception of the Eucharist marks a child's transition into a fuller practice of the faith. *Photo courtesy of Mérida M. Rúa Cruz*

Petronila Delgado holds her great-grandson on the day of his baptism in 2002. Celebrations of Catholic rites are often an intergenerational affair, commemorating a family's commitment to their faith. *Author's collection*

This flyer for the author's lecture in the community, "From Migrant to Residents," represents an aspect of "intellectual reciprocity." Research findings were shared and discussed with Puerto Rican community members, among them persons interviewed by the author, in the Logan Square branch of the Chicago Public Library, March 2007. *Author's collection*

6 COMMUNITIES OF RECIPROCAL KNOWLEDGE

HOME WORK, FIELDWORK: RESEARCH AND ACCOUNTABILITY

"Home" was the site of my fieldwork, the locus of my historical and ethnographic study. I was a "native" researcher. What kinds of responsibilities were required of me I as engaged with the people who inhabited my home, the Puerto Ricans of Chicago? In the dissertation, I wrote of my own identity—"*La Nena* Comes Home" ("The Young Girl Comes Home")—and how it informed my scholarship, and first raised the question of accountability that would come to challenge me throughout the process of this book.

> I am one of "those people" who literally conducted research at "home." I went back to live in the neighborhood of my youth, Logan Square, on the North Side of the city—this kind of specificity matters. I became reacquainted with people from my childhood—imposing figures that I had memories of but did not really know—like the women who scolded me in church for chewing gum or not paying attention during the homily. For most of them, I remained *la nena*, the young girl, who came back home after studying away at the university. Over time, I met other residents for whom I came to develop a deep respect and appreciation as they recounted their life histories, situated the neighborhood in the past and in the present, and expressed their sense of community. The dilemmas I encountered as a "native" researcher emerged as I tried to create and sustain a distinction between the long-time resident of the area and the researcher. I could not distance myself from the research site, even when I ended the period of data collection. The research site was and is home. As a result, I do not have the luxury of leaving the site without facing the consequences of what I write. And yet, that very accountability has made this undertaking a worthwhile project.[1]

What were these consequences I had spoken of, and how, specifically, would I be accountable? I had framed my task as between an "embedded" resident of the area and a "detached" social science researcher. In reassessing my "self-revelatory maneuvers," I realized, for the most part, that it was nothing like the "rigorous reflexivity" anthropologist John L. Jackson calls for to unsettle artificial categories of analysis—that is, not an endeavor to get at the heart of issues of power and control over what scholars are able to see and how we choose to write about what we see.[2] Stretching and deepening my framing of this undertaking, I wondered: How did people respond to a researcher among them? Did they make a distinction between me as researcher and me as community member? Or was that my own distinction? Under what conditions, if any, did they allow me to investigate their lives? How much of an advantage or disadvantage was it to be of the same ethnoracial background as the people under study? Was I more circumspect, more protective? Or more diffident, less engaged?[3]

Anthropologist Virginia Dominguez has called into question the indiscriminant coupling of "rescue projects," scholarship intended to correct the historical record, and "salvage projects," scholarship driven not by desire to understand, but to preserve certain cultural practices believed to be on the brink of disappearance. Dominguez raises critical questions about "native" researchers: "*All* scholars who write about people they really care about face serious editorial dilemmas, not just those born, raised, and active in local, re-gional, or national communities of which they have long been members. Let us not make the mistake of assuming that only longtime 'insiders' are ever driven by love—or even that they are always driven by love."[4] What is scholar-ship "driven by love"? Is it taboo? Would it affect collection and interpreta-tion of evidence? Would it hide secrets? Perhaps Dominguez means by "love," knowledge produced not to "give voice" or convey pity or romanticize a com-munity or individuals under study but to show "real love and respect for real people."[5] What is at stake when readers detect love in a scholar's work as op-posed to when they cannot? Will other scholars insist on "detachment" as an indication of "objectivity," and a sense of engagement as evidence of "subjec-tivity," of "soft" not "hard" data, and hence, of unreliability? For Dominguez and Jackson not to challenge assumptions would make all scholarship sus-pect. Respect ought to mean not camouflage or concealment but intellectu-ally rigorous work courageous enough to present individuals and collectives one cares about in the full complexity and contradictions all communities have: compassionate and callous, reactionary and progressive, dutiful and negligent, demoralized and fulfilled. In short, all dimensions of personhood.

"First Entry"

Conventional discussions of how the researcher is perceived by the subjects of study often begin with the obligatory "first entry" into the field: how admittance into the community was negotiated and rapport established. Few discuss what I learned of a process of constant negotiation and renegotiation throughout the fieldwork process, or the process of the researcher's exit and the community's subsequent response, as well as what a community makes of the scholarship produced from the stories of their lives. Scholars who have no "first entry" because they are members of the community of study face particular dilemmas of their own.[6] John Langston Gwaltney, a blind "sagacious observer" of ordinary black urban life and a theorist of native research,[7] testified that "the fact that some participants in this project had known me since the hour of my birth certainly did not prove to be a hindrance."[8]

I, however, found the cause and effect more complicated than did Gwaltney. My experiences resonated more with anthropologist Faye Harrison's "outsider within," a refinement of Gwaltney's "native research."[9] My "informants," "interlocutors," "cultural consultants,"—that is, the community folk of Puerto Rican Chicago—interviewed me as much as I interviewed them, the older ones taking control of the interview. We were both subjects and both objects, all engaged in a shared endeavor. Some who declined to be formally interviewed were, in the end, my best sources, but they kept control and some insisted on keeping their interview tapes to cherish as historical records. Some asked that I protect their identities; others *wanted* to be identified. Before William Rios, my landlady's older brother, would reveal his own life history to me, he posed a few questions: "Why do you live alone?" "Why do you need so much space for one person?" "You don't have a family?" I responded that my parents lived a few blocks away, but this did not satisfy him. Gina Bishop later told me that her brother had scolded her, questioning, "What business do you have to rent to her all alone?" She then added, "He hasn't asked how many men I see going up there." Perhaps William had questions about my "respectability." His daughter-in-law tried to assure me that this was not the case, but Gina knew her brother's old-fangled thoughts about women who live alone. William was researching and analyzing *me*.

"Valeria Girón," a one-time resident of the Shakespeare building in Palmer Square, mulled over signing the consent form that allowed me to record our interview. "*Si te ayuda*" ("if it helps you"), she said, yet when she walked with me to her front door, she bade me not to give the information, the tapes, to anyone. "Otilia Irizarry," a neighborhood activist who puzzled over how to create and sustain an inclusive sense of community, came to several of my public presentations of my research, on occasion revealing her ethnographic alter ego, proudly explaining that she had selected her pseudonym for my use in honor of her favorite aunt. Some refused to take part in my research, even people who had known me as a child, and with whose children I had grown up. They avoided me after I approached to ask for an interview or when I talked about the project. One woman I saw often asked my thoughts on gentrification, affordable housing, and urban education but declined to offer her own. My subjects' attitudes toward my purpose in this study were at times in keeping with my own, other times in conflict with my own.

Dominguez proposes "a politics of love and rescue" from the perspective of scholars writing in scholarly defense of the people they love. Such a politics can be extended outside the academy, as to the neighborhood intellectuals I came to know and respect from past and present Puerto Rican neighborhoods.[10] Gina and Julius Bishop, Ana La Luz, Otilia Irizarry, and Elena Padilla, and many other women and men, expressed a desire to help me with my "homework" but reminded me to be discrete. Their cautions were not a ploy to have me showcase "favorable" aspects of community or themselves but rather evidence of the experiences these women and men have had to the state, to academic and popular depictions of who they are and the places they come from. They know what has been said and written about Puerto Rican communities, by "outsiders" and "insiders" alike, and they know what is wrong with it. Their own politics of love and rescue included much pride, but also a strong critique of their/our community and of what I needed to pay attention to as a scholar.

Elena Padilla may have learned a similar lesson half a century earlier from her exchanges with Muna Muñoz Lee, Jesús Colón, and the contract workers who shared their lives and perspectives with her. My own fascination with Padilla's scholarly activism inspired another project—extracting her from the buried footnotes of the discipline of anthropology and the field of Puerto Rican studies. This important pioneering scholar had been cast as a marginal figure by the academy; I planned a book to reclaim her and to provide her with a say in how she has been reclaimed.[11] Hence, before I began my own work, I edited a volume titled *Latino Urban Ethnography and the Work of Elena Padilla* as a critical introduction to her. Social sciences must vulnerably engage with the "subjects" of their research, lest the complicated relationship between the academy and communities of study not be reconciled, and lest scholars lose the capacity to discover, understand, and convey the dimensions of personhood.

John Langston Gwaltney afforded those who had "donated" their life histories a forum from which to talk back to him and hence to social science.[12] Elva Noble, one of Gwaltney's "cultural consultants," believed she had a say in what was to be done with her donation and his role in making it happen: "I'm not trying to tell you your job, but if you ever do write a book about us, then I hope you really do write about things as they really are. I guess that depends on you to some extent."[13] The persons who animate the story of Puerto Rican life in Chicago as I write of it here, pointed to what Political Theorist Iris Marion Young terms "asymmetrical reciprocity," that is, taking the perspectives of others into account without assuming that one has adopted or shares their positions.[14] It is necessary to recognize and acknowledge the distinct history and social position that make relations unequal, especially among those of similar background. Differences in experience matter. Puerto Ricans in Chicago who contributed their diverse experiences and life histories to my own work did so knowing they had limited control over how the story would return to them (if it ever reaches them) but nonetheless set certain expectations for me to meet. They came to my public presentations in a variety of community settings, demonstrating that they hold me accountable to them in exchange for making my work possible. Indeed, their support *required* accountability.

The "Outsider Within"

Historian Earl Lewis noted that black residents of Norfolk, Virginia, trusted him because, in his own memories of Norfolk, they recognized "the value of my personal and scholarly memory"; for some residents, "my memory was important to them as their memory was essential for me." Further, Lewis wrote that, "Residents, who valued examples of prodigious research, sound judgments, and keen analytical skills, embraced me because I was one of their own coming home to tell their story."[15] My own "outsider *within*" status had stimulated some in Chicago's Puerto Rican neighborhoods to take an interest in my framing of my project and in my findings, even as they left me free to reach my own conclusions. Still, the reality that ideas about identity and community are of fundamental importance to Puerto Ricans in Chicago because of their positioning at the social and structural hem of society was made painfully clear to me when community members challenged my own "*outsider within*" status. When I pushed Gina Bishop for a conversation about my findings in *Vida Latina*, a bilingual monthly magazine of the 1950s, Gina protested, if with a smile, "You're like the FBI investigating my life!" Considering the history of Puerto Ricans with federal institutions, particularly with the FBI, I knew she was not complimenting my research skills. Like anthropologist Faye Harrison, I learned that "social research is often seen as comparable to intelligence gathering in support of state surveillance containment."[16] I overheard Gina once telling some visitors, "she's studying the old Puerto Ricans," by which she meant the pioneros, and every now and then she laughed about having to watch herself around me. Her signed consent form had given me permission to use her funeral home as a "field site" and to interview her, but she was always "too busy" for a formal interview. Yet, Gina's spontaneous stories and our conversations at public and private functions proved to be, as I should have known they would, incredibly rich. They were, I believe, a gift—on her terms.

In anthropology, and in some sociology, it has become almost standard to consider a researcher's participation in the field, the relationship to and contacts with the place and the people who animate the ethnography. Less standard is it, however, to seek to understand a scholar's relationship and experience with an archival institution or a living archive and how both shape the history scholars write.[17] All archives hold stories, and these, too, are part of the chronicle. Thus, *A Grounded Identidad* began with my childhood experiences exploring the city with my father as my guide. His life history served as a living repository of working-class ways of knowing and ways of being, a rich source of information not widely available in the archives. "For marginalized communities constantly involved in struggles for visibility, political identity and space," Latina/o studies scholar Horacio Roque Ramírez contends, life histories "about their existence are critical acts of documentation."[18] Archives may be found in unexpected places. The Newberry Library in Chicago I first encountered had not sought to preserve the history of the poor and immigrant and migrant communities that shared its proximity. Thus, instead, I reconstructed elements of Puerto Rican life in Chicago through an archive more than 2,000 miles away in the home of Gloria Arjona, one of Elena Padilla's classmates from the University of Puerto Rico.

On a research trip to Puerto Rico, I had gone to visit Gloria Arjona, retired professor of Spanish literature of the University of Puerto Rico and daughter of Rafael Arjona Siaca, senator, advocate of independence, and political rival of her father-in-law, Luis Muñoz Marín, first elected governor of the island. I was on a journey to explore the archive of Puerto Rican social and political history she had compiled in her own home. (She had married Luis Muñoz Lee in 1944, two months after Muñoz Marín, then president of the Puerto Rican Senate, derailed her father's nomination for resident commissioner.)[19]

Before my trip, I phoned from Chicago to introduce myself and to express interest in working with Arjona's archive of Muna Muñoz Lee's time as a graduate student at the University of Chicago. After asking me a few questions, she agreed to grant me access. However, upon my arrival in Puerto Rico a few weeks later, she seemed to have changed her mind, complaining on the phone of ailments and of having no one to help her organize and maintain the archive. I should, she said, get in touch the following week to see if she could find someone to pull out the boxes I needed. Although I had come to the island for only a few days and for this single purpose, I decided not to push the matter, and simply listened (having already learned my lesson with Gina). After we were on the phone for about an hour, she abruptly asked, "So when do you want to come over?" We arranged to meet the next day.

Archivists at the *Fundación Luis Muñoz Marín* were surprised Arjona had agreed to meet with me since she was so selective about whom she allowed in. I think it may have been because I was not there to explore her fight to restore the honor and political legacy of her father, whom she felt Muñoz Marín had undermined. But, fearful she might change her mind, I asked no details when she supplied Puerto Rican-style directions to her home (markers instead of road numbers); I wrote as quickly as I could; later, I could hardly make out my chicken scratch notes: *La Muda: Carretera de Caguas, derecha garaje de gasolina, dobla para la carretera de la casas, Barrio Mamey 1, parque de pelota, pregunta en el Colmado Meléndez la entrada a la casa*. (La Muda: road that goes to Caguas, right at the gas station, follow the road toward the houses, Barrio Mamey 1, ballpark, at the grocery store Meléndez ask where to find the driveway to her house). Carlos Alamo, a colleague who was researching race and national identity on the island and knew how to get around better than I did, accompanied me to the remote area of Caguas where Arjona lives. We stopped here and there to ask locals about some of the markers. Once we arrived we were welcomed with kisses.

Big blue bins and boxes filled the floors; a path led to a workstation (with a desk, a table with a desktop photocopy machine, and a few mismatched chairs) and on to the kitchen. Arjona had pulled out what she thought I might find useful, such as a folder of personal letters from Muñoz Lee's mother and from friends and acquaintances, and, of course, papers from the University of Chicago (syllabi, qualifying examine questions, course assignments). There was also a plastic bag of pamphlets from organizations on Chicago's South Side (Urban League, NAACP, and a neighborhood association). She made some copies for me and gave me some originals of things she had in duplicate. We "should not jump to conclusions about the things we find," she said, and began to talk. "This isn't like an archive that's quiet and where you're left alone." Carlos and I appreciated her spending time with us; we knew it was her way of checking us out and judging our intentions. She pointed out, for example, that Muna Muñoz Lee's membership in the NAACP cannot be confirmed (though she had a button and a card with her name indicating membership); hence, we could only speculate that she was sympathetic to its purpose and program. She made sure that we put things back in place and that nothing was missing. Like the countless persons I interviewed in Chicago, Gloria Arjona was evaluating me, deciding whether I could handle the story of which she possessed important pieces.[20]

Intellectual Reciprocity: Real Life as Theory

In the 2000–01 academic year, at the University of Illinois at Chicago, Latina/o Studies scholar Frances R. Aparicio, recently hired chair of the Latin American and Latino Studies program, initiated a "Lectures in the Community Series," its purpose to strengthen the relationship between the university and the city's Latina/o communities. Aparicio inaugurated the series by an invitation to Francisco Scarano, a prominent historian of the Caribbean and Latin America, specialist in Puerto Rico, to speak at the Pedro Albizu Campos Museum along *Paseo Boricua* in Humboldt Park. A mile-long belt, Paseo Boricua, along Division Street is marked at the entrance and exit by two towering Puerto Rican flags forged of steel. Community groups near the museum brought in folding chairs to accommodate the overflow, eager to engage with scholars who wrote about "people like us." The Lectures in the Community Series also sponsored panel discussions, musical performances, poetry and literary readings, and film showings held in various community settings: Association House, Hispanic Housing, the Juan Antonio Corretjer Puerto Rican Cultural Center in Humboldt Park, the Instituto del Progreso Latino, Orozco Academy, the Rudy Lozano Library in Pilsen.[21]

I was one of a panel of nine at Hispanic Housing in Humboldt Park invited to talk about a special issue of *Centro: Journal of the Center for Puerto Rican Studies*, edited by anthropologist Gina M. Pérez, dedicated to the Puerto Rican community in Chicago. I would report to that community about what I had learned and hear their response. It was, for me, the beginning of accountability. The special journal issue on Chicago set the Puerto Rican community within the city's sociocultural history and within the emerging academic domains of Latina/o studies, ethnic studies, and Puerto Rican studies, and urban ethnography, more broadly.[22] In my March 2002 field notes about the event, I wrote:

At Hispanic Housing, the journal issue ran out even before the lecture began . . . I don't think the Center for Puerto Rican Studies expected people to buy multiple copies. The place was packed, people from St. Sylvester [Church] taking up at least the first four rows on both sides. People from the PRCC [Puerto Rican Cultural Center] made up the majority of those in attendance. The Bishops [including Mr. Bishop] came to see me present. As well as some of the people I had interviewed for my article.

Carlos Flores [an accomplished photographer and occasional contributor to "Eight Forty-Eight" on Chicago Public Radio] . . . wanted to have the last word . . . When he got up to speak he had the "elders" of the community stand to honor them . . . the two elders were my grandmother and my godfather. My godfather [Inocencio] stood with tears in his eyes . . . receiving the kind of acknowledgement I think he has always thought he deserved. My grandmother just liked being noticed. She stood and waved to the crowd.

Still in the throes of my research, I spoke of my interest in the Near West Side and the need for historical research on Chicago's pioneering Puerto Rican communities. I appealed to the audience, especially those from, or with roots in, the Near West Side, to allow me to interview them. Lena Sandoval, an administrator at a health-care center in Pilsen who had grown up on Harrison Street, said she was thrilled I was "thinking about that community." "Our community is more than one section," Lena said, an objection to *Paseo Boricua* as *the* dominant space that defines *puertorriqueñidad* in Chicago. She wondered if I had heard of or if anyone I had interviewed mentioned *el aguacate* (the avocado). I had not. Was it a restaurant or bar? "It was a well-known building on Harrison Street where many Puerto Ricans lived. It was the building of newcomers," Lena explained. She agreed to an interview and to recruit others from her family and friends. Since none of my books on Chicago referred to el aguacate, I asked Gina Bishop if she had ever heard of it; a few days later, Gina handed me an annual directory of community businesses with a who's who of the Latino community. On one page I read: "We remember those who lived in Harrison and Loomis, in a building called 'The avocado tree,' because that's where the newly-arrived from the island turned up, all very good people."[23] Months after the panel discussion, I was interviewing Lena along with Ada, her mother, and Rosa, her older sister—the first in her family to migrate to Chicago, arriving as a teenager in 1953. El aguacate was "a huge building with a store and a barbershop, and above were the apartments," Rosa remembered.

Lena thought it was named for the "green *jíbaro*" (rural peasant)—similar to the avocado, her mother said: "All who came from Puerto Rico were called avocados . . . the avocados arrived in a bunch." I was reading a living archive. I found many others.

The success of the "Lectures in the Community," several weeks later, led to a radio program on "Eight Forty-Eight," Chicago Public Radio's award-winning news magazine, about the *Centro Journal's* issue on Puerto Rican Chicago hosted by Carlos Flores. I, though still a doctoral candidate, was one of only two native Chicagoans from among the journal's contributors and so was asked to take part.[24] My reporting back to the community was continuing. The other Chicagoan was sociologist Marixsa Alicea, who had studied displacement and segregated communities, the kind of communities out of which Latina/o identities emerged. "As far as I can remember," Flores said, "the displacement of Puerto Ricans first began when I was growing up as a young kid in Lincoln Park, on Armitage and Sheffield. And it was probably one of the first communities that actually felt the impact of the displacement of Puerto Ricans from that community to other parts of the city." Now I was getting more evidence from a living archive in a reciprocal encounter. Alicea pointed to "the diminishing number of . . . decent low-income housing" as once default neighborhoods became desirable, race and racism no doubt steering people to certain areas and away from others.

Flores was intrigued with my focus on *latinidad* and especially on the tensions between Mexicans and Puerto Ricans. "Growing up . . . Puerto Rican," I said, "it was always very natural to see the mixture of Latino groups. . . . I try and talk about . . . what this . . . means for . . . the Puerto Rican identity of the generation that grows up in what we would call Latino neighborhoods." But were these identities "natural," or rather the result of exclusion, the sort of structural exclusion Alicea had written about? And what did people make of their circumstances? Considering the scholarship of critical race theorist and legal scholar Lani Guinier and of historian Earl Lewis and anthropologist Steven Gregory, I recognized that the negative aspects of race as category of difference "do not stand in for the entire experience of being 'raced.'"[25] Lewis had reminded us that black—and I would add Latino—communities "discovered that even though they could not always secure the range of improvements desired, they modified the political language so that segregation became congregation."[26] And, most important, people of color claimed a sense of community because they fought back as communities of color.[27] The combination of state-sanctioned exclusion and grassroots alternatives, under certain constraints, was underscored by those who had shared their stories with me. It had taken me time to listen to, and make sense of, their perspectives. They were teaching me about the fine line between recognizing the problems of a community and criticizing a community. They were pushing me to bring my work to life, to reflect the breadth and depth of their daily lives, to avoid either an idealistic, romanticized portrait, or a negative and corrosive template. They could not see themselves in either kind of narrative. They were compelling me to write about them as real people.

Five years later, as a Rockefeller Foundation postdoctoral fellow, and after follow-up archival and ethnographic research, I presented my research, "From Migrants to Residents: Puerto Ricans in the City of Neighborhoods," in yet another community lecture. After fruit and cheese in the meeting room of the Logan Square branch of the Chicago Public Library, I was invited to speak, with historian Nancy R. Mirabal from San Francisco State University commenting on my work. In the audience were public school teachers and administrators, faculty and staff from the University of Illinois, a few individuals I had interviewed, some neighborhood families, and my own family. I spoke of my interest in how Puerto Ricans took the identity of a city, became Chicago Puerto Ricans, and, in turn, transformed the city's own identity. I wanted to hear their opinions of the meaning to Puerto Ricans of a Latino identity. Did a Puerto Rican identity still matter in this "Latino" moment? "Of course, it does," said a woman in the front (I found out later that she was a teacher). Others nodded. The teachers, the neighborhood folks, the people I had interviewed, and my own family, for the most part, were convinced of the power and potential in claiming a Latina/o identity, but assured me that the meaning and value of a Puerto Rican identity was also significant. For the same reasons that home is critical for generations of migrants and their descendants, identity matters. Place was about social relations and about social mobility, not about assimilation, at least not in the sense of discarding one's past or melting away but in the sense of a recognizable identity and a continuation of the larger community.

I found most interesting, especially in the pioneering generation, the prominence it gave to stories of adversity and defeat. Such stories had been told, and retold, as lessons of the need to remain vigilant because community is fragile and fleeting. To some, stories of defeat proved that things would never change; to others, the stories demonstrated that daily life should, and could, be different. Through these inquiries and explorations, I was gaining a more complex appreciation of the nexus of the identity, community, and place. Beyond the world that had traditionally been defined by those in power, I began to look at the alternative versions or social worlds my "subjects" as coresearchers created against a background of limitation.

To understand the historical meanings of Puerto Rican identity over time, as perhaps of all ethnoracial identities, it had become imperative to consider the relationships not only with those they lived among but with the state, and imperative to consider the communities produced for Puerto Ricans compared with Puerto Ricans' own ideas of community. The distinction made between Chicago's residency and US citizenship, for example, had exposed the dichotomy between theoretical citizenship and lived reality and its consequences for personhood. Puerto Ricans had been categorized as citizens, in the abstract, in formalizing a relationship, however limited, to the state, but their actual citizenship status, as real persons in need of real resources, not honored or remaining in dispute. Their demands and struggles over place and memory (a grounded identidad) had been and have been efforts to make evident the unique and historically specific vestiges of colonialism not reconciled by the granting of citizenship, a status that captured neither all social relations nor all social realities. Understandings of place and processes of memory are a means of articulating a sense of personhood: the insistence on respect as ordinary, imperfect living contradictions who reach to do better than is imagined of them and who are more human than their circumstances.

So, too, I have recorded here not only what I thought I got right but also my own miscues, missteps, and mishaps. The process itself enriched me, an experience in intellectual reciprocity, in real life as theory. Scholars must take more seriously theoretical and methodological exchanges with community members. Those who shared their lives and stories with me may recognize more of themselves than in other narratives of the history and politics of Puerto Rican identity and community life, yet there are still parts of themselves they will not recognize. Whether scholars are strangers or persons coming home, a book can become a means of reimagining the relationship between scholars and communities of study, of living history, and of the responsibilities each owes the other.

ESSAY ON METHODOLOGY AND SOURCES

A Grounded Identidad is an interdisciplinary work, of ethnographic and historical methodology. The project had been simmering in my head since my first high school research assignment (a poster board for the Chicago History Fair on Puerto Ricans in city politics) and later in my undergraduate history courses. But it took shape when, as a graduate student at the University of Illinois at Urbana Champaign, I discovered Elena Padilla's 1947 University of Chicago master's thesis, "Puerto Rican Immigrants in New York and Chicago." I first envisioned a study similar to, or updating, Padilla's master's thesis, comparing identity formation and community building among Puerto Ricans in Chicago and New York, but funding and time constraints in my research for a dissertation at the University of Michigan led to a decision to focus on an ethnographic study of Puerto Ricans in Chicago, a study that would attend to their history. I started with ethnographic research and worked my way into the archives, seeking to maintain a flow from the present to the past and back for an account of Puerto Rican urban life.

Trained by a historian in an interdisciplinary doctoral program, I had been accustomed to hearing that "sometimes the story is in the footnotes." Padilla's master's footnotes became, for me, a roadmap to archives in Puerto Rico and New York City, connecting the island and the East Coast's principle port of entry to the United States, to the Midwest metropolis of Chicago. Later, as an assistant professor at Williams College and a Rockefeller postdoctoral fellow at the University of Illinois at Chicago, I conducted archival research in both New York and Puerto Rico and further ethnographic research and archival work in Chicago.

Drawing on qualitative research techniques, I explored, in-depth, nuanced relationships and meanings of complex ethnoracial dimensions of identity and space in relation to ideas about community. Ethnographers carry out intimate and systematic investigations of urban social life and culture by compiling detailed accounts of direct observation, by conducting formal and informal interviews with willing participants, and by consulting documentation (pamphlets, newsletters, leaflets, and periodicals). I asked individuals about what they believe, how they practice those beliefs, and observed how those beliefs were confirmed or contradicted in the day-to-day. My grounded methodology included semistructured interviews, ethnographic observations, archival research, textual criticism—and personal experience—over a four-year period, from September 2000 through March 2003 and from June 2006 to December 2007. I interviewed residents of Chicago's Near West Side, West Side, Humboldt Park, and Logan Square, selecting, first, from families I knew. They, in turn, suggested others, in what the social sciences call a "snowball approach." I prepared consent forms in Spanish and English and bilingual documents describing the project, and discovered that people preferred an oral summary, in Spanish, English, or Spanglish (code-switching). Those from the pioneering generation of Puerto Rican migration to Chicago were my most engaged participants—they gave many hours. I interviewed those who were active in the community life on the Near Northwest Side, and individuals who had attended a community function, festival, protest, or meeting, or who had worked with a community organization.

My most important field site was the Caribe Funeral Home, owned and operated by Julius and Gina Bishop. Gina was central in helping me make contacts among the older generation, and often vouched for me. She would walk me around at a wake or other gathering, explaining that I was studying Puerto Ricans in Chicago, or she would suggest that I talk to so-and-so. Sitting in the funeral home itself, I gathered information in spontaneous, informal "focus groups," in which people shared opinions about local happenings or about the community in general. But, I usually let conversations flow in their own directions, occasionally interjecting a question or two to gauge opinions on subjects of community debate or to ask for an elaboration on particular topics or memories. I arranged for formal interviews in peoples' homes as well as several interviews in my own temporary apartment above the funeral home. There were informal interviews too, usually taking place in a local diner or neighborhood restaurant. I conducted few group interviews: two, in pairs (best friends and a husband and wife) and one with three members of a family to accommodate peoples' busy schedules.

In these open-ended, semistructured interviews, we talked of family histories, of the neighborhoods they had lived in, their daily life, past and current neighborhood, city, and national debates, and institutional and social experiences that informed and influenced their life histories. Members of the pioneering generation of Puerto Rican migrants to Chicago, who came in the 1950s (about a third of forty-five interviews), provided especially revealing accounts of their lives in Puerto Rico, why they migrated, and what their memories were of early Puerto Rican life in Chicago. I talked with Elena Padilla about her thesis, her scholarly activism, and her time at the University of Chicago. I took extensive notes and talked to folks in a variety of social settings, among them birthday parties, baby showers, and memorial services, and participated in a wide array of neighborhood-wide, citywide, and out-of-state activities from religious services to community meetings, and neighborhood festivals, to political protests and rallies. Casual interviews initiated during social and political activities were followed up, when possible, with semistructured interviews.

All who took part received consent forms describing the purpose of the study and explaining that participation was voluntary (See Appendix A). Those formally interviewed signed these forms and, except for public figures, were assigned or selected fictitious names (to my knowledge, no persons of these given names exist). Public figures are defined as well-known or notable persons involved in public affairs—local and national politicians and leaders at the forefront of public debates and concerns. When I began my study, my intension was to conduct only confidential life history interviews; I had no intention of using actual names and, therefore, I do not cite individual interviews. But, since in light of the visibility of the Caribe Funeral Home in Chicago's Puerto Rican and Latino community and in my narrative, I could not guarantee confidentially, the Bishop-Rios family have given their consent for the book to include their real names.

My participant observation concentrated on recording observable data of everyday practices as part of living in the community over a sustained period of time; my notes were more detailed/targeted or specific when of a community event, festival, or protest. I was especially eager to observe how people related to one another and to the spaces they inhabit, to learn what they remembered or reminisced about, what they fought over, and what they celebrated. I collected community newspapers and ephemera from activities I had attended, including flyers, buttons, and leaflets, and mailings.

In analyzing the data, I used a grounded theory approach, the researcher actively suspending her preconceived assumptions about what the data would reveal, inductively developing arguments and theories from material collected. This requires the researcher to rely on data as a guide to sense-making, to detect meanings and associations within the data, and to generate theory.[1] I reviewed field notes and interview transcripts, noting emergent or recurring themes, and began to develop explanations and analysis of these themes, an approach that allowed me to immerse myself in evidence through a reflexive effort to understand my own intentions in conducting the research, as well as my thematic categories and my interpretation of the data. I considered how my research was in conversation or debate with other scholarship.

As others have noted before me, the researcher's social location informs the production of data, the kinds of questions asked, what one pays heed to, and interpretation.[2] As the daughter of working-class migrants from Puerto Rico and as a native Chicagoan, I am, necessarily, invested in questions of identity and space, what ordinary people make of their circumstances. And, as the daughter of a welder and of a public school lunchroom supervisor, I am interested in working-class identities and communities. Having grown up in mixed Latino neighborhoods and experienced inter-Latino relations at the level of the day-to-day, I have been eager to understand how a Latina/o identity was mobilized for social and political purposes. These personal interests formed a pattern that framed the dimensions and boundaries through which I came to understand the daily lives, past and present, of Chicago's Puerto Rican neighborhoods and urban life. The theme of this book emerged as much from the people I spoke with as from the kinds of questions I posed. At the same time, the multipositionality of my identity as an "outsider within" during both the data collection and the analytical process was evident.

I complemented ethnographic investigation with wide-ranging archival study in Chicago, New York, and Puerto Rico. In Chicago, I mined public, private, and university archives, some with conveniently catalogued materials on Puerto Ricans. But, most often, I had to think creatively of where to find materials on Puerto Rican life. Knowing the neighborhoods where Puerto Ricans lived made the Chicago Public Library a good starting place. I found useful, though not extensive, information on Near Northwest Side neighborhood histories and community newspapers in the Neighborhood History Research Collection of the Sulzer Regional Library. The General Information Services Department, Newspapers and General Periodicals, in the Harold Washington Library Center houses neighborhood newspapers and a wide range of Chicago newspaper microfilm holdings from 1833 to the present.

The Chicago History Museum's Archives and Manuscript Holdings (formerly The Chicago Historical Society) include records of the Welfare Council of Metropolitan Chicago. I examined pamphlets, reports, memoranda, and correspondence directed to and from local Chicago agencies concerned with Puerto Rican migration and settlement. In the University of Illinois at Chicago Daley Library, Special Collections Department, I found the Martin Bickham Papers and Immigrant Protective League Papers especially helpful for the agendas, reports, memoranda, case histories, newspaper clippings, articles, and reports on the status of Puerto Ricans in Chicago, who were citizens but foreign in many respects.

Access to the Special Collections Research Center, University of Chicago Library allowed me to consult the papers of noted faculty members of the anthropology and sociology departments. The *Sol Tax Papers* include personal and professional correspondence, memoranda, reports, proposals and a preliminary questionnaire for a "Puerto Rican Immigrants Project." The *Mary Bolton Wirth Papers* contain correspondence, manuscripts, brief case reports, memoranda, interviews, notes, and notebooks. (Bolton Wirth, wife of University of Chicago Sociologist Louis Wirth, was a social worker who specialized in public housing; she served as supervisor of community and tenant relations with the Chicago Housing Authority from 1952 to 1958.)

In New York, Pedro Juan Hernández was especially accommodating in helping me obtain materials from the Archives of the Puerto Rican Diaspora, Centro de Estudios Puertorriqueños, Hunter College, City University of New York, including the *Jesús Colón Papers* correspondence, pamphlets, newsletters, leaflets, and essays, constituting a centerpiece of the Centro's archive on early Puerto Rican and Latino life in the United States. I found correspondence from Elena Padilla, mainly on the situation of Puerto Rican workers in Chicago, but no record of Colón's responses to Padilla. I also found *The Records of The Offices of the Government of Puerto Rico In the United States, 1930–1993*, with field, regional, and the central office records of the Migration Division, vital resources on the Puerto Rican diaspora in New York, and beyond. No official records of the Chicago Regional Office are extant, but information on Chicago can be gleaned from monthly and yearly reports submitted to the national director, available in the New York central office records. Missing documents from the Chicago Regional Office include minutes, agendas, speeches, detailed case records, and weekly reports; resource files, such as newspaper clippings, newsletters, brochures, flyers, and other ephemera; and correspondence with community agencies, private corporations and government agencies that collaborated with the Chicago office. Although we have important information from the collection at the Centro, the Centro provides a view of the diaspora from the perspective of what policy makers found useful in making their case about migration as a tool of economic development; I was unable to locate evidence of more mundane aspects of Puerto Rican urban life in Chicago, notes that did not make pages of official reports or details behind monthly or annual summaries. Such material would have been invaluable in understanding what made life in Chicago both unique as well as similar to other diasporic communities, as in Cleveland and Philadelphia. I was able to consult newspaper microfilms, including *El Imparcial* and *El Mundo*, at the Center for Puerto Rican Studies Archive.

In Puerto Rico I acquired and processed items from La Fundación Luis Muñoz Marín, which holds the papers of the island's first elected Puerto Rican governor (1949–1965), previous president of the Puerto Rican Senate (1941–1949), and correspondence, confidential reports, newspaper clippings, and reports collected from various agencies concerned with Puerto Rican migration to the United States. Through Elena Padilla, I was able to gain access to previously unused personal papers of Muñoz Marín's daughter, Muna Muñoz Lee (correspondence, course syllabi from the University of Chicago, and other memorabilia) held in a personal archive of Dr. Gloria Arjona in Caguas, Puerto Rico. Due to time constrains, I was unable to visit the National Anthropological Archives in Washington, DC, to examine the *John Victor Murra Papers*, including correspondence between Murra and Padilla, during and after Padilla's time at Chicago, and other research associates from Julian Steward's project in Puerto Rico, out of which *The People of Puerto Rico* was produced.

Dr. Carolina A. Villarroel, now director of research for Recovering the US Hispanic Literary Heritage at the University of Houston, provided valuable assistance in helping me obtain a microfilm copy of the *Vida Latina* collection (February 1952—Vol. 1 No. 1 through July 1963—Vol. 12 No. 6.) Under the direction of Dr. Nicolás Kanellos, this national research program identifies, preserves, and publishes literary contributions of US Latinos from colonial times through the 1960s. I consulted Chicago newspapers, *Chicago Tribune*, *Chicago Defender*, *Chicago Sun-Times*, *Chicago Daily News*, *Chicago Herald-American*, but more work is needed with local and discontinued papers located in the Harold Washington Center of the Chicago Public Library.

Secondary Sources

Although Chicago has served as a premier site of urban community studies, most of this valuable earlier scholarship has framed racial formations in Chicago along a rigid black/white polarity consistent with US predominant understandings of race. Seminal works on race, space, and identity in Chicago include St. Clair Drake and Horace R. Cayton, *Black Metropolis: A Study of Negro Life in a Northern City*, revised and enlarged ed. (New York: Harcourt, Brace and Company, 1945; Chicago: The University of Chicago Press, 1993); Arnold R. Hirsch, *Making the Second Ghetto: Race and Housing in Chicago, 1940–1960* (Chicago: University of Chicago Press, 1983); and James Grossman, *Land of Hope: Chicago, Black Southerners, and the Great Migration*

(Chicago: University of Chicago, 1989). Otherwise, people who do not neatly fit into a black or white category have been neglected by the scholarship. Gregory D. Squires et al., *Chicago: Race, Class, and the Response to Urban Decline* (Philadelphia: Temple University Press, 1987) and, more recently, Andrew J. Diamond, *Mean Streets: Chicago Youths and the Everyday Struggle for Empowerment in the Multiracial City, 1908–1969* (Berkeley: University of California Press, 2009) acknowledge this gap in the literature.

Projects investigating the intersection between urban studies and critical race/ethnicity theories, especially those gesturing away from black/white modes of interpreting city life and struggles for rights, include Felix Padilla, *Latino Ethnic Consciousness: The Case of Mexican Americans and Puerto Ricans in Chicago* (University of Notre Dame Press, 1985) an important early work exploring pan-ethnic identity formation (Latinismo) for political purposes. Later anthropological studies examine the ways in which Puerto Ricans, and Latinos more broadly, unsettle conventional narratives of migration and settlement and black and white views of urban life in the United States and underscore complex negotiations of latinidad, the shared identity as Latinos among people of diverse Latin American and Caribbean backgrounds. Arlene Dávila, *Barrio Dreams: Puerto Ricans, Latinos, and the Neoliberal City* (University of California Press, 2004) investigates the relationship of Puerto Rican identity to latinidad in everyday and institutional settings. Urban ethnographies concerned with Latinas and Latinos in Chicago include Ana Yolanda Ramos-Zayas, *National Performance: The Politics of Class, Race, and Space in Puerto Rican Chicago* (Chicago: University of Chicago Press, 2003); Nicholas De Genova and Ana Yolanda Ramos-Zayas, *Latino Crossings: Mexicans, Puerto Ricans, and the Politics of Race and Citizenship* (Routledge, 2003); Gina M. Pérez, *The Near Northwest Side Story: Migration Displacement and Puerto Rican Families* (Berkeley: University of California Press, 2004); Nicholas De Genova, *Working the Boundaries: Race, Space, and "Illegality" in Mexican Chicago* (Durham: Duke University Press 2005); and Gina M. Pérez, ed. *Centro: Journal of the Center for Puerto Rican Studies*, Special issue on the Puerto Rican Community in Chicago (2001).

While ethnographers have undertaken studies of Puerto Rican diaspora communities, historical accounts of this community are wanting. Existing historical studies on the development of the Puerto Rican diaspora include Virginia Sanchez Korrol, *From Colonia to Community: The History of Puerto Ricans in New York City* (Berkeley: University of California Press, 1983); Carmen T. Whalen's *From Puerto Rico to Philadelphia: Puerto Rican Workers and Postwar Economies* (Philadelphia: Temple University Press, 2001); Carmen T. Whalen and Víctor Vázquez-Hernández, ed., *The Puerto Rican Diaspora: Historical Perspectives* (Philadelphia: Temple University Press, 2005); and, now, Lorrin Thomas's *Puerto Rican Citizen: History and Political Identity in Twentieth Century New York City* (Chicago: University of Chicago Press, 2010). Lilia Fernandez's forthcoming comparative race history, *Brown in the Windy City: Mexicans and Puerto Ricans in Postwar Chicago*, promises to be a welcome addition to the scholarship.

Studies that explore how the migration process shaped poor and working-class racial identities and notions of citizenship rights and privileges in the context of limited opportunities include Earl Lewis, *In Their Own Interests: Race, Class, and Power in Twentieth-Century Norfolk, Virginia* (Berkeley: University of California Press, 1991); James Grossman, *Land of Hope: Chicago, Black Southerners, and the Great Migration* and Carmen T. Whalen, *From Puerto Rico to Philadelphia*. For useful studies on Puerto Rican labor migration and citizenship, see Edwin Maldonado, "Contract Labor and the Origins of Puerto Rican Communities in the United States," *International Migration Review* 13, no. 1 (1979): 103–21; *Centro de Estudios Puertorriqueños*, History Task Force, *Labor Migration Under Capitalism: The Puerto Rican Experience* (New York: Monthly Review Press, 1979); Maura I. Toro-Morn, "Boricuas En Chicago: Gender and Class in the Migration and Settlement of Puerto Ricans," in *The Puerto Rican Diaspora: Historical Perspectives*, ed. Carmen Teresa Whalen and Víctor Vázquez-Hernández (Philadelphia: Temple University Press, 2005); and Lilia Fernandez, "Of Immigrants and Migrants: Mexican and Puerto Rican Labor Migration in Comparative Perspective, 1942–1964" *Journal of American Ethnic History* 29, no. 3 (2010): 6–39.

For helpful literature on Latina/o identity and latinidad, see Frances R. Aparicio, "Reading the 'Latino' in Latino Studies: Toward Reimagining Our Academic Location," *Discourse* 21, no. 3 (1999): 3–18; Frances Aparicio and Susana Chávez-Silverman, ed., *Tropicalizations: Transcultural Representations of Latinidad* (Hanover: University Press of New England, 1997); Suzanne Oboler, *Ethnic Labels, Latino Lives: Identity and the Politics of (Re)Presentation in the United States* (Minneapolis: University of Minnesota Press, 1995); William V. Flores and Rina Benmayor, ed., *Latino Cultural Citizenship: Claiming Identity, Space and Rights* (Boston: Beacon Press, 1997); Nicholas De Genova and Ana Yolanda Ramos Zayas, *Latino Crossings: Mexicans, Puerto Ricans, and the Politics of Race and Citizenship* (Routledge, 2003); and Horacio N. Roque Ramírez, "'That's My Place!': Negotiating Racial, Sexual, and Gender Politics in San Francisco's Gay Latino Alliance, 1975–1983," *Journal of the History of Sexuality*, Special Issue: Sexuality and Politics since 1945, 12, no. 2, (2003): 224–58.

On native researchers and self-reflexivity in research, see John Langston Gwaltney, *Drylongso: A Self-Portrait of Black America* (New York: Random House, 1980); John Langston Gwaltney, "Common Sense and Science: Urban Core Black Culture," in *Anthropologists at Home in North America: Methods and Issues in the Study of One's Own Society*, ed. Donald A. Messerschmidt (New York: Cambridge University Press, 1981); Ruth Behar, *The Vulnerable Observer: Anthropology that Breaks Your Heart* (Boston: Beacon Press, 1996); Virginia R. Dominguez, "For a Politics of Love and Rescue," *Cultural Anthropology* 15, no. 3 (2000): 365–66; Patricia Hill Collins, *Black Feminist Thought: Knowledge, Consciousness, and the Politics of Empowerment*, rev. 10th anniversary ed. (New York: Routledge, 2000); John L. Jackson, *Real Black: Adventures in Racial Sincerity* (Chicago: The University of Chicago Press, 2005); and Faye V. Harrison, *Outsider Within: Reworking Anthropology in the Global Age* (Urbana: University of Illinois Press, 2008).

CONSENT FORM

I have agreed to participate in this project that will explore the views of Latinas and Latinos on the changing social, cultural, and political nature of life in Chicago. The objective of this project is to gain an understanding of individual and group ethnic/racial identity, neighborhood relations, and perceptions about the areas in which Latinos live.

I understand that my participation in this interview is entirely voluntary, that I may refuse to answer any questions or stop my participation at any time. I have been informed the interview will be no more than 2 hours in length and that I may end the interview at any time along the way.

I understand that my responses are confidential and that confidentiality will be maintained to the extent allowable by local, state, and federal law. I am aware that I will be assigned a pseudonym and only this name will appear on all transcripts and relevant data. Pseudonyms (made up names) will also be assigned to any person I may mention during data collection. Further, I have been informed that when findings are reported only these pseudonyms will be used and all identifying characteristics will be deleted or altered to maintain my anonymity and that of others.

I agree to participate in this project: _____YES _____NO

_____

Print Full Name   Print Full Name
(Parent/Guardian if under 18)

_____

Signature   Signature

I understand that I have been asked if the interview can be tape-recorded and/or video-recorded. I am aware that I can still participate in this project even if I decide not to be audiotaped or videotaped. If I do consent to having my interview recorded, I am aware that I can ask to have the recorder turned off at any point during the interview and that the tape will be destroyed once the project is complete.

I agree to be audiotaped: _____YES _____NO
I agree to be videotaped: _____YES _____NO

_____

Print Full Name   Print Full Name
(Parent/Guardian if under 18)

_____

Signature   Signature

FORMULARIO DE CONSENTIMIENTO

Voy a participar en este proyecto que explorará la visión de los latinos/latinas sobre el cambio social, cultural, y político de la vida en Chicago. El objetivo de este proyecto es obtener conocimientos sobre los individuos y grupos étnicos, la identidad racial, las relaciones en las comunidades, y las percepciones en las respectivas zonas donde viven los latinos.

Entiendo que mi participación en esta entrevista es voluntaria, que puedo negarme a contestar cualquier pregunta e interrumpir mi participación en cualquier momento. Se me ha informado que mi entrevista no durará más de 2 horas y que puedo negarme a participar en cualquier momento.

Entiendo que mis respuestas serán confidenciales y que la confidencialidad será mantenida según lo que permitan las leyes local, estatal, y federal. Entiendo que me asignaré o me asignarán un seudónimo (nombre fictico), y que será el nombre que ha de aparecer en las transcripciones y en otras informaciones. Un seudónimo le será asignado a cualquier persona que yo mencione. Se me ha sido informado que cuando se use este informe solamente se utilizáran estos seudónimos y se eliminarán o alterarán todas las características identificadas a fin de mantener mi anonimato y el de otros.

Consiento participar en este proyecto: _____SI _____NO

_____   _____
Nombre Completo   Nombre Completo
(Padre/Madre de familia/guardián si menos de 18 años)

_____   _____
Firma   Firma

Se me ha informado que dicha entrevista será grabada. Entiendo que todavía puedo participar en este proyecto aunque no consienta a que la entrevista se grabe. Si permito la grabación de la entrevista estoy consciente de que puedo pedir que se detenga la grabadora en cualquier momento durante la entrevista. La grabación será destruida una vez terminado el proyecto.

Consiento en que se me grabe: _____SI _____NO
Consiento en el video: _____SI _____NO

_____   _____
Nombre Completo   Nombre completo
(Padre/Madre de familia/guardián si menos de 18 años)

                                                                  _____
Firma   Firma

PRELIMINARY QUESTIONS TO BE ASKED IN FORMAL AND INFORMAL INTERVIEWS

1. How old are you?
2. How far along did you get in school (HS diploma, associates degree, BA, MA)? What do you do for a living?
3. Tell me about your siblings' education and current work status.
4. What type of work does your father/mother/guardian do for a living?
5. What is your racial/ethnic background?
6. What does this (racial/ethnic definition) mean to you?
7. Does this (racial/ethnic definition) change depending on who you are with? Where you are?
8. Describe your family to me. (What do you do together? When do you get together? How do you get along? Are there any members of the family of a different race/ethnicity? Informants will be asked to diagram their family on a sheet of paper.)
9. Tell me about people considered part of your family who are not blood-related.
10. How did they become family? (How did they become a part of your family?)
11. Describe your friends. (Tell me the story of how you became friends.)
12. Tell me about where you were born? (If not the United States, at what age did you come to the United States? Why?)
13. Can you name and tell me about the places/neighborhoods in which you lived (before Chicago and once in Chicago)?
14. Do you remember which years and for how long you lived there?
15. Can you tell me about the people that lived around you? (What were they like? How well did you know them?)
16. What was it like living there?
17. Why did you move?
18. What does this place look like today? (Informants will be asked to draw a map.)
19. Do you still go back to your old neighborhood(s)? (For what reasons or why not?)
20. Where do you currently live? (How close do you live to your family?)
21. Can you describe your current neighborhood for me (buildings, people, parks, etc.)? (Informants will be asked to draw a map.)

22. What is it like living there?
23. Describe the people who live around you. (What are they like? How well do you know them?)
24. What can you tell me about Humboldt Park (buildings, people, parks, *ambiente*, etc.)? Pilsen? Little Village/26th Street?
25. On what occasions do you visit Humboldt Park? Pilsen? Little Village/ 26th Street?
26. Are these areas any different from your neighborhood? How?
27. What does the word "community" mean to you?
28. Do you know about current debates happening in your community? What are they?
29. Do people in your family hold different views about these debates? What happens when you talk politics at home?
30. What would you like to see different about your neighborhood? What would you change? What would you keep the same?
31. What do you know about the situation in Vieques?
32. From where do you get your information? (Newspapers, radio, television, friends, family?)
33. On the basis of what you know, have you participated in any public events?
34. What do you know about the campaigns for amnesty?
35. From where do you get your information? (Newspapers, radio, television, friends, family?)
36. On the basis of what you know have you participated in any public events?
37. Did you follow the elections in Mexico? What can you tell me about the elections? What can you tell me about Vicente Fox?
38. From where do you get your information? (Newspapers, radio, television, friends, family).
39. Did you follow the elections in Puerto Rico? What can you tell me about the elections? What can you tell me about Sila Calderón?
40. From where do you get your information? (Newspapers, radio, television, friends, family).
41. Did you follow the US presidential and congressional elections? What can you tell me about the elections? Did you vote? What can you tell me about Congressman Luis Gutierrez?
42. How is your political participation different from the last election? How is it different from the first time Gutierrez ran for Congress? The first time Gutierrez ran for alderman?
43. What do you think about the movement of Latinos outside of Humboldt Park? Pilsen? Logan Square? Chicago?
44. What do you see as the future of your community?
45. How do you envision this place for your children/next generation?
46. What do you see as the future of Latinos in Chicago?

PREGUNTAS PRELIMINARES QUE HACER EN ENTREVISTAS FORMALES Y EN ENTREVISTAS INFORMALES

1. ¿Edad?
2. ¿Años de escuela (diploma de escuela superior, bachillerato, etc)? ¿Clase de trabajo?
3. Háblame de tu familia (educación, trabajo).
4. ¿Clase de trabajo de padre/madre/guardián?
5. ¿Clase de antecedentes étnicos?
6. ¿Qué significan para ti estos antecedentes étnicos/raciales?
7. ¿Esta definición de tus antecedentes étnicos/raciales cambia dependiendo de con quién estás o dónde estás?
8. Descríbeme tu familia (¿Qué hacen juntos? ¿Cuándo se reúnen? ¿Se llevan bien? ¿Es alguien de tu familia miembro alguno de algún grupo étnico distinto? (Al informante se le pedirá que haga un diagrama de su familia en un papel).
9. Háblame de la gente que consideras parte de tu familia pero que no es pariente consanguíneo/de sangre ni político.
10. ¿Cómo llegaron ser familia? (¿Cómo llegaron a formar parte de tu familia?)
11. Describe a tus amigos (cuéntame cómo se hicieron amigos).
12. ¿Dónde naciste? (Si no en los Estados Unidos, a qué edad viniste a los Estados Unidos y por qué.)
13. ¿Me puedes hablar sobre los barrios en que has vivido antes y después de haber venido a Chicago?
14. ¿Recuerdas los años exactos y la cantidad tiempo que viviste ahi?
15. Cuéntame de la gente que vivía a tu alrededor.
16. ¿Cómo era vivir ahi?
17. ¿Por qué te mudaste?
18. ¿Cómo se ve este sitio ahora? (Se le pide que dibuje un mapa).
19. ¿Visitas tu antiguo barrio? ¿Por qué razones o por qué no?
20. ¿Dónde vives actualmente? (¿Vives lejos de tus familiares?)

21. Describe dónde vives actualmente (edificios, gente, parques). (Se le pide que dibuje un mapa).
22. ¿Cómo es vivir ahi?
23. Describe la gente que vive a tu alrededor. ¿Cómo son? ¿Qué bien los conoces?
24. ¿Qué me puedes decir de Humboldt Park (los edificios, el parque, la gente, el ambiente, etc)? ¿De Pilsen, la villlita/la calle 26?
25. ¿En qué ocasiones visitas Humboldt Park/Pilsen/la villita/la calle 26?
26. ¿Estas zonas son diferentes a tu vecindario? ¿Cómo?
27. ¿La palabra comunidad, qué significa para ti?
28. ¿Sabes/estas al tanto de algún debate que esté ocurriendo en tu comunidad? ¿Cuáles son?
29. ¿Alguien de tu familia tiene una visión u opinion diferente sobre estos debates? ¿Qué pasa cuando hablas de política en tu hogar?
30. ¿Qué quieres ver diferente en tu vecindario? ¿Qué cambiarías tú, o es que lo mantendrías igual?
31. ¿Qué sabes de la situación en Vieques?
32. ¿De dónde consigues tu información (periódicos, radio, televisión, amigos, familia)?
33. A base de lo que conoces, ¿has participado en algún evento público?
34. ¿Qué sabes de la campaña de amnistía?
35. ¿De dónde consigues tu información (periódicos, radio, televisión, amigos, familia)?
36. ¿A base de lo que conoces, has participado en algún evento público?
37. ¿Seguiste las elecciones en México? ¿Qué me puedes decir de las elecciones? ¿Qué me puedes decir acerca de Vicente Fox?
38. ¿De dónde consigues tu información (periódicos, radio, televisión, amigos, familia)?
39. ¿Seguiste las elecciones en Puerto Rico? ¿Qué me puedes decir de las elecciones? ¿Qué me puedes decir acerca de Sila Calderón?
40. ¿De dónde consigues tu información (periódicos, radio, televisión, amigos, familia)?
41. ¿Seguiste las elecciones presidenciales y congresionales en los Estados Unidos? ¿Qué me puedes decir de las elecciones? ¿Votaste? Qué me puedes decir del congresista Luis Gutiérrez?
42. ¿Cuánto de diferente ha sido tu participación política desde las últimas elecciones? ¿Es diferente a la primera vez que corrió Gutiérrez para el congreso? ¿La primera vez que Gutiérrez corrió para alderman?
43. ¿Qué piensas del movimiento Latino fuera del Humboldt Park? Fuera de Pilsen? Fuera de Logan Square? Fuera de Chicago?
44. ¿Cómo ves tú el futuro de tu comunidad?
45. ¿Cuál es tu visión de este lugar para tus hijos y la próxima generación?
46. ¿Cómo ves el futuro de los latinos en Chicago?

NOTES

PROLOGUE

1. Felix Padilla, *Latino Ethnic Consciousness: The Case of Mexican Americans and Puerto Ricans in Chicago* (South Bend, IN: University of Notre Dame Press, 1985), 41.
2. Unless otherwise noted, all translations are the author's.
3. Frances Aparicio, "Cultural Twins and National Others: Allegories of Intralatino Subjectivities in U.S. Latino/a Literature," *Identities* 16, no. 5 (2009): 622–41.
4. John Langston Gwaltney, *Drylongso: A Self-Portrait of Black America* (New York: Random House, 1980), xix.
5. I am drawing from Avery Gordon's concept of complex personhood: "Complex personhood means that all people (albeit in specific forms whose specificity is sometimes everything) remember and forget, are beset by contradiction, and recognize and misrecognize themselves and others. Complex personhood means that people suffer graciously and selfishly too, get stuck in the symptoms of their troubles, and also transform themselves. Complex personhood means that even those called 'Other' are never never that. . . . At the very least, complex personhood is about conferring the respect on others that comes from presuming that life and people's lives are simultaneously straightforward and full of enormously subtle meaning." See Avery Gordon, *Ghostly Matters: Haunting and the Sociological Imagination* (Minnesota: University of Minnesota Press, 1997), 4–5.

    I also take heed of Gordon's critique of those of us who attempt to interpret the lives of everyday people: "It has always baffled me why those most interested in understanding and changing the barbaric domination that characterizes our modernity often—not always—withhold from the very people they are most concerned with the right to complex personhood." Ibid.
6. Faye V. Harrison, *Outsider Within: Reworking Anthropology in the Global Age* (Urbana: University of Illinois Press, 2008).

CHAPTER 1

1. Manuel Martinez, *Chicago: Historia De Nuestra Communidad Puertorriqueña—Photographic Documentary* (Chicago: Privately printed, 1989).
2. Elena Padilla, "Puerto Rican Immigrants in New York and Chicago: A Study in Comparative Assimilation" (master's thesis, Anthropology, University of Chicago, 1947).

3. "Puerto Ricans Charge Exploitation in US" *Chicago Defender*, November 30, 1946, 7. Also see letter from Elena Padilla to Jesús Colón, December 9, 1946 (Box 3 Folder 5, Jesús Colón Papers, Archives of the Puerto Rican Diaspora, Centro de Estudios Puertorriqueños, Hunter College, CUNY); letter from Muna Muñoz Lee to Luis Muñoz Marín, December 9, 1947 (Section IV, Series 2, Sub-series 9B, Folder 277, Fundación Luis Muñoz Marín).

4. The University of Puerto Rico was to play a central role in preparing islanders for Puerto Rican Senate President Luis Muñoz Marín's plan to modernize Puerto Rico's political and economic status.

5. The island's first popularly elected governor in 1948, Luis Muñoz Marín, earlier a proponent of Puerto Rican independence, in the 1940s began to negotiate considerable changes in the island's colonial status, developing economic relationships with the US government and US investors interested in Puerto Rico. He no longer envisioned independence as a complete resolution of the island's economic and political dilemmas. However, while statehood would establish entrance to a US market, it would also carry the onus of taxation. In addition, Muñoz Marín still believed that Puerto Ricans had a "distinct personality" (i.e., culture) inherently incompatible with US statehood. He therefore came to favor an alternative political status, proposing that Puerto Rico cease to be a colony but become neither an independent nation nor a state of the union but something in-between, a Free Associated State (*Estado Libre Asociado*). In 1952 Puerto Rico became a Commonwealth of the United States.

Puerto Rico's status as an "unincorporated dependent territory" allows residents of the island, as of 2010, to elect the island's executive and legislative branches of government, and one nonvoting delegate to the US House of Representatives. They are not entitled to vote for President of the United States (although they do vote in the primaries) or to elect a member of the US Senate. The political and economic plan led to the rise of the Popular Democratic Party (*populares*) hegemonic bloc, in power in Puerto Rico until 1968, after which the *populares* have alternated power with the New Progressive Party (*progresistas*), advocates of statehood. Referenda on the political status of the island were held in 1963, 1967, and 1998. See Rafael Bernabe and Cesar Ayala, *Puerto Rico in the American Century: A History Since 1898* (Chapel Hill: University of North Carolina Press, 2007).

6. Katharine M. Donato, Donna Gabaccia, Jennifer Holdaway, Martin Manalansan, IV, and Patricia R. Pessar "A Glass Half Full? Gender in Migration Studies," *International Migration Review* 40, no. 1 (2006): 4, 6.

7. Maura Toro-Morn, "The Gender and Class Dimensions of Puerto Rican Migration to Chicago" (PhD diss., Sociology, Loyola University of Chicago, 1993). Also see Carmen Teresa Whalen, *From Puerto Rico to Philadelphia: Puerto Rican Workers and Postwar Economies* (Philadelphia: Temple University Press, 2001); Laura Briggs, *Reproducing Empire: Race, Sex, Science, and U.S. Imperialism in Puerto Rico* (Berkeley: University of California Press, 2002).

8. Héctor Alvarez Silva, Anne Duvendeck, Henry Goodman, Muna Muñoz, Milton Pabon, Elena Padilla, Albert Rees, Manuel Zambrana, "Preliminary Report on the Puerto Rican Contract Workers in the Chicago Area," November 25, 1946. Also see letter from Muna Muñoz Lee to Luis Muñoz Marín, December 9, 1947 (Section IV, Series 2, Sub-series 9B, Folder 277, Fundación Luis Muñoz Marín); letter from Elena Padilla to Jesús Colón, December 9, 1946 (Box 3 Folder 5, Jesús Colón Papers, Archives of the Puerto Rican Diaspora, Centro de Estudios Puertorriqueños, Hunter College, CUNY).

9. Judith Friedenberg, ed. *The Anthropology of Lower Income Urban Enclaves: The Case of East Harlem* (New York: New York Academy of Sciences, 1995); Gina M. Pérez, ed. *Centro: Journal of the Center for Puerto Rican Studies* 13, no. 2 (2001); Mérida M. Rúa, ed., *Latino Urban Ethnography and the Work of Elena Padilla* (Urbana: University of Illinois Press, 2011), see chapter by Ana Y. Ramos-Zayas, "Gendering 'Latino Public Intellectuals' Personal Narratives in the Ethnography of Elena Padilla."

10. John Sullivan, "Puerto Rican Maids—a Successful Experiment," *Chicago Herald American*, October 5, 1946.

11. John Sullivan, "Puerto Rican Maids—a Successful Experiment," *Chicago Herald American*, October 5, 1946.

12. "Fly Puerto Ricans to Chicago to Fill Jobs as Domestics," *Chicago Daily Tribune*, September 17, 1946, 24.

13. Eliseo Melendez, Jefe Int. Servicio de Empleos, "A Los Trabajadores de servicio domestico que se contraten con la agencia de empleos Castle, Barton & Associates, Para ir a Chicago," Gobierno de Puerto Rico, Departamento del Trabajo, Servicio de Empleos, septiembre 1946, (Section IV, series 2, sub-series 9B, folder 277, Fundación Luis Muñoz Marín).

14. Laura Briggs, *Reproducing Empire: Race, Sex, Science, and U.S. Imperialism in Puerto Rico* (Berkeley: University of California Press, 2002).

15. The Chicago experiment arose from profound changes in Puerto Rico's economy in the post-World War II era, which had set in motion migration waves from rural to urban areas in Puerto Rico, and, later, from the island to the United States. Displacement of rural residents and the poor was compounded by a collapse of the agricultural and home needlework industries, by economic development models based on exportation, and by government policies that proposed migration as a means of population control. See Centro de Estudios Puertorriqueños, History Task Force, *Labor Migration Under Capitalism: The Puerto Rican Experience* (New York: Monthly Review Press, 1979); Maura Toro-Morn, "The Gender and Class Dimensions of Puerto Rican Migration to Chicago" (PhD diss., Sociology, Loyola University of Chicago, 1993); Carmen Teresa Whalen, *From Puerto Rico to Philadelphia: Puerto Rican Workers and Postwar Economies* (Philadelphia: Temple University Press, 2001); Laura Briggs, *Reproducing Empire: Race, Sex, Science, and U.S. Imperialism in Puerto Rico* (Berkeley: University of California

Press, 2002); Gina M. Pérez, *The Near Northwest Side Story: Migration, Displacement, and Puerto Rican Families* (Berkeley: University of California Press, 2004).

16. Cited in Maura I. Toro-Morn, "Boricuas En Chicago: Gender and Class in the Migration and Settlement of Puerto Ricans," in *The Puerto Rican Diaspora: Historical Perspectives*, ed. Carmen Teresa Whalen and Víctor Vázquez-Hernández (Philadelphia: Temple University Press, 2005), 113.

17. Cited in Carmen Teresa Whalen, *From Puerto Rico to Philadelphia: Puerto Rican Workers and Postwar Economies* (Philadelphia: Temple University Press, 2001), 58.

18. Lois Thrasher, "52 Pct. Success Marks Experiment of Imported Maids: Overworked or Dissatisfied, 172 Puerto Rican Girls Quit," *Chicago Daily News*, March 7, 1947 (Section IV, Series 2, Sub-series 9B, Folder 277, Fundación Luis Muñoz Marín).

19. "Fly Puerto Ricans to Chicago to Fill Jobs as Domestics," *Chicago Daily Tribune*, September 17, 1946, 24.

20. Lois Thrasher, "52 Pct. Success Marks Experiment of Imported Maids: Overworked or Dissatisfied, 172 Puerto Rican Girls Quit," *Chicago Daily News*, March 7, 1947 (Section IV, Series 2, Sub-series 9B, Folder 277, Fundación Luis Muñoz Marín). Also see Elena Padilla, "Puerto Rican Immigrants in New York and Chicago: A Study in Comparative Assimilation" (master's thesis, Anthropology, University of Chicago, 1947), 85.

21. Carmen Isales, "Report on Cases of Puerto Rican Laborers Brought to Chicago to Work as Domestics and Foundry Workers Under Contract with Castle, Barton and Associates, Inc." (Confidential), March 22, 1947 (Section IV, series 2, subseries 9B, folder 277, Fundación Luis Muñoz Marín). Tea times at the YWCA became a common social activity for Puerto Rican domestic workers in other US urban centers as well. Historian Carmen Whalen documents tea times in Philadelphia as a time and space where Puerto Rican women exchanged information and formed relationships. See Carmen Teresa Whalen, *From Puerto Rico to Philadelphia: Puerto Rican Workers and Postwar Economies* (Philadelphia: Temple University Press, 2001).

22. See Elena Padilla, "Puerto Rican Immigrants in New York and Chicago: A Study in Comparative Assimilation" (master's thesis, Anthropology, University of Chicago, 1947), 84–86; Edwin Maldonado, "Contract Labor and the Origins of Puerto Rican Communities in the United States," *International Migration Review* 13, no. 1 (1979): 103–21; Maura I. Toro-Morn, "Género, trabajo y migración: las empleadas domésticas puertorriqueñas en Chicago," *Revista de Ciencias Sociales* 7 (1999): 102–25.

23. Héctor Alvarez Silva, Anne Duvendeck, Henry Goodman, Muna Muñoz, Milton Pabon, Elena Padilla, Albert Rees, Manuel Zambrana, "Preliminary Report on the Puerto Rican Contract Workers in the Chicago Area," November 25, 1946.

24. Carmen Isales, "Situación de los Obreros Puertorriqueños Contratados por la Agencia de Empleos Castle, Barton and Assoc." December 1946 (Section IV, series 2, sub-series 9B, folder 277, Fundación Luis Muñoz Marín).

25. Armando Armindo Cadilla, "Consideran 'Indeseables' a Boricuas Obreros De Chicago Por Su 'Competencia Desleal,'" *El Imparcial*, December 31, 1946. Also see Carmen Isales, "Situación de los Obreros Puertorriqueños Contratados por la Agencia de Empleos Castle, Barton and Assoc." December 1946 (Section IV, series 2, sub-series 9B, folder 277, Fundación Luis Muñoz Marín). *Borinquen* is the indigenous Taino name of the island of Puerto Rico; Boricua is the name derived to describe the people of and from Puerto Rico.

26. Carmen Isales, "Report on Cases of Puerto Rican Laborers Brought to Chicago to Work as Domestics and Foundry Workers Under Contract with Castle, Barton and Associates, Inc." (Confidential), March 22, 1947 (Section IV, series 2, sub-series 9B, folder 277, Fundación Luis Muñoz Marín).

27. Carmen Isales, "Report on Cases of Puerto Rican Laborers Brought to Chicago to Work as Domestics and Foundry Workers Under Contract with Castle, Barton and Associates, Inc." (Confidential), March 22, 1947 (Section IV, series 2, sub-series 9B, folder 277, Fundación Luis Muñoz Marín).

28. Lois Thrasher, "52 Pct. Success Marks Experiment of Imported Maids: Overworked or Dissatisfied, 172 Puerto Rican Girls Quit," *Chicago Daily News*, March 7, 1947 (Section IV, Series 2, Sub-series 9B, Folder 277, Fundación Luis Muñoz Marín).

29. Lois Thrasher, "52 Pct. Success Marks Experiment of Imported Maids: Overworked or Dissatisfied, 172 Puerto Rican Girls Quit," *Chicago Daily News*, March 7, 1947 (Section IV, Series 2, Sub-series 9B, Folder 277, Fundación Luis Muñoz Marín).

30. Lois Thrasher, "52 Pct. Success Marks Experiment of Imported Maids: Overworked or Dissatisfied, 172 Puerto Rican Girls Quit," *Chicago Daily News*, March 7, 1947 (Section IV, Series 2, Sub-series 9B, Folder 277, Fundación Luis Muñoz Marín).

31. John Sullivan, "Puerto Rican Maids—a Successful Experiment," *Chicago Herald American*, October 5, 1946.

32. Carmen Isales, "Report on Cases of Puerto Rican Laborers Brought to Chicago to Work as Domestics and Foundry Workers Under Contract with Castle, Barton and Associates, Inc." (Confidential), March 22, 1947 (Section IV, series 2, sub-series 9B, folder 277, Fundación Luis Muñoz Marín).

33. "Castle-Barton Copy 'Not in Public Interest,'" *The Report: Chicago Better Business Bureau* March 6, 1947, 3. (Section IV, series 8, sub-series 13, folder Illinois, Fundación Luis Muñoz Marín).

34. Lois Thrasher, "52 Pct. Success Marks Experiment of Imported Maids: Overworked or Dissatisfied, 172 Puerto Rican Girls Quit," *Chicago Daily News*, March 7, 1947 (Section IV, Series 2, Sub-series 9B, Folder 277, Fundación Luis Muñoz Marín).

35. Carmen Isales, "Report on Cases of Puerto Rican Laborers Brought to Chicago to Work as Domestics and Foundry Workers Under Contract with Castle, Barton

and Associates, Inc." (Confidential), March 22, 1947 (Section IV, series 2, sub-series 9B, folder 277, Fundación Luis Muñoz Marín).

36. Carmen Isales, "Report on Cases of Puerto Rican Laborers Brought to Chicago to Work as Domestics and Foundry Workers Under Contract with Castle, Barton and Associates, Inc." (Confidential), March 22, 1947 (Section IV, series 2, sub-series 9B, folder 277, Fundación Luis Muñoz Marín).

37. Armando Armindo Cadilla, "Periodista De Chicago Revela Que Se Intimida Y Se Explota a Sirvientes Puertorriqueños," *El Imparcial*, December 26, 1946, 31. Charneco's case had been discussed among social service workers in Chicago. Her name was found scribbled on a fact sheet from the Immigrants' Protective League. "Fact Sheet Porto Rican, Immigrants' Protective League," December 1946 (Immigrants' Protective League Papers, Puerto Rico—Employment Issues, 1940—August 1947, Box 9, Folder 100, UIC Special Collections).

38. Carmen Isales, "Report on Cases of Puerto Rican Laborers Brought to Chicago to Work as Domestics and Foundry Workers Under Contract with Castle, Barton and Associates, Inc." (Confidential), March 22, 1947 (Section IV, series 2, sub-series 9B, folder 277, Fundación Luis Muñoz Marín).

39. Personal communication with Elena Padilla, October 20, 2005. Also see Carmen Dolores Hernández, *Ricardo Alegría: Una Vida* (Puerto Rico: Centro de Estudios Avanzados de Puerto Rico y el Caribe, Fundación Puertorriqueña de las Humanidades, Instituto de Cultura Puertorriqueña, Academia Puertorriqueña de Historia, 2002), Pedro A. Reina Pérez, *La Semilla Que Sembramos: Autobiografía Del Proyecto Nacional* (Puerto Rico: Centro de Estudios Avanzados de Puerto Rico y El Caribe, 2003).

40. Personal communication with Elena Padilla, October 20, 2005. Padilla also enrolled in courses with Robert Redfield, Lloyd Warner, FayeCopper Cole, and John V. Murra.

41. In both cases, Quintero Alfaro's and Pabón's offspring have also become prominent figures in Puerto Rican Studies and the University of Puerto Rico. Angel G. Quintero Rivera is a professor at the Center for Social Research at the University of Puerto Rico, known for his work on salsa music, and Carlos Pabón is known for his work as part of the postmodern "radical statehood" camp of Puerto Rican studies.

42. Colón penned more than 400 hundred essays and was a regular contributor to many New York City newspapers, including the *Daily Worker* and *Daily World*. He amassed books and other written materials (pamphlets, newsletters, leaflets, and periodicals) documenting Puerto Rican daily life in New York City and other parts of the country, devoting his life to advancing grassroots leadership, to unionizing workers, and to shedding light on the dire straits of Puerto Rican and Latino communities as he argued for sociopolitical change. Today, the Jesús Colón collection, consisting of his personal archive, correspondence, and essays, is a centerpiece of the Center for Puerto Rican Studies archive on early Puerto Rican and Latino life in the United States.

43. Letter from Elena Padilla to Jesús Colón, October 3, 1946 (Box 3, Folder 5, Jesús Colón Papers, Archives of the Puerto Rican Diaspora, Centro de Estudios Puertorriqueños, Hunter College, CUNY).

44. John Sullivan, "Puerto Rican Maids—a Successful Experiment," *Chicago Herald American*, October 5, 1946.

45. Letter from Muna Muñoz Lee to Luis Muñoz Marín, December 9, 1947 (Section IV, Series 2, Sub-series 9B, Folder 277, Fundación Luis Muñoz Marín); letter from Elena Padilla to Jesús Colón, December 9, 1946 (Box 3 Folder 5, Jesús Colón Papers, Archives of the Puerto Rican Diaspora, Centro de Estudios Puertorriqueños, Hunter College, CUNY).

46. Handwritten statement by Leonides Algarín and Miguel Rivera (Personal collection of Gloria Arjona, Caguas, Puerto Rico).

47. Pérez had earlier attributed workers' complaints to acclimating to a new environment and to industrial labor, of which they had been warned in the contract they had freely signed. In the October 21 letter, Pérez replied to Baiz Miró that "Protests and complaints should be expressed when specific violations to contracts really happen, in those cases the Department would adopt the advisable measures." Letter from Manuel A. Pérez to Enrique Baiz Miró, October 29, 1946 (Section IV, Series 2, Sub-series 9B, Folder 277, Fundación Luis Muñoz Marín).

48. Notarized statement by Leonard C. Lewin, December 20, 1946 (Section IV, Series 2, Sub-series 9B, Folder 277, Fundación Luis Muñoz Marín).

49. In my archival research in Chicago, New York, and Puerto Rico, I found Padilla, and to a lesser extent Muñoz Lee, the only individuals identified in relation to the report and its distribution.

50. "Puerto Ricans Charge Exploitation in US," *Chicago Defender*, November 30, 1946, 7; "Plight of Puerto Ricans Starts Dispute, 'Deplorable Conditions' Denied by Employers," *Chicago Daily Tribune*, December 11, 1946, 30; "Protesta de los obreros de P.R. en Chicago, Ill.," *La Prensa*, December 11, 1946; "Revelan atropellos a obreros boricuas llevados a Chicago," *El Imparcial*, December 12, 1946.

51. Letter from Elena Padilla to Jesús Colón, December 9, 1946 (Box 3 Folder 5, Jesús Colón Papers, Archives of the Puerto Rican Diaspora, Centro de Estudios Puertorriqueños, Hunter College, CUNY); letter from Muna Muñoz Lee to Luis Muñoz Marín, December 9, 1947 (Section IV, Series 2, Sub-series 9B, Folder 277, Fundación Luis Muñoz Marín).

52. "Puerto Ricans Charge Exploitation in US," *Chicago Defender*, November 30, 1946, 7.

53. Letter from Elena Padilla to Jesús Colón, December 9, 1946 (Box 3 Folder 5, Jesús Colón Papers, Archives of the Puerto Rican Diaspora, Centro de Estudios Puertorriqueños, Hunter College, CUNY).

54. Letter from Muna Muñoz Lee to Luis Muñoz Marín, December 9, 1947 (Section IV, Series 2, Sub-series 9B, Folder 277, Fundación Luis Muñoz Marín).

55. "Plight of Puerto Ricans Starts Dispute, 'Deplorable Conditions' Denied by Employers," *Chicago Daily Tribune*, December 11, 1946, 30.

56. "Free Puerto Rico," *Chicago Daily Tribune*, December 15, 1946.

57. "Alaska and Puerto Rico," *Chicago Daily Tribune*, October 15, 1946. The *Chicago Tribune* had previously published editorials advocating Puerto Rican Independence. See "Puerto Rico's Future," *Chicago Daily Tribune*, October 18, 1945; "Free Puerto Rico," *Chicago Daily Tribune*, April 19, 1946.

58. "Free Puerto Rico," *Chicago Daily Tribune*, December 15, 1946.

59. Letter from Manuel A. Pérez to Luis Muñoz Marín, December 18, 1946 (Section IV, series 2, sub-series 9, folder 251, Fundación Luis Muñoz Marín).

60. Letter from Manuel A. Pérez to Muna Muñoz Lee, December 17, 1946 (Series 2, sub-series 9, folder 251, Fundación Luis Muñoz Marín).

61. Notas Editoriales, "Nuestros Emigrantes Desamparados," *El Imparcial*, December 16, 1946, 16.

62. Jose Armindo Cadilla, "Estudiantes Chicago Contestan a Comisionado Pérez Señalando Caso De Violación De Contrato," *El Imparcial*, December 28, 1946, 6–7.

63. Elena Padilla, "Puerto Rican Immigrants in New York and Chicago: A Study in Comparative Assimilation" (master's thesis, Anthropology, University of Chicago, 1947), 94.

64. Elena Padilla, "Puerto Rican Immigrants in New York and Chicago: A Study in Comparative Assimilation" (master's thesis, Anthropology, University of Chicago, 1947), 68–71.

65. Elena Padilla, "Puerto Rican Immigrants in New York and Chicago: A Study in Comparative Assimilation" (master's thesis, Anthropology, University of Chicago, 1947), 82.

66. Elena Padilla, "Puerto Rican Immigrants in New York and Chicago: A Study in Comparative Assimilation" (master's thesis, Anthropology, University of Chicago, 1947), 69–70.

67. "Fly Puerto Ricans to Chicago to Fill Jobs as Domestics," *Chicago Daily Tribune*, September 17, 1946, 24; "Foundry Solves Problem: Hires Puerto Ricans!" *Chicago Daily News* September 28, 1946, 3; Lois Thrasher, "52 Pct. Success Marks Experiment of Imported Maids: Overworked or Dissatisfied, 172 Puerto Rican Girls Quit," *Chicago Daily News*, March 7, 1947 (Section IV, Series 2, Sub-series 9B, Folder 277, Fundación Luis Muñoz Marín).

68. Elena Padilla, "Puerto Rican Immigrants in New York and Chicago: A Study in Comparative Assimilation" (master's thesis, Anthropology, University of Chicago, 1947).

69. Letter from Elena Padilla to Jesús Colón, December 9, 1946 (Box 3 Folder 5, Jesús Colón Papers, Archives of the Puerto Rican Diaspora, Centro de Estudios Puertorriqueños, Hunter College, CUNY).

70. Dolores Hernández, *Ricardo Alegría: Una Vida* (Puerto Rico: Centro de Estudios Avanzados de Puerto Rico y el Caribe, Fundación Puertorriqueña de las Humanidades, Instituto de Cultura Puertorriqueña, Academia Puertorriqueña de

Historia, 2002), 96–97. Also see Pedro A. Reina Pérez, *La Semilla Que Sembramos: Autobiografía Del Proyecto Nacional* (Puerto Rico: Centro de Estudios Avanzados de Puerto Rico y El Caribe, 2003).

71. Personal communication with Elena Padilla, November 2, 2005.
72. Letter from Evangelina Serrano to Muna Muñoz Lee, May 19, 1947 (Private collection of Dr. Gloria Arjona, Puerto Rico).
73. Letter from Elena Padilla to Jesús Colón, July 3, 1947 (Folder 5, Jesús Colón Papers, Archives of the Puerto Rican Diaspora, Centro de Estudios Puertorriqueños, Hunter College, CUNY).
74. Letter from Muna Muñoz Lee to Luis Muñoz Marín, December 9, 1947 (Section IV, Series 2, Sub-series 9B, Folder 277, Fundación Luis Muñoz Marín); letter from Muna Muñoz Lee to Luis Muñoz Marín, nd (circa January–February 1947) (Section IV, Series 3, Folder 397a Fundación Luis Muñoz Marín).
75. Personal communication with Elena Padilla, November 2, 2005.
76. Letter from Muna Muñoz Lee to Luis Muñoz Marín, December 9, 1947 (Section IV, Series 2, Sub-series 9B, Folder 277, Fundación Luis Muñoz Marín)
77. Letter from Muna Muñoz Lee to Luis Muñoz Marín, December 9, 1947 (Section IV, Series 2, Sub-series 9B, Folder 277, Fundación Luis Muñoz Marín)
78. See Carlos Alamo Pastrana, "Racializing the Research Laboratory: Puerto Rico and the African American Intellectual Imaginary 1940–1950" (8th International Congress of the Puerto Rican Studies Association, San Juan, PR, October 3, 2008).
79. Elena Padilla, "Puerto Rican Immigrants in New York and Chicago: A Study in Comparative Assimilation" (master's thesis, Anthropology, University of Chicago, 1947), 91–92.
80. Letter from Elena Padilla to Jesús Colón, December 9, 1946 (Box 3 Folder 5, Jesús Colón Papers, Archives of the Puerto Rican Diaspora, Centro de Estudios Puertorriqueños, Hunter College, CUNY).
81. Letter from Elena Padilla to Jesús Colón, October 3, 1946 (Box 3, Folder 5, Jesús Colón Papers, Archives of the Puerto Rican Diaspora, Centro de Estudios Puertorriqueños, Hunter College, CUNY).
82. "Maid Problem," *The New Republic*, April 28, 1947, 7.
83. Pedro A. Reina Pérez, *La Semilla Que Sembramos: Autobiografía Del Proyecto Nacional* (Puerto Rico: Centro de Estudios Avanzados de Puerto Rico y El Caribe, 2003), 79.
84. Letter from Luis Muñoz Marín to Munita Muñoz Lee, February 14, 1947 (Section IV, series 3, folder 397a, Fundación Luis Muñoz Marín).
85. Carmen Isales, "Situación de los Obreros Puertorriqueños Contratados por la Agencia de Empleos Castle, Barton and Assoc." December 1946 (Section IV, series 2, sub-series 9B, folder 277, Fundación Luis Muñoz Marín). Also see "'Y' Names Adviser For Puerto Rican Girls in Chicago," *Chicago Sun-Times*, nd. (Section IV, series 2, sub-series 9B, folder 277, Fundación Luis Muñoz Marín).

86. Carmen Isales, "Report on Cases of Puerto Rican Laborers Brought to Chicago to Work as Domestics and Foundry Workers Under Contract with Castle, Barton and Associates, Inc." (Confidential), March 22, 1947 (Section IV, series 2, sub-series 9B, folder 277, Fundación Luis Muñoz Marín).

87. Carmen Isales, "Report on Cases of Puerto Rican Laborers Brought to Chicago to Work as Domestics and Foundry Workers Under Contract with Castle, Barton and Associates, Inc." (Confidential), March 22, 1947 (Section IV, series 2, sub-series 9B, folder 277, Fundación Luis Muñoz Marín).

88. Mary A. Young, "Minutes of the meeting of sub-committee re Importation and Employment of Porto Ricans," January 10, 1947 (Immigrants' Protective League Papers, Puerto Rico—Employment Issues, 1940—August 1947, Box 9, Folder 100, UIC Daley Library Special Collections Department).

89. Fact Sheet: Porto Ricans (Immigrants' Protective League, December 1946, Immigrants' Protective League Papers, Puerto Rico—Employment Issues, 1940—August 1947, Box 9, Folder 100, UIC Daley Library Special Collections Department).

90. Carmen Isales, "Report on Cases of Puerto Rican Laborers Brought to Chicago to Work as Domestics and Foundry Workers Under Contract with Castle, Barton and Associates, Inc." (Confidential), March 22, 1947 (Section IV, series 2, sub-series 9B, folder 277, Fundación Luis Muñoz Marín).

91. Carmen Isales, "Situación de los Obreros Puertorriqueños Contratados por la Agencia de Empleos Castle, Barton and Assoc." December 1946 (Section IV, series 2, sub-series 9B, folder 277, Fundación Luis Muñoz Marín).

92. Carmen Isales, "Situación de los Obreros Puertorriqueños Contratados por la Agencia de Empleos Castle, Barton and Assoc." December 1946 (Section IV, series 2, sub-series 9B, folder 277, Fundación Luis Muñoz Marín).

93. Letter from Carmen Isales to Luis Muñoz Marin, March 11, 1947 (Section IV, series 3, folder 275, Fundación Luis Muñoz Marín).

94. Carmen Isales, "Report on Cases of Puerto Rican Laborers Brought to Chicago to Work as Domestics and Foundry Workers Under Contract with Castle, Barton and Associates, Inc." (Confidential), March 22, 1947 (Section IV, series 2, sub-series 9B, folder 277, Fundación Luis Muñoz Marín).

95. Letter from Carmen Isales to Luis Muñoz Marin, March 11, 1947 (Section IV, series 3, folder 275, Fundación Luis Muñoz Marín).

96. Carmen Isales, "Report on Cases of Puerto Rican Laborers Brought to Chicago to Work as Domestics and Foundry Workers Under Contract with Castle, Barton and Associates, Inc." (Confidential), March 22, 1947.

97. Carmen Isales, "Report on Cases of Puerto Rican Laborers Brought to Chicago to Work as Domestics and Foundry Workers Under Contract with Castle, Barton and Associates, Inc." (Confidential), March 22, 1947 (Section IV, series 2, sub-series 9B, folder 277, Fundación Luis Muñoz Marín).

98. Letter from Carmen Isales to Luis Muñoz Marin, March 11, 1947 (Section IV, series 3, folder 275, Fundación Luis Muñoz Marín).

99. Carmen Isales, "Report on Cases of Puerto Rican Laborers Brought to Chicago to Work as Domestics and Foundry Workers Under Contract with Castle, Barton and Associates, Inc." (Confidential), March 22, 1947 (Section IV, series 2, subseries 9B, folder 277, Fundación Luis Muñoz Marín).

100. Letter from Carmen Isales to Luis Muñoz Marin, March 11, 1947 (Section IV, series 3, folder 275, Fundación Luis Muñoz Marín).

101. "60 Puerto Rican Women Hunted by Vice Squads," *Chicago Daily Tribune*, March 5, 1947, 17.

102. "60 Puerto Rican Women Hunted by Vice Squads," *Chicago Daily Tribune*, March 5, 1947, 17; letter from Carmen Isales to Luis Muñoz Marin, March 11, 1947.

103. Letter from Carmen Isales to Luis Muñoz Marin, March 11, 1947 (Section IV, series 3, folder 275, Fundación Luis Muñoz Marín).

104. Carmen Isales, "Report on Cases of Puerto Rican Laborers Brought to Chicago to Work as Domestics and Foundry Workers Under Contract with Castle, Barton and Associates, Inc." (Confidential), March 22, 1947 (Section IV, series 2, subseries 9B, folder 277, Fundación Luis Muñoz Marín).

105. Letter from Carmen Isales to Luis Muñoz Marin, March 11, 1947 (Section IV, series 3, folder 275, Fundación Luis Muñoz Marín).

106. Letter from Carmen Isales to Luis Muñoz Marín, April 3, 1947 (Section IV, series 3, folder 275, Fundación Luis Muñoz Marín).

107. Letter from Carmen Isales to Luis Muñoz Marín, April 3, 1947 (Section IV, series 3, folder 275, Fundación Luis Muñoz Marín).

108. Letter from Carmen Isales to Luis Muñoz Marín, April 3, 1947 (Section IV, series 3, folder 275, Fundación Luis Muñoz Marín).

109. Earl Lewis, "Connecting Memory, Self, and the Power of Place in African American Urban History," *Journal of Urban History* 21, no. 3 (1995), 363. Lewis draws on the work of Elsa Barkley Brown in his analysis of the backstage activism of African American women. See Elsa Barkley Brown, "Negotiating and Transforming the Public Sphere: African American Political Life in the Transition from Slavery to Freedom," *Public Culture* 7, no. 1 (1994): 107–46.

110. Muñoz Lee left Chicago without completing her thesis, but she never left the world of scholarship; Oscar Lewis thanked her for her assistance in translating data and reading chapters of his book, *La Vida*. In the acknowledgements section of the book, Lewis wrote, "To Muna Muñoz Lee I am deeply grateful for her excellent translation of the field data upon which this volume is based." Oscar Lewis, *La Vida: A Puerto Rican Family in the Culture of Poverty—San Juan and New York* (New York: Random House, 1966).

111. Western Union Cable from Vincente Géigel Polanco to Luis Muñoz Marín, January 12, 1947 (Section IV, series 8, sub-series 13, folder Illinois, Fundación Luis Muñoz Marín).

112. Clarence Senior, *Puerto Rican Emigration* (Río Piedras, PR: Social Science Research Center, University of Puerto Rico, 1947), 38.

From 1945 to 1948 Clarence Senior was director of the Social Science Research Center of the University of Puerto Rico, and from 1948 to 1949 he was director of fieldwork for the study of Puerto Rican migrants in New York City based out of Columbia University.

113. Elena Padilla, "Puerto Rican Immigrants in New York and Chicago: A Study in Comparative Assimilation" (master's thesis, Anthropology, University of Chicago, 1947), 92.

114. "Maid Problem," *The New Republic*, April 28, 1947, 7.

115. "Agency to Stop Importing Girls for Housework," *Chicago Daily Tribune*, May 17, 1947, 12.

116. Felix Padilla, *Latino Ethnic Consciousness: The Case of Mexican Americans and Puerto Ricans in Chicago* (Indiana: University of Notre Dame Press, 1985), 43–44.

117. Marion F. Houstoun, Roger G. Kramer, and Joan Mackin Barrett, "Female Predominance in Immigration to the United States Since 1930: A First Look," *International Migration Review*, Special Issue: Women in Migration 18, no. 4 (1984): 908–63.

118. C. Wright Mills, Clarence Senior, and Rose Kohn Goldsen, *The Puerto Rican Journey: New York's Newest Migrants* (New York: Harper & Row, 1950), 23–26. In the late 1940s, 63 percent of Puerto Rican migrants to New York were women, 37 percent men. According to Mills et al., the preponderance of women was a defining characteristic of Puerto Rican migration to New York City.

119. C. Wright Mills, Clarence Senior, and Rose Kohn Goldsen, *The Puerto Rican Journey: New York's Newest Migrants* (New York: Harper & Row, 1950), 48, 54–55.

120. Elena Padilla, "Puerto Rican Immigrants in New York and Chicago: A Study in Comparative Assimilation" (master's thesis, Anthropology, University of Chicago, 1947), 98–99.

121. Elena Padilla, "Puerto Rican Immigrants in New York and Chicago: A Study in Comparative Assimilation" (master's thesis, Anthropology, University of Chicago, 1947), 98. Anthropologist Nicholas De Genova contends that "one must consider whether the hypothetical increase of 'Puerto Rican migration' was in fact presumed to signify an increased migration of Puerto Rican *men*, inasmuch as it was precisely their absence that seemed to truncate the prospects for young Puerto Rican women alone to constitute a veritable 'community' of their own, and doom their Puerto Rican-ness to disintegration." Nicholas De Genova, "'White' Puerto Rican Migrants, the Mexican Colony, 'Americanization' and Latino History," in *Latino Urban Ethnography and the Work of Elena Padilla*, ed. Mérida M. Rúa (Urbana: University of Illinois Press, 2011), 168.

122. C. Wright Mills, Clarence Senior, and Rose Kohn Goldsen, *The Puerto Rican Journey: New York's Newest Migrants* (New York: Harper & Row, 1950), 87.

123. John V. Murra, review of *The Puerto Rican Journey: New York's Newest Migrants*, *The Hispanic American Historical Review* 31, no. 4 (1951): 680–81. The following articles were collected and filed for President of the Puerto Rican Senate Luis Muñoz Marin: "Puerto Rican Drift to Mainland Gains," *New York Times*, July 31,

1947; Albert J. Gordon, "Officials Worried by Influx of Migrant Puerto Ricans," *New York Times*, August 2, 1947; Albert J. Gordon, "Crime Increasing in 'Little Spain,'" *New York Times*, August 3, 1947; "Puerto Rican Progress," *New York Times*, August 7, 1947; "Economy of Puerto Rico," *New York Times*, August 7, 1947; "Governor of Puerto Rico Planning Study by Columbia of Migration," *New York Times*, August 8, 1947; "Columbia Accepts Puerto Rico Study," *New York Times*, August 10, 1947; "Puerto Rican Governor Calls Influx a Trifle," *New York Herald Tribune*, August 10, 1947; "Sugar-Bowl Migrants," *Time*, August 11, 1947; "Columbia is Ready for Migrant Study," *New York Times*, October 14, 1947. (Section IV, Sub-Section 1, Series 2, Sub-Series 1C, Fundación Luis Muñoz Marin).

124. C. Wright Mills, Clarence Senior, and Rose Kohn Goldsen, *The Puerto Rican Journey: New York's Newest Migrants* (New York: Harper & Row, 1950). For more on the construction and representation of a "Puerto Rican problem" in New York City in this era, see Lorrin Thomas, *Puerto Rican Citizen: History and Political Identity in Twentieth Century New York City* (Chicago: The University of Chicago Press, 2010), chapter 4.

125. C. Wright Mills, Clarence Senior, and Rose Kohn Goldsen, *The Puerto Rican Journey: New York's Newest Migrants* (New York: Harper & Row, 1950), x.

126. Anthropologist Gina M. Pérez notes, "The nexus of University of Chicago researchers and Puerto Rican government officials has important historical precedents. Rexford Tugwell, governor of Puerto Rico from 1941 to 1946, was also a professor at the University of Chicago, and Jaime Benítez, one of the founders of the Center for Social Science Research at the University of Puerto Rico in 1945, was a University of Chicago student." Gina M. Pérez, *The Near Northwest Side Story: Migration Displacement and Puerto Rican Families*. (Berkeley: University of California Press, 2004), 216, n20. Clarence Senior was director of the Center in Puerto Rico from 1945 to 1948 and the one who proposed the Puerto Rico project to Steward; both men were at Columbia University (Senior was director of fieldwork for *The Puerto Rican Journey* study from 1948 to 1949). Julian Steward, Robert A. Manners, Eric R. Wolf, Elena Padilla Seda, Sidney W. Mintz, and Robert L. Scheele, *The People of Puerto Rico: A Study in Social Anthropology* (Urbana: University of Illinois Press, 1956).

127. From the late 1940s and throughout the 1950s, US social scientists used Puerto Rico as a social laboratory to study economic development and cultural change, and to promote the island as a "showcase for democracy" in the American hemisphere. See Michael Lapp, "The Rise and Fall of Puerto Rico as a Social Laboratory, 1945–1965," *Social Science History* 19, 2 (1995): 169–99.

128. Clarence Senior, *Puerto Rican Emigration* (Río Piedras, PR: Social Science Research Center, University of Puerto Rico, 1947). Also see Michael Lapp, "The Rise and Fall of Puerto Rico as a Social Laboratory, 1945–1965," *Social Science History* 19, 2 (1995): 169–99.

129. Puerto Rican Immigrants to Chicago Project, Memo to Social Science Research Committee from Everett Hughes and Sol Tax, Re: Funds to compile records on recent Porto Rican [sic] immigrants to Chicago, n.d. (Sol Tax Papers, box 256, Folder 4, Special Collections Research Center, University of Chicago Library).

130. Puerto Rican Immigrants to Chicago Project, Memo to Social Science Research Committee from Everett Hughes and Sol Tax, Re: Funds to compile records on recent Porto Rican [sic] immigrants to Chicago, n.d. (Sol Tax Papers, box 256, Folder 4, Special Collections Research Center, University of Chicago Library).

The Social Science Research Committee appropriated $550 to the Puerto Rican Immigrants to Chicago Project. See Puerto Rican Immigrants to Chicago Project, Memo from Louis Wirth to E.C. Hughes and Sol Tax, May 12, 1947 (Sol Tax Papers, box 256, Folder 4, Special Collections Research Center, University of Chicago Library).

131. Letter from Ruth M. Senior to Sol Tax, July 22, 1947 (Sol Tax Papers, box 256, Folder 4, Special Collections Research Center, University of Chicago Library).

132. Letter from Sol Tax to Clarence Senior, July 15, 1947 (Sol Tax Papers, box 256, Folder 4, Special Collections Research Center, University of Chicago Library); letter from Ruth M. Senior to Sol Tax, July 22, 1947 (Sol Tax Papers, Box 256, Folder 4, Special Collections Research Center, University of Chicago Library); letter from Sol Tax to Ruth M. Senior, August 5, 1947 (Sol Tax Papers, box 256, Folder 4, Special Collections Research Center, University of Chicago Library); letter from Ruth M. Senior to Sol Tax, August 8, 1947 (Sol Tax Papers, box 256, Folder 4, Special Collections Research Center, University of Chicago Library). Correspondence between Ruth Senior and Sol Tax, and newspaper articles from the Fundación Luis Muñoz Marín archive, indicate that Clarence Senior aided little toward Tax's efforts to obtain information from the Puerto Rican government.

133. Julian Steward, Robert A. Manners, Eric R. Wolf, Elena Padilla Seda, Sidney W. Mintz, and Robert L. Scheele, *The People of Puerto Rico: A Study in Social Anthropology* (Urbana: University of Illinois Press, 1956). John V. Murra, an instructor in anthropology at the University of Chicago during Padilla's time there, had recommended her for the Steward study.

134. The project, a cultural historical approach, investigated ecological patterns of the island manifested in community studies on tobacco, coffee, sugar (government-owned plantation and a US absentee-owned plantation), and on the urban milieu of Puerto Rico's prominent families. To the dismay of Muñoz Marín's Popular Democratic Party, which was interested in propagandizing a united island society with a coherent culture, the Steward study claimed that Puerto Rico could most appropriately be described and understood as "several partially similar subcultures." Julian Steward, Robert A. Manners, Eric R. Wolf, Elena Padilla Seda, Sidney W. Mintz, and Robert L. Scheele, *The People of Puerto Rico: A Study in Social Anthropology* (Urbana: University of Illinois Press, 1956), 504–5. Also see Antonio Lauria-Perricelli,

"A Study in Historical and Critical Anthropology: The Making of 'The People of Puerto Rico'" (PhD diss., Political and Social Science, New School for Social Research, 1989); Michael Lapp, "The Rise and Fall of Puerto Rico as a Social Laboratory, 1945–1965," *Social Science History* 19, 2 (1995): 169–99.

135. Despite the fact that Padilla had completed all of her coursework for the dissertation, while Sidney Mintz and Eric Wolf had yet to obtain their master's degrees, Mintz and Wolf gained international prominence for their contributions to the discipline of anthropology, whereas Elena Padilla's contributions have remained at the far fringes of the discipline. See also Antonio Lauria-Perricelli and Robert Duncan for a more extensive discussion of *The People of Puerto Rico* project. Antonio Lauria-Perricelli, "A Study in Historical and Critical Anthropology: The Making of 'The People of Puerto Rico'" (PhD diss., Political and Social Science, New School for Social Research, 1989); Ronald Duncan, ed., *The Anthropology of the People of Puerto Rico* (Puerto Rico: Inter American University of Puerto Rico, 1979).
    Arlene Torres, in her effort to rehistoricize the discipline of anthropology, has reviewed and critically assessed the work and contributions of Elena Padilla to the field. Arlene Torres, "Re-Articulating Hidden Histories: Puerto Rican Ethnography in the Late Twentieth Century," paper presented at New Perspectives in Latino/Latina Studies Lecture Series, University of Michigan, February 1999. Also see Joan Vincent, *Anthropology and Politics: Visions, Traditions, and Trends* (Tucson: The University of Arizona Press, 1990); Mérida M. Rúa, ed., *Latino Urban Ethnography and the Work of Elena Padilla* (Urbana: University of Illinois Press, 2011).

136. Letter from Elena Padilla to Sol Tax, January 3, 1948 (Sol Tax Papers, Box 256, Folder 4, Special Collections Research Center, University of Chicago Library)

137. Personal communication with Elena Padilla, May 29, 2010. Padilla believed that people gave great importance to ritual and the social and economic relations that were structured out of those rituals in the formation and transformation of culture.

138. Elena Padilla, "Nocorá: An Agrarian Reform Sugar Community" (PhD diss., Anthropology, Columbia University, 1951). In retirement, Padilla was a scholar-in-residence at Saint Barnabas Hospital in the Bronx and as of 2009 she is a fellow at the New York Academy of Medicine.

139. Faye V. Harrison and Ira E. Harrison, "Introduction: Anthropology, African Americans, and the Emancipation of a Subjugated Knowledge," in *African-American Pioneers in Anthropology*, ed. Ira E. Harrison and Faye V. Harrison (Urbana: University of Illinois Press, 1999), 11.

140. Elena Padilla, "Looking Back and Thinking Forward: Puerto Ricans in Chicago and in New York," in *Latino Urban Ethnography and the Work of Elena Padilla*, ed. Mérida M. Rúa (Urbana: University of Illinois Press, 2011), 30, n5.

141. Elena Padilla, *Up from Puerto Rico* (New York: Columbia University Press, 1958), xiii. Also see Judith Friedenberg, ed., *The Anthropology of Lower Income Urban Enclaves: The Case of East Harlem* (New York: The New York Academy of Sciences, 1995).

CHAPTER 2

1. Albert J. Gordon, "Officials Worried by Influx of Migrant Puerto Ricans," *New York Times*, August 2, 1947; Albert J. Gordon, "Crime Increasing in 'Little Spain,'" *New York Times*, August 3, 1947; "Governor of Puerto Rico Planning Study by Columbia of Migration," *New York Times*, August 8, 1947; "Columbia Accepts Puerto Rico Study," *New York Times*, August 10, 1947; "Puerto Rican Governor Calls Influx a Trifle," *New York Herald Tribune*, August 10, 1947; "Sugar-Bowl Migrants," *Time*, August 11, 1947; "Columbia is Ready for Migrant Study," *New York Times*, October 14, 1947. (Section IV, Sub-Section 1, Series 2, Sub-Series 1C, Fundación Luis Muñoz Marin). Also see Clarence Senior, "Migration and Puerto Rico's Population Problem," *Annals of the American Academy of Political and Social Science* 285, Puerto Rico a Study in Democratic Development (1953), 130–36.
2. Memo from Anthony Vega to Mary Young, April 22, 1954 (Welfare Council of Metropolitan Chicago, Chicago Historical Society, box 148, folder 3).
3. Gerald Suttles's study of the Near West Side contended that group formation depended on carefully demarcated territories, but these boundaries were permeable: "Informants tell me that there was originally an 'understanding' that the Negroes would have the projects south of Taylor while Italians were to retain those to the north. However, this never really worked, and the Negroes soon took over the entire Jane Addams Projects." He cited two likely factors: local politicians' inability to resist pressure from "militant Negro political action," and Italians moving out "once the project had been defined as a 'place for Negroes.'" At the time he wrote, he said more than "92 percent of Chicago Public Housing . . . [was] occupied by Negroes." Gerald D. Suttles, *The Social Order of the Slum: Ethnicity and Territory in the Inner City* (Chicago: The University of Chicago Press, 1968), 16, n5. Also see Thomas A. Guglielmo, *White on Arrival: Italians, Race, Color, and Power in Chicago, 1890–1945* (New York: Oxford University Press, 2003); Andrew Diamond, *Mean Streets: Chicago Youths and the Everyday Struggle for Empowerment in the Multiracial City, 1908–1968* (Berkeley: University of California Press, 2009). For an in-depth analysis of "the second ghetto" and the connection of redevelopment, renewal, and public housing to racial violence and increased racial segregation, consult Arnold Hirsch, *Making the Second Ghetto: Race and Housing in Chicago, 1940–1960* (Chicago: University of Chicago Press, 1983).
4. Andrew Diamond, *Mean Streets: Chicago Youths and the Everyday Struggle for Empowerment in the Multiracial City, 1908–1968* (Berkeley: University of California Press, 2009), 198.
5. Interestingly, Drake and Cayton acknowledge that the presence of Mexicans, Puerto Ricans, and Latin Americans made it "more difficult to detect persons with considerable Negro blood." St. Clair Drake and Horace R. Cayton, *Black Metropolis: A Study of Negro Life in a Northern City*, revised and enlarged ed. (New York: Harcourt, Brace and Company, 1945; Chicago: The University of Chicago Press, 1993), 163–64. Citations refer to the University of Chicago Press edition.

6. Gerald Suttles, *The Social Order of the Slum: Ethnicity and Territory in the Inner City* (Chicago: University of Chicago Press, 1968), 16, n5.

7. Bernardo Vega, *Memoirs of Bernardo Vega: A Contribution to the History of the Puerto Rican Community in New York*, ed. César Andreu Iglesias, trans. Juan Flores (New York: Monthly Press, 1984), 181.

8. Community Area 28—The Near West Side, Report, October 1953 (Welfare Council of Metropolitan Chicago, Chicago Historical Society, box 92, folder 4).

9. Deportation of Mexicans with US citizenship revived shameful memories of the 1930s. "Operation Wetback," when more than 3.7 million Latinos—more than a million Mexican nationals and an unknown number of US citizens—were deported between 1954 and 1959, more than 63,000 had formal deportation proceedings, the remainder departing "willingly." Néstor P. Rodríguez, "Social Construction of the US-Mexico Border," in *Immigrants Out: The New Nativism and the Anti-Immigrant Impulse in the United States*, ed. Juan F. Perca (New York: New York University Press, 1996); Gilbert Paul Carrasco, "Latinos in the United States: Invitation and Exile," in *Immigrants Out: The New Nativism and the Anti-Immigrant Impulse in the United States*, ed. Juan F. Perea (New York: New York University Press, 1996).

10. Pedro Cabán, "Subjects and Immigrants During the Progressive Era," *Discourse* 23, no. 3 (2001), 37.

11. Cited in Pedro Cabán, "Subjects and Immigrants During the Progressive Era," *Discourse* 23, no. 3 (2001), 32.

12. Cited in Pedro Cabán, "Subjects and Immigrants During the Progressive Era," *Discourse* 23, no. 3 (2001), 38. See Rafael Bernabe and Cesar Ayala, *Puerto Rico in the American Century: A History Since 1898* (Chapel Hill: University of North Carolina Press, 2007), 177; Christina Duffy Burnett and Burke Marshall, "Between the Foreign and the Domestic: The Doctrine of Territorial Incorporation, Invented and Reinvented," in *Foreign in a Domestic Sense: Puerto Rico, American Expansion, and the Constitution*, ed. Christina Duffy Burnett and Burke Marshall (Durham: Duke University Press, 2001), 1–36.
   It was the same Supreme Court membership that upheld the doctrine of "separate but equal," *Plessey v. Ferguson* in 1896 by a vote of 5 to 4, with three majority opinions. Justice Henry B. Brown delivered the judgment of the Court. Justices Brown, Edward D. White, and Horace Gray writing majority opinions; Justices Melville W. Fuller and John M. Harlan wrote the dissenting opinions. See José Trías Monge, *Puerto Rico: The Trials of the Oldest Colony in the World* (New Haven: Yale University Press, 1997), 45–51; Efrén Rivera Ramos, *The Legal Construction of Identity: The Judicial and Social Legacy of American Colonialism in Puerto Rico* (Washington, DC: American Psychological Association, 2001), 79–85.

13. José A. Cabranes, "Citizenship and the American Empire: Notes on the Legislative History of the United States Citizenship of Puerto Ricans," *University of Pennsylvania Law Review* 127, no. 2 (1978): 396–97n12. Also see Frederic R.

Coudert, Jr., "Our New Peoples: Citizens, Subjects, Nationals or Aliens," *Columbia Law Review* 3, no. 1 (1903): 13–32. Also see Sam Erman, "Meanings of Citizenship in the U.S. Empire: Puerto Rico, Isabel Gonzalez, and the Supreme Court, 1898 to 1905." *Journal of American Ethnic History* 27, no. 4 (2008): 5–33.

14. "Women Want Freedom, Too," *New York Times*, February 22, 1917, 20.

15. Pedro Cabán, "Subjects and Immigrants During the Progressive Era," *Discourse* 23, no. 3 (2001): 44.

16. Torresola was mortally wounded during the attack; Collazo was wounded and arrested. He was sentenced to the electric chair, but President Truman converted his sentence to life imprisonment. In 1979 President Carter pardoned Collazo. Bernabe and Ayala suggest that the goal of Nationalists was to create a political crisis on the island to discredit the United States before a world stage and, thus, to press foreign governments to question the validity of Public Law 600, authorizing Puerto Rico to draft its own constitution as a procedure of decolonization. Rafael Bernabe and Cesar Ayala, *Puerto Rico in the American Century: A History Since 1898* (Chapel Hill: University of North Carolina Press, 2007), 168.

17. Rafael Bernabe and Cesar Ayala, *Puerto Rico in the American Century: A History Since 1898* (Chapel Hill: University of North Carolina Press, 2007), 159.

18. Rafael Bernabe and Cesar Ayala, *Puerto Rico in the American Century: A History Since 1898* (Chapel Hill: University of North Carolina Press, 2007), 172–73.

19. Orlando Patterson, "Migration in Caribbean Societies: Socioeconomic and Symbolic Resource," in *Human Migration: Patterns and Policies*, edited by William McNeil and Ruth S. Adams (Bloomington: University of Indiana Press, 1978), 122.

20. "Un Amigo en Chicago," Migration Division Films, 1952–1956, 1970, Archives of the Puerto Rican Diaspora, Centro de Estudios Puertorriqueños, The Records of the Offices of the Government of Puerto Rico in the United States (OGPRUS), Public Relations Program, 1945–1993.

21. See Michael Lapp, "Managing Migration: The Migration Division of Puerto Rico and Puerto Ricans in New York City, 1948–1968" (PhD diss., History, Johns Hopkins University, 1990); Carmen Teresa Whalen, *From Puerto Rico to Philadelphia: Puerto Rican Workers and Postwar Economies* (Philadelphia: Temple University Press, 2001); Jorge Duany, *The Puerto Rican Nation on the Move: Identities on the Island and in the United States* (Chapel Hill: The University of North Carolina Press, 2002); Gina M. Pérez, *The Near Northwest Side Story: Migration, Displacement, and Puerto Rican Families* (Berkeley: University of California Press, 2004); Lorrin Thomas, *Puerto Rican Citizen: History and Political Identity in Twentieth Century New York City* (Chicago: The University of Chicago Press, 2010).

22. Carmen Teresa Whalen, *From Puerto Rico to Philadelphia: Puerto Rican Workers and Postwar Economies* (Philadelphia: Temple University Press, 2001), 68.

23. Carmen Teresa Whalen, *From Puerto Rico to Philadelphia: Puerto Rican Workers and Postwar Economies* (Philadelphia: Temple University Press, 2001), 68.

24. "Puerto Rican Influx Brings New Inquiry," *Chicago Daily Tribune*, February 3, 1954, 22.

25. Midwest Office, Monthly Report, Director, February 1954 (Archives of the Puerto Rican Diaspora, Centro de Estudios Puertorriqueños, OGPRUS, Migration Division, box 2744, folder 3).

26. "Devolverán A Boricuas De Chicago," *El Mundo*, Enero 28, 1954, 1, 16.

27. "Devolverán A Boricuas De Chicago," *El Mundo*, Enero 28, 1954, 16.

28. Madelon Golden, "Welfare Council to Weigh Puerto Ricans' Plight," *Chicago Sun-Times*, February 2, 1954, 13 (Martin Bickham Papers, Puerto Rico Clippings—1954, box 130, folder 1044, UIC Daley Library Special Collections Department).

29. "Puerto Ricans, for discussion in Cabinet, February 2, 1954," Mary A. Young to Robert H. MacRae, January 28, 1954 (Welfare Council of Metropolitan Chicago, Chicago Historical Society, box 148, folder 3).

30. Mary A. Young to Joseph L. Moss, April 2, 1954 (Welfare Council of Metropolitan Chicago, box 148, folder 3, Chicago Historical Society, box 148, folder 3).

31. "Puerto Rican Influx Brings New Inquiry," *Chicago Daily Tribune*, February 3, 1954, 22.

32. "Puerto Ricans Pour Into City and Ask Dole," *Chicago Daily Tribune*, February 2, 1954, 1.

33. "Puerto Ricans, for discussion in Cabinet, February 2, 1954," Mary A. Young to Robert H. MacRae, January 28, 1954 (Welfare Council of Metropolitan Chicago, Chicago Historical Society, box 148, folder 3).

34. "Puerto Ricans Pour Into City and Ask Dole," *Chicago Daily Tribune*, February 2, 1954, 1.

35. "Puerto Rican Influx Brings New Inquiry," *Chicago Daily Tribune*, February 3, 1954, 22.

36. "Puerto Ricans Pour Into City and Ask Dole," *Chicago Daily Tribune*, February 2, 1954, 1.

37. "Puerto Ricans Pour Into City and Ask Dole," *Chicago Daily Tribune*, February 2, 1954, 1.

38. "Puerto Ricans Pour Into City and Ask Dole," *Chicago Daily Tribune*, February 2, 1954, 1. Also see "Boricuas Piden Ayuda en Chicago," *El Mundo*, Febrero 3, 1954, 1.

39. "Rose to Seek Migration End in Puerto Rico," *Chicago Sun-Times*, February 4, 1954, 52. (Martin Bickham Papers, Puerto Rico Clippings—1954, box 130, folder 1044, UIC Daley Library Special Collections Department).

40. Annual Report 1953–1954 (Archives of the Puerto Rican Diaspora, Centro de Estudios Puertorriqueños, OGPRUS, Migration Division, box 2733, folder 1).

41. "Seeks to Curb Migration of Puerto Ricans," *Chicago Daily Tribune*, February 4, 1954, 3.

42. Luis Sanchez Cappa, "Funcionario Chicago Vino a Discutir su Plan De Repatriar a Obreros." *El Mundo*, Febrero 5, 1954, 1.

43. "Agree to Stem Puerto Rican Immigration," *Chicago Daily Tribune*, February 8, 1954, 8.

44. Rafael A. Barreto, "Rose Tratará se de Ayuda a Boricuas: Enviado Chicago Cambia Actitud," *El Mundo*, Febrero 9, 1954, 12.

45. Luis Sanchez Cappa, "Chicago Enviará a la Isla Grupo de 50 Boricuas: Sufren Escasez de Empleos Allí," *El Mundo*, Febrero 6, 1954, 20.

46. "Agree to Stem Puerto Rican Immigration," *Chicago Daily Tribune*, February 8, 1954, 8.

47. "Agree to Stem Puerto Rican Immigration," *Chicago Daily Tribune*, February 8, 1954, 8.

48. See St. Clair Drake and Horace R. Cayton, *Black Metropolis: A Study of Negro Life in a Northern City*, revised and enlarged ed. (New York: Harcourt, Brace and Company, 1945; Chicago: The University of Chicago Press, 1993), 65–76. William M. Tuttle, *Race Riot: Chicago in the Red Summer of 1919* (New York, Atheneum, 1970). Also see Thomas A. Guglielmo, *White on Arrival: Italians, Race, Color, and Power in Chicago, 1890–1945* (New York: Oxford University Press, 2003), 39–45; Andrew Diamond, *Mean Streets: Chicago Youths and the Everyday Struggle for Empowerment in the Multiracial City, 1908–1968* (Berkeley: University of California Press, 2009), 17–64.

49. Florette Hendri, *Black Migration: Movement North, 1900–1920* (Garden City, New York: Anchor Press/Double Day, 1975), 77.

50. Florette Hendri, *Black Migration: Movement North, 1900–1920* (Garden City, New York: Anchor Press, 1975), 77.

51. See Carol Stack, *A Call to Home: African Americans Reclaim the Rural South* (New York: BasicBooks, 1996).

52. James Grossman, *Land of Hope: Chicago, Black Southerners and the Great Migration* (Chicago: University of Chicago Press, 1989), 19.

53. "Rose to Seek Migration End in Puerto Rico," *Chicago Sun-Times*, February 4, 1954, 52. (Martin Bickham Papers, Puerto Rico Clippings—1954, box 130, folder 1044, UIC Daley Library Special Collections Department; Annual Report 1953–1954, Archives of the Puerto Rican Diaspora, Centro de Estudios Puertorriqueños, OGPRUS, Migration Division, box 2733, folder 1).

54. "Puerto Rico to Help Curb Chicago Trek," *Chicago Sun-Times,* February 6, 1954 (Martin Bickham Papers, Puerto Rico Clippings—1954, box 130, folder 1044, UIC Daley Library Special Collections Department).

55. Vega said that the week before, "at least 90 percent of the men and women daily crowding his offices . . . represented layoffs." Madelon Golden, "Welfare Council to Weigh Puerto Ricans' Plight," *Chicago Sun-Times*, February 2, 1954, 13 (Martin Bickham Papers, Puerto Rico Clippings—1954, box 130, folder 1044, UIC Daley Library Special Collections Department).

56. "Puerto Rico to Help Curb Chicago Trek," *Chicago Sun-Times,* February 6, 1954 (Martin Bickham Papers, Puerto Rico Clippings—1954, box 130, folder 1044, UIC Daley Library Special Collections Department).

57. "Puerto Rican Influx Brings New Inquiry," *Chicago Daily Tribune,* February 3, 1954, 22; "Boricua en Chicago: Preside Comité ha Ayudar a Grupo Minoría sin Empleos," *El Mundo,* Febrero 8, 1954, 1, 16.

58. "Boricua en Chicago: Preside Comité ha Ayudar a Grupo Minoría sin Empleos," *El Mundo,* Febrero 8, 1954, 16.

59. "Boricua en Chicago: Preside Comité ha Ayudar a Grupo Minoría sin Empleos," *El Mundo,* Febrero 8, 1954, 16.

60. "Boricua en Chicago: Preside Comité ha Ayudar a Grupo Minoría sin Empleos," *El Mundo,* Febrero 8, 1954, 16.

61. "Puerto Rican 'Tide' Ebbs Here: Tugwell," *Chicago Daily News,* February 4, 1954, 7 (Martin Bickham Papers, Puerto Rico Clippings—1954, box 130, folder 1044, UIC Daley Library Special Collections Department; Annual Report 1953–1954, Archives of the Puerto Rican Diaspora, Centro de Estudios Puertorriqueños, OGPRUS, Migration Division, box 2733, folder 1); "Señala Boricuas Tienen Derecho a ir a Chicago," *El Mundo,* Febrero 6, 1954, 1. Tugwell was one of a trio of Columbia University law professors in the original "Brain Trust," which played a central part in shaping the policies of the New Deal.

62. "Imported Reliefers," *Chicago Daily Tribune,* February 4, 1954.

63. Frances Fox Piven and Richard A. Cloward, *Regulating the Poor: The Functions of Public Welfare* (New York: Pantheon Books, 1971), 133.

64. "Puertorriqueños en Chicago," *El Mundo,* February 4, 1954, 7.

65. Carlos Renta "La Voz del Lector: Carta de Chicago," *El Mundo,* Febrero 12, 1954, 6.

66. "Enviaría Boricuas al Suroeste de EU," *El Mundo,* Febrero 10, 1954, 1.

67. "Enviaría Boricuas al Suroeste de EU," *El Mundo,* Febrero 10, 1954, 16.

68. L. R. Stinson, "Farm Labor Source," *Chicago Daily Tribune,* February 24, 1954, 20.

69. For a more in-depth discussion of the conflict over Puerto Ricans as transient workers or permanent community members, see Carmen Teresa Whalen, *From Puerto Rico to Philadelphia: Puerto Rican Workers and Postwar Economies* (Philadelphia: Temple University Press, 2001).

70. Commissioner Alvin Rose, transcript of talk recorded in Spanish, February 9, 1954 (Welfare Council of Metropolitan Chicago, Chicago Historical Society, box 148, folder 3).

71. Luis Sanchez Cappa, "Boricuas Devueltos Por Chicago Se Muestran Reacios a Relatar Sus Experiencias," *El Mundo,* Febrero 10, 1954, 16.

72. "Chicago's Puerto Ricans," *New Republic,* February 22, 1954, 4.

73. Midwest Office, Monthly Report, Director, February 1954 (Archives of the Puerto Rican Diaspora, Centro de Estudios Puertorriqueños, OGPRUS, Migration Division, box 2744, folder 2).

74. Midwest Office, Monthly Report, Director, February 1954 (Archives of the Puerto Rican Diaspora, Centro de Estudios Puertorriqueños, OGPRUS, Migration Division, box 2744, folder 2).

75. Midwest Office, Monthly Report, Director, April 1954 (Archives of the Puerto Rican Diaspora, Centro de Estudios Puertorriqueños, OGPRUS, Migration Division, box 2744, folder 4).

76. John Fisher, "5 Congressmen Shot Down: Puerto Ricans Fire from House Gallery," *Chicago Daily Tribune*, March 2, 1954, 1.

77. "$100,000 Bail Set for Each in Gun Attack," *Chicago Daily Tribune*, March 2, 1954, 4.

78. John Fisher, "5 Congressmen Shot Down: Puerto Ricans Fire from House Gallery," *Chicago Daily Tribune*, March 2, 1954, 1. The Resident Commissioner is a nonvoting member of the US House of Representatives elected by the people of Puerto Rico every four years.

79. John Fischer, "Four Indicted for Congress Gun Assault," *Chicago Daily Tribune*, March 4, 1954, 6.

80. John Fischer, "Four Indicted for Congress Gun Assault," *Chicago Daily Tribune*, March 4, 1954, 6.

81. John Fischer, "Four Indicted for Congress Gun Assault," *Chicago Daily Tribune*, March 4, 1954, 1; "$100,000 Bail Set for Each in Gun Attack," *Chicago Daily Tribune*, March 2, 1954, 4.

82. "Dulles to Tell U.S. Policy Toward Latin Americans," *Chicago Daily Tribune*, March 4, 1954, 7.

83. "Bare Puerto Rican Terrorism in Chicago: Family Gets Threatening Phone Calls," *Chicago Daily Tribune*, March 3, 1954, 1, 7.

84. "Police Squads Round Up Five Puerto Ricans, Reputed Leader of Unit Here Among Them," *Chicago Daily News*, March 4, 1954, 7.

85. "Police Squads Round Up Five Puerto Ricans, Reputed Leader of Unit Here Among Them," *Chicago Daily News*, March 4, 1954, 7.

86. "Terrorist Roundup Ordered Here," *Chicago Sun-Times*, March 3, 1954, 3.

87. "Police Squads Round Up Five Puerto Ricans, Reputed Leader of Unit Here Among Them," *Chicago Daily News*, March 4, 1954, 7; Madelon Golden, "Sun-Times Finds Girl Terrorist's Brother," *Chicago Sun-Times*, March 3, 1954, 3; "Terrorist Roundup Ordered Here," *Chicago Sun-Times*, March 3, 1954, 3. After the attempt to assassinate President Truman in 1950, Gonzalo Lebrón Sotomayor had been brought in for questioning and admitted he was a member of the Nationalist party.

88. Madelon Golden, "Sun-Times Finds Girl Terrorist's Brother," *Chicago Sun-Times*, March 3, 1954, 3. Lebrón Sotomayor emerged as the state's leading witness against his sister and twelve other Nationalists. Under oath, he admitted to arranging "the purchase in Chicago of the pistols that were used by four party members" in the attack on Congress at the request of New York Nationalist leaders. "Terrorist Guns Bought in Chicago," *Chicago Daily News*, September 16, 1954, 20; Robert M. Hallet, "Slaying Plot Cites Puerto Rico Group," *Christian Science Monitor*, September 14, 1954, 1. The four Nationalists received life

sentences, becoming heroes in the eyes of pro-independence sympathizers. Lebrón and her Nationalist compañeros were granted amnesty by the Carter Administration in 1979. On their release, the four Nationalists visited Chicago before any other US city.

89. "Terrorist Roundup Ordered Here," *Chicago Sun-Times*, March 3, 1954, 3.

90. "Puerto Ricans Seized by Cops are Released," *Chicago Daily Tribune*, March 16, 1954, 7. Also see "Puerto Rican Nationalists: Order Roundup of Fanatics Here," *Chicago Daily News*, March 3, 1954, 8; "8 More Seized in Roundup of Puerto Ricans," *Chicago Daily News* March 5, 1954, 9.

91. "6 held for N.Y. in Puerto Rico Plot Roundup," *Chicago Daily Tribune*, March 29, 1954, B7.

92. "30 Islanders Offer Blood as Sympathy Sign," *Chicago Daily News*, March 3, 1954, 8.

93. Midwest Office, Monthly Report, Director, March 1954 (Archives of the Puerto Rican Diaspora, Centro de Estudios Puertorriqueños, OGPRUS, Migration Division, box 2744, folder 3). Also see "Puerto Rican Nationalists: Order Roundup of Fanatics Here," *Chicago Daily News*, March 3, 1954, 8; "Terrorist Roundup Ordered Here," *Chicago Sun-Times*, March 3, 1954, 3. Brief news stories about the blood drive, supported by the Midwest Migration Division office, appeared in the *New York Times* and the *Hartford Courier*, as well as *El Diario de Nueva York*. "Puerto Ricans Donate To Illinois Blood Bank," *New York Times*, March 4, 1954, 10; "Don't Blame All The Puerto Ricans," *The Hartford Courant*, March 4, 1954, 10. "Puertorriqueños Donan Sangre," *El Diario de Nueva York*, Marzo 5, 1954.

94. "30 Islanders Offer Blood as Sympathy Sign," *Chicago Daily News*, March 3, 1954, 8.

95. "Mexican Group Decries Attack by Terror Gang," *Chicago Tribune*, March 8, 1954, 2.

96. "Protest 'Mass Arrest' of Puerto Ricans," *Chicago Tribune*, March 8, 1954, 3.

97. Midwest Office, Monthly Report, Director, March 1954 (Archives of the Puerto Rican Diaspora, Centro de Estudios Puertorriqueños, OGPRUS, Migration Division, box 2744, folder 3).

98. As Puerto Ricans began to gain access to state and federal resources in the United States and to make connections to the civil rights movement, anthropologist Jorge Duany contends that the diaspora "became increasingly alienated from the Commonwealth's political agenda and organized separately from the Migration Division, which lost much of its authority over New York's Puerto Rican community in the mid-1960s." Jorge Duany, *The Puerto Rican Nation on the Move: Identities on the Island and in the United States* (Chapel Hill: The University of North Carolina Press, 2002), 169.

99. Midwest Office, Monthly Report, Director, April 1954 (Archives of the Puerto Rican Diaspora, Centro de Estudios Puertorriqueños, OGPRUS, Migration Division, box 2744, folder 4).

100. Midwest Office, Monthly Report, Director, May 1954 (Archives of the Puerto Rican Diaspora, Centro de Estudios Puertorriqueños, OGPRUS, Migration Division, box 2744, folder 5).

101. Midwest Office, Monthly Report, Director, June 1954 (Archives of the Puerto Rican Diaspora, Centro de Estudios Puertorriqueños, OGPRUS, Migration Division, box 2744, folder 6). For more on the Trumbull Park Homes Race Riot see Arnold R. Hirsch, *Making the Second Ghetto: Race and Housing in Chicago, 1940–1960* (Chicago: University of Chicago Press, 1983), Andrew J. Diamond, *Mean Streets: Chicago Youths and the Everyday Struggle for Empowerment in the Multiracial City, 1908–1968* (Berkeley: University of California Press, 2009). Mary Bolton Wirth, wife of famed Chicago sociologist Louis Wirth, wrote, in her "Reminiscences of My Assignment as an 'Aide'—1953–1954," of a Puerto Rican Nationalist who was living in public housing: "There was one, a Puerto Rican, alone in the apartment on Sunday morning, hostile and menacing. When he was told that CHA was not urging him to sign [a loyalty oath]—only making sure that he understood, and the aide was backing out of the apartment (thinking at last there was a communist in our midst) he grabbed the lease rider and signed it. Later in the year, showing how little we knew of our tenants, he was arrested and convicted for being a member of the Puerto Rican *Nationalist* organization that had attempted to assassinate President Truman in Washington." Mary Bolton Wirth, "Reminiscences of My Assignment as an 'Aide'—1953–1954," n.d. (Mary Bolton Wirth Papers, box 2, folder 14, Special Collections Research Center, University of Chicago Library).

102. Midwest Office, Monthly Report, Director, August 1954 (Archives of the Puerto Rican Diaspora, Centro de Estudios Puertorriqueños, OGPRUS, Migration Division, box 2744, folder 8); Mary A. Young to Hollis Vick, Memorandum, September 16, 1954 (Welfare Council of Metropolitan Chicago, Chicago Historical Society, box 148, folder 3); Midwest Office, Monthly Report, Director, November 1954 (Archives of the Puerto Rican Diaspora, Centro de Estudios Puertorriqueños, OGPRUS, Migration Division, box 2744, folder 11).

103. Thomas A. Guglielmo, *White on Arrival: Italians, Race, Color, and Power in Chicago, 1890–1945* (New York: Oxford University Press, 2003).

104. Anthony Vega to Mary Young, April 22, 1954 (Welfare Council of Metropolitan Chicago, Chicago Historical Society, box 148, folder 3).

105. Anthony Vega to Mary Young, April 22, 1954 (Welfare Council of Metropolitan Chicago Papers, Chicago Historical Society, box 148, folder 3).

106. "*Necesidad imperiosa de asociarse,*" *Vida Latina*, Abril 1953, 5.

107. Manuel Martinez, *Chicago: Historia De Nuestra Communidad Puertorriqueña—Photographic Documentary* (Chicago: Privately printed, 1989), 75.

108. For more on the effects of the federal repatriation programs to Mexico in Chicago, see Gabriela F. Arredondo, *Mexican Chicago: Race, Identity and Nation, 1916–39* (Urbana: University of Illinois Press, 2008) and Nicholas De Genova,

Working the Boundaries: Race, Space, and Illegality in Mexican Chicago (Durham: Duke University Press, 2005).

109. Virginia E. Sánchez Korrol, "Latinismo among Early Puerto Rican Migrants in New York City: A Sociohistoric Interpretation," in *The Hispanic Experience in the United States: Contemporary Issues and Perspectives*, ed. Edna Acosta-Belén and Barbara R. Sjostrom (New York: Praeger, 1988).

110. Elena Padilla, *Up from Puerto Rico* (New York: Columbia University Press, 1958), 32–33.

111. Martin Ortiz to Hollis Vick, March 19, 1953 (Welfare Council of Metropolitan Chicago Papers, Chicago Historical Society, box 147, folder 10).

112. Suzanne Oboler, *Ethnic Labels, Latino Lives: Identity and the Politics of (Re) Presentation in the United States* (Minneapolis: University of Minnesota Press, 1995).

113. Some estimates had the number Puerto Ricans residing in Chicago at 30,000. "Rose to Seek Migration End in Puerto Rico," *Chicago Sun-Times*, February 4, 1954, 52; "Puerto Rican 'Tide' Ebbs Here: Tugwell," *Chicago Daily News*, February 4, 1954, 7 (Martin Bickham Papers, Puerto Rico Clippings—1954, box 130, folder 1044, UIC Daley Library Special Collections Department); Annual Report 1953–1954 (Archives of the Puerto Rican Diaspora, Centro de Estudios Puertorriqueños, OGPRUS, Migration Division, box 2733, folder 1).

CHAPTER 3

1. "Chicago Fights Gang Wars," *The Washington Post*, April 24, 1979, A4, George De Lama, "Neighbors Protest a Senseless War," *Chicago Tribune*, April 30, 1979, 5.

2. Henry Bacon designed the monument erected in 1918.

3. "L.N.S.A. March Mourns Death of Affordable Housing," *The Eagle News*, Fall/Winter 2001, 10.

4. "L.N.S.A. March Mourns Death of Affordable Housing," *The Eagle News*, Fall/Winter 2001, 10.

5. Janet L. Abu-Lughod, *New York, Chicago, Los Angeles: America's Global Cities* (University of Minnesota Press: Minneapolis, 1999).

6. Carl Smith, *The Plan of Chicago: Daniel Burnham and the Remaking of the American City* (Chicago: University of Chicago Press, 2006); Robert Bruegmann, "Built Environment of the Chicago Region," in *The Encyclopedia of Chicago*, ed. James R. Grossman, Ann Durkin Keating, and Jeff L. Reiff (Chicago: University of Chicago Press), 101–5.

7. Sudhir Alladi Venkatesh, "Chicago's Pragmatic Planners: American Sociology and the Myth of Community," *Social Science History* 25, 2 (2001): 275–317.

8. Robert E. Park and Ernest W. Burgess, *The City* (1925; reprint, Chicago: The University of Chicago Press, 1968).

9. St. Clair Drake and Horace R. Cayton, *Black Metropolis: A Study of Negro Life in a Northern City*, revised and enlarged ed. (New York: Harcourt, Brace and Company, 1945; Chicago: The University of Chicago Press, 1993).

10. Elena Padilla, "Puerto Rican Immigrants in New York and Chicago: A Study in Comparative Assimilation" (master's thesis, Anthropology, University of Chicago, 1947). For a consideration of how Asian and Asian American scholars at the University of Chicago documented and analyzed constructions of race and space during the era of exclusion, see Henry Yu, *Thinking Orientals: Migration, Contact and Exoticism in Modern America* (New York: Oxford University Press, 2001).

11. Charles N. Wheeler III and Jerome Watson, "Wellsprings of the Latin Tide: From Tiny Clusters, Whole Communities Spring," *Chicago Sun-Times*, September 12–20, 1971 (Hull House Association Records, Box 105, Folder 1285, UIC Daley Library Special Collections Department).

12. See Felix M. Padilla, *Puerto Rican Chicago* (Notre Dame, Ind.: University of Notre Dame Press, 1987); Ana Yolanda Ramos-Zayas, *National Performances: The Politics of Class, Race, and Space in Puerto Rican Chicago* (Chicago: University of Chicago Press, 2003).

13. For an examination of Young Lord social and political actions in other US cities with significant Puerto Rican population, see Ruth Glasser, *Aquí Me Quedo: Puerto Ricans in Connecticut/Puertorriqueños En Connecticut* (Connecticut: Connecticut Humanities Council, 1997); Iris Morales, "¡Palante, Siempre Palante! The Young Lords," in *The Puerto Rican Movement: Voices from the Diaspora*, ed. Andrés Torres and José Velásquez (Philadelphia: Temple University Press, 1998); Carmen Teresa Whalen, *From Puerto Rico to Philadelphia: Puerto Rican Workers and Postwar Economies* (Philadelphia: Temple University Press, 2001); Carmen Teresa Whalen, "Bridging Homeland and Barrio Politics: The Young Lords in Philadelphia," in *The Puerto Rican Movement: Voices from the Diaspora*, ed. Andrés Torres and José Velásquez (Philadelphia: Temple University Press, 1998).

14. David Hernández, "Armitage Street," in *Unsettling America: An Anthology of Contemporary Multicultural Poetry*, ed. Maria Mazziotti Gillian and Jennifer Gillian (New York: Viking Press, 1994), 271–272.

15. Janet L. Abu-Lughod, *New York, Chicago, Los Angeles: America's Global Cities* (University of Minnesota Press: Minneapolis, 1999).

16. Alexander Von Hoffman, *House by House, Block by Block: The Rebirth of American Urban Neighborhoods* (New York: Oxford University Press, 2003), 9. Historian Ruth Glasser provides a compelling account of how Puerto Rican communities in Connecticut rebounded from urban renewal. Carmen T. Whalen documents similar developments in Philadelphia. Ruth Glasser, *Aquí Me Quedo: Puerto Ricans in Connecticut/Puertorriqueños En Connecticut* (Connecticut: Connecticut Humanities Council, 1997); Carmen Teresa Whalen, *From Puerto Rico to Philadelphia: Puerto Rican Workers and Postwar Economies* (Philadelphia: Temple University Press, 2001). For the case of Mexicans/Mexican Americans/Chicanos in Los Angeles, see Raúl Villa, *Barrio-Logos: Space and Place in Urban Chicano Literature and Culture*, 1st ed. (Austin, TX: University of Texas Press, 2000).

17. Michael Katz, "Reframing the 'Underclass' Debate," in *The "Underclass" Debate: Views from History*, ed. Michael Katz (Princeton: Princeton University Press, 1993).

18. Carmen Teresa Whalen, "Colonialism, Citizenship, and the Making of the Puerto Rican Diaspora: An Introduction," in *The Puerto Rican Diaspora: Historical Perspectives*, ed. Carmen Teresa Whalen and Víctor Vázquez-Hernández (Philadelphia: Temple University Press, 2005), 31–32. Also see Maura I. Toro-Morn, "Boricuas En Chicago: Gender and Class in the Migration and Settlement of Puerto Ricans," in *The Puerto Rican Diaspora: Historical Perspectives*, ed. Carmen Teresa Whalen and Víctor Vázquez-Hernández (Philadelphia: Temple University Press, 2005).

19. John J. Betancur, Teresa Cordova, and Maria de los Angles Torres, "Economics Restructuring and the Process of Incorporation of Latinos into Chicago," in *Latinos in a Changing US Economy: Comparative Perspectives on Growing Inequality*, ed. Rebecca Morales and Frank Bonilla (New York: SAGE Publications, 1993). Taking into account economic restructuring's varying impact on diverse Latino national-origin groups (Cubans and South Americans fairing best, Central Americans midway, and Mexican and Puerto Ricans fairing worse), Betancur et al.'s data suggests that, in Chicago, Latino groups that have traditionally faired better in the labor market have not approached the average conditions of whites and are increasingly approximating the average conditions of Mexicans and Puerto Ricans.

20. The Housing Act of 1949, the first major federal program to rebuild the central city, provided federal loans and grants for the acquisition of land, allotting a hundred million dollars to help public agencies or private companies to redevelop the land with the purpose of constructing low-income housing to replace "slum dwellings." Private investors determined which projects were worth developing and decided on the design. See Alexander Von Hoffman, *House by House, Block by Block: The Rebirth of American Urban Neighborhoods* (New York: Oxford University Press, 2003).

21. Gregory D. Squires et al., *Chicago: Race Class, and the Response to Urban Decline* (Philadelphia: Temple University Press, 1987); Pauline Lipman, "Chicago School Reform: Advancing the Global City Agenda," in *The New Chicago: A Social and Cultural Analysis*, ed. John P. Koval, et al. (Philadelphia: Temple University Press, 2006).

22. Thomas M. Gray, "Housing Battle Fought Hard, and They're Winning," *Chicago Sun-Times*, September 1971, 12–20 (Hull House Association Records, Box 105, Folder 1285, UIC Daley Library Special Collections Department).

23. Larry Green, "Chicago's Latins Get the Housing Leftovers," *The Chicago Daily News*, August 3, 1971. (Hull House Association Records, Box 105, Folder 1285, UIC Daley Library Special Collections Department).

24. See Arjun Appadurai, "The Production of Locality," in *Modernity at Large: Cultural Dimensions of Globalization* (Minneapolis: University of Minnesota Press, 1996).

25. The distinction made between *levantar comunidad* and *subir la vecindad* conveys a vernacular understanding of the relationship, and the dividing line, of use value and exchange value in urban space economy. See John R. Logan and Harvey Molotch, *Urban Fortunes: The Political Economy of Place* (Berkeley: University of California Press, 1987); Raúl Villa, *Barrio-Logos: Space and Place in Urban Chicano Literature and Culture*, 1st ed. (Austin, TX: University of Texas Press, 2000). Both Logan and Molotch as well as Villa draw on David Harvey's interpretation of how use and exchange values in urban land-use theory are distinct, linked, and collide. See David Harvey, *Social Justice and the City* (Baltimore: Johns Hopkins University Press, 1973).

26. Thomas M. Gray, "Housing Battle Fought Hard, and They're Winning," *Chicago Sun-Times*, September 1971, 12–20 (Hull House Association Records, Box 105, Folder 1285, UIC Daley Library Special Collections Department).

27. Historian Carmen T. Whalen documented an earlier Puerto Rican riot in the Spring Garden neighborhood of Philadelphia in the summer of 1953. See Carmen Teresa Whalen, *From Puerto Rico to Philadelphia: Puerto Rican Workers and Postwar Economies* (Philadelphia: Temple University Press, 2001).

28. Chicago columnist Mike Royko explained the causes of the riot as follows: "the usual job and housing discrimination, coupled with the city's indifference and the police's habitual harshness." See Mike Royko, *Boss: Richard J. Daley of Chicago* (New York: Plume, 1971), 152.

29. Arjun Appadurai, "The Production of Locality," in *Modernity at Large: Cultural Dimensions of Globalization* (Minneapolis: University of Minnesota Press, 1996).

30. Larry Bennett, *Fragments of Cities: The New American Downtowns and Neighborhood* (Columbus, OH: Ohio State University Press, 1990).

31. See Felix Padilla, "The Quest for Community: Puerto Ricans in Chicago," in *In the Barrios: Latinos and the Underclass Debate*, ed. Joan Moore and Raquel Pinderhughes (New York: Russell Sage Foundation, 1993); Ray Suarez, *The Old Neighborhood: What We Lost in the Great Suburban Migration, 1966–1999* (New York: The Free Press, 1999). A prosperous, predominantly white, population remained in the area, although quite separate, along the Logan Square segment of the City's boulevard system.

A 1981 Latino Institute and University of Chicago study of the Logan Square and Avondale (area north of Logan Square) communities indicated that approximately 35 percent of Latinos owned their homes. John McCarron and Stanley Ziemba, "Hispanics' Growth Makes Them Major Component of City, Suburbs," *Chicago Tribune*, April 21, 1981, 11.

32. Thomas M. Gray, "Housing Battle Fought Hard, and They're Winning," *Chicago Sun-Times*, September 1971, 12–20 (Hull House Association Records, Box 105, Folder 1285, UIC Daley Library Special Collections Department).

33. Chicago Fact Book Consortium, ed., *Local Community Fact Book Chicago Metropolitan Area Based on the 1970 and 1980 Censuses* (Chicago: The University of Illinois at Chicago, 1984), George De Lama, "Neighbors Protest a Senseless War," *Chicago Tribune*, April 30, 1979, 5; Janet L. Abu-Lughod, *New York, Chicago, Los Angeles: America's Global Cities* (University of Minnesota Press: Minneapolis, 1999). Also see, John J. Betancur, "The Settlement Experience of Latinos in Chicago: Segregation, Speculation, and the Ecology Model," *Social Forces* 74, no. 4 (1996): 1299–324.

34. Thomas M. Gray, "Housing Battle Fought Hard, and They're Winning," *Chicago Sun-Times*, September 1971, 12–20. (Hull House Association Records, Box 105, Folder 1285, UIC Daley Library Special Collections Department).

35. Thomas M. Gray, "Housing Battle Fought Hard, and They're Winning," *Chicago Sun-Times*, September 1971, 12–20. (Hull House Association Records, Box 105, Folder 1285, UIC Daley Library Special Collections Department).

36. Appadurai's consideration of the production of locality proves useful in revealing the tensions betweens resistance and complicity in struggles over place within the context of uneven and ever-changing power relations. For Appadurai, "locality is a structure of feeling produced by particular forms of intentional activity and that yields particular sorts of material effects." See Arjun Appadurai, "The Production of Locality," in *Modernity at Large: Cultural Dimensions of Globalization* (Minneapolis: University of Minnesota Press, 1996), 182. Also see Robin D. G. Kelley and Earl Lewis, eds., *To Make Our World Anew: A History of African Americans* (New York: Oxford University Press, 2000).

37. Ray Suarez, *The Old Neighborhood: What We Lost in the Great Suburban Migration, 1966–1999* (New York: The Free Press, 1999).

38. For Naples, an examination of activist mothering enables a fresh understanding of the intertwined roles of labor, politics, and mothering. These are components of women's social lives traditionally investigated as separate spheres. Nancy Naples, "Activist Mothering: Cross-Generational Continuity in the Community Work of Women from Low-Income Urban Neighborhoods," *Gender and Society* 6, no. 3 (1992): 441–63. For more on the concept of "cooperative self-help" see Ruth Wilson Gilmore's chapter, "Mother Reclaiming Our Children. Ruth Wilson Gilmore, *Golden Gulag: Prisons, Surplus, Crisis, and Opposition in Globalizing California* (Berkeley: University of California Press, 2007). Although Ana, and many of the other women I came to know on Chicago's Near Northwest Side, would hesitate or flat out refuse to be identified as feminist, and would argue that motherhood and commitment to family are ideals not valued in feminism, I interpret their activism and consciousness as evidence of a grounded Latina feminism. Sociologist Mary Pardo makes a similar point in her study of Mexican-American mother activists in California: "These women based their theories about grassroots activism in everyday life and in their work as wives and mothers. Rather than allow themselves to be constricted by them, they used traditional and social identities in community

action." Mary S. Pardo, *Mexican American Women Activists: Identity and Resistance in Two Los Angeles Communities* (Philadelphia: Temple University Press, 1998), 230.

39. Robin D. G. Kelley and Earl Lewis, eds., *To Make Our World Anew: A History of African Americans* (New York: Oxford University Press, 2000).

40. Similarly, Vicky Muñiz observed Puerto Rican women in Brooklyn, New York, using a variety of small-scale strategies to defend their homes, their neighborhood, and their sense of place. Vicky Muñiz, *Resisting Gentrification and Displacement: Voices of Puerto Rican Women of the Barrio* (New York: Garland Publishing, 1998).

41. Ana Yolanda Ramos-Zayas, "Delinquent Citizenship, National Performances: Racialization, Surveillance, and the Politics of 'Worthiness' in Puerto Rican Chicago," *Latino Studies* 2, no. 1 (2004): 26–44.

42. Marixsa Alicea, "Cuando Nosotros Vivíamos . . .: Stories of Displacement and Settlement in Puerto Rican Chicago," *Centro: Journal of the Center for Puerto Rican Studies* 13, no. 2 (2001): 167–95.

43. E.R. Shipp, "Chicago's Hispanic Parents Protest 70 percent Dropout Rate," *The New York Times*, March 28, 1984, A16; Pauline Lipman, "Chicago School Reform: Advancing the Global City Agenda," in *The New Chicago: A Social and Cultural Analysis*, ed. John P. Koval, et al. (Philadelphia: Temple University Press, 2006).

44. See Ruth Wilson Gilmore, *Golden Gulag: Prisons, Surplus, Crisis, and Opposition in Globalizing California* (Berkeley: University of California Press, 2007); Sudhir Alladi Venkatesh and Alexandra K. Murphy, "Policing Ourselves: Law and Order in the American Ghetto," in *Youth, Globalization, and the Law*, ed. Sudhir Alladi Venkatesh and Ronald Kassimir (Stanford: Stanford University Press, 2007); Christian Parenti, *Lockdown America: Police and Prisons in the Age of Crisis* (New York: Verso, 1999). I thank Carlos Alamo for introducing me to this literature.

45. Anthropologist Gina Pérez examines the adoption of exile as a means to rid communities of "problem" youth in her work on Puerto Ricans in Chicago. Gina M. Pérez, "The Other 'Real World': Gentrification and the Social Construction of Place in Chicago," *Urban Anthropology* 31, no. 1 (2002): 37–68.

46. Cherri Moraga and Gloria Anzaldúa, eds., *This Bridge Called My Back: Writings by Radical Women of Color* (Watertown, MA: Persephone Press, 1981).

47. John J. Betancur, "The Politics of Gentrification: The Case of West Town in Chicago," *Urban Affairs Review* 37, no. 6 (2002): 780–814.

48. The nuanced approach to community activism undertaken by Otilia Irizarry and Ana La Luz reveals a more complex understanding of community than the one presented by Felix Padilla in which community actions and the signs posted in the neighborhood are interpreted as a simplistic battle between good and evil, and a wholesale demonization of gang members and their friends. See Felix Padilla, "The Quest for Community: Puerto Ricans in Chicago," in *In the Barrios: Latinos and the Underclass Debate*, ed. Joan Moore and Raquel Pinderhughes (New York: Russell Sage Foundation, 1993). I thank Lorena Garcia for this observation.

49. Patricia Hill Collins, *Black Feminist Thought: Knowledge, Consciousness, and the Politics of Empowerment*, rev. 10th anniversary ed. (New York: Routledge, 2000).

50. Ray Suarez, *The Old Neighborhood: What We Lost in the Great Suburban Migration, 1966–1999* (New York: The Free Press, 1999), 214.

51. Ray Suarez, *The Old Neighborhood: What We Lost in the Great Suburban Migration, 1966–1999* (New York: The Free Press, 1999), 219.

52. Ray Suarez, *The Old Neighborhood: What We Lost in the Great Suburban Migration, 1966–1999* (New York: The Free Press, 1999), 215.

53. Ray Suarez, *The Old Neighborhood: What We Lost in the Great Suburban Migration, 1966–1999* (New York: The Free Press, 1999), 217.

54. Ray Suarez, *The Old Neighborhood: What We Lost in the Great Suburban Migration, 1966–1999* (New York: The Free Press, 1999), 217.

55. Ray Suarez, *The Old Neighborhood: What We Lost in the Great Suburban Migration, 1966–1999* (New York: The Free Press, 1999), 218.

56. See Patricia Leeds, "Task Force Patrols in Arson Crackdown," *Chicago Tribune*, August 7, 1976, S6; Richard Phillip, "Federal Probe of Arsons on N.W. Side Under Way," *Chicago Tribune*, November 25, 1976, C1.

57. Barry Pearce, "Logan Square," July 23, 1993. (Logan Square folder, Neighborhood History Research Collection, The Harold Washington Library Center).

58. See Ray Suarez, *The Old Neighborhood: What We Lost in the Great Suburban Migration, 1966–1999* (New York: The Free Press, 1999); Bill Cunniff, "Touring Logan Square," *Chicago Sun-Times*, September 5, 1997.

    In 1985, sections of Logan Square were designated as a National Historic District through lobbying efforts of the Logan Square Preservation Council, a nonprofit neighborhood group that sponsors an annual house walk.

59. The 1974 Housing and Community Development Act ended funding for the controversial urban renewal program, replacing it with community development block grants administered under Housing and Urban Development (HUD). As part of the law, a voucher program known as Section 8 authorized construction of new housing and rehabilitation of existing housing for low-income families. Those who qualify for federal governmental rental assistance were not to pay more than 30 percent of their income for rent, with the option of renting privately owned housing that meets the (HUD) standards. See Alexander Von Hoffman, *House by House, Block by Block: The Rebirth of American Urban Neighborhoods* (New York: Oxford University Press, 2003).

    A 2006 Loyola University study on the differential impact of gentrification for African Americans and Latino areas found that, in Latino neighborhoods, development had largely consisted of teardowns and conversion of subsidized and low-income rental units to upscale apartments or luxury condominiums, whereas in predominantly African American neighborhoods, development tends to be of empty lots or abandoned buildings. See Philip Nyden, Emily Edlynn, and Julie Davis, "The Differential Impact of Gentrification on Communities in Chicago," (Chicago: Loyola University Center for Urban Research and Learning, 2006).

60. The La Luz family was able to move within the same neighborhood, literally across the street from the first home they purchased in Logan Square, but theirs is a rare case in the current market, where upsizing or even downsizing within the same neighborhood is almost impossible for poor-, low-, or moderate-income families. As of 2002, Chicago had a tight rental market with a 4 percent vacancy rate, a housing deficit of more than 182,000 affordable dwellings for low-income families, and is at risk of losing thousands of Section 8 units to market rate housing. Chicago Rehab Network, "Present Realities and Future Prospects: Chicago's Low Income Housing Tax Credit Portfolio, Summer Report" (Chicago: Chicago Rehab Network, 2002).

    The average rent in Logan Square increased by more than 97 percent from 1980 ($216) to 1990 ($426), while from 1990 to 2000 there was another 50 percent increase ($639) in the median rent in the area. In 2005 the median residential sales prices in Logan Square ranged between $300,000–349,000. Nathalie P. Voorhees Center for Neighborhood and Community Improvement, "Affordable Housing Conditions and Outlook in Chicago: An Early Warning for Intervention," (Chicago: Voorhees Center, 2006).

    The City's housing program uses regional family income figures (over $75,000 for a family of four); however, Chicago's medium family income falls almost $45,000 short (for Latinos in Logan Square the disparity is even greater) resulting in a housing policy that targets above the income of many Chicagoans. Consult the Chicago Rehab Network's website, "Housing Set-Asides," Chicago Rehab Network, http://www.chicagorehab.org/. Accessed January 24, 2012.

61. In a study on immigration and gentrification, Taylor and Puente note that Latinos leaving gentrifying areas are moving to working-class areas where the white population is on the decline and "in almost every case . . . the increase in Latino population was accompanied by moderate improvement in economic circumstance of the neighborhood. Nonetheless, areas with growing Latino populations are experiencing increasing overcrowding rates." See D. Garth Taylor and Sylvia Puente, "Immigration, Gentrification and Chicago: Race Ethnic/Relations in the New Global Era," Chapin Hall Center for Children at the University of Chicago, www.about.chapinhall.org/uuc/presentations/TaylorPuentePaper.pdf. Accessed on October 1, 2004.

62. The 27 percent of African Americans and 39 percent of Latinos in the metropolitan area who reside in "suburbs" are segregated from the suburbs where whites live. So, too, African Americans and Latinos in those separate suburbs are buying homes segregated from each other. Guy Stuart, "Integration or Segregation: Metropolitan Chicago at the Turn of the New Century," paper presented at the Race, Place, and Segregation: Redrawing the Color Line in Our Nation's Metros Symposium, The Civil Rights Project at Harvard University, May 2002.

63. Raymond Williams, *Marxism and Literature* (Oxford: Oxford University Press, 1977); Pierre Bourdieu, *Outline of a Theory of Practice*, trans. Richard Nice (Cambridge: University of Cambridge Press, 1998); Arjun Appadurai, "The Production

of Locality," in *Modernity at Large: Cultural Dimensions of Globalization* (Minneapolis: University of Minnesota Press, 1996).

64. John R. Logan and Harvey Molotch, *Urban Fortunes: The Political Economy of Place* (Berkeley: University of California Press, 1987), 99. Also see Raúl Villa, *Barrio-Logos: Space and Place in Urban Chicano Literature and Culture*, 1st ed. (Austin, TX: University of Texas Press, 2000), 8–16.

65. Nyden et al. documented "half joking" references to the decrease of children and increase of dogs in discussions with community leaders in rapidly gentrifying Chicago neighborhoods. See Philip Nyden, Emily Edlynn, and Julie Davis, "The Differential Impact of Gentrification on Communities in Chicago," (Chicago: Loyola University Center for Urban Research and Learning, 2006).

66. These three communities had 458 residential units in thirty-one buildings in 1989, more than 22,000 units in more than 1,300 buildings in 2004, approximately 13 percent of the City's condos, an increase from 0.6 percent in 1989. Julie Lynn Davis and David F. Merriman, "One and a Half Decades of Apartment Loss and Condominium Growth: Changes in Chicago's Residential Building Stock," Loyola University Center for Urban Research and Learning, *www.luc.edu/curl/pdfs/one_and_a_half_decades.pdf*. Accessed on January 24, 2012.

67. Ben LeFort, "Condo Controversy," *Extra*, August 30, 2001.

68. Urban Studies scholar Dana Cuff contends, "When a group of dwellings are planned, they embody a figure of the neighbor that can be discerned, an intended figure that stands in relation to the practiced figure." Dana Cuff, "The Figure of the Neighbor: Los Angeles Past and Future," *American Quarterly* 56, no. 3 (2004), 560.

69. The Logan Square Neighborhood Association supported this platform even though few low- and moderate-income residents in Logan Square would directly benefit from set-asides because of the small number of affordable units and their income ceiling. However, it supported this platform in context of a broader campaign that entails "new affordable home ownership programs, support for rental subsidies, property tax abatements, and advocacy for public housing residents." See Suzanne Blanc, Matthew Goldwasser, and Joanna Brown, "From the Ground Up: The Logan Square Neighborhood Association's Approach to Building Community Capacity," Research for Action, http://www.researchforaction.org/publication-listing/?id=9. Accessed on January 24, 2012.

70. The Quiñones Delgado family represents Latina/o middle class aspirations to place and offer some insight into how these ambitions and investments are tied to urban development initiatives. See Arlene Dávila's *Barrio Dreams: Puerto Ricans, Latinos, and the Neoliberal City* (University of California Press, 2004).

71. This will most likely be the fate of a number of young men in the nearby Lathrop Homes, a low-rise public housing complex with a racially diverse population (in comparison to other less desirable Chicago Public Housing facilities). In 2006 the Lathrop Homes was slated for a controversial transformation to a mixed-income

development, with a quota of subsidized and low-income slots as part of the housing authority's general transformation plan.

72. In a rethinking of the afamilial character of gentrification, Lia Karsten looked at middle-class professional families with children (or "yupps," young urban professional parents) in the Netherlands who held a strong preference for urban areas as places to live, in strong connection with the city as a place of work. She contends that professional mothers are driving the process of family gentrification, viewing the city as having a more "liberal climate" than the suburbs, and that thus this movement is also transforming male and female identities within the family. The study argues for a design of cities that considers families, yet the idea of families presented, or rather the view points that are given serious attention in making cities "family friendly," upholds a hegemonic notion of family as a white, middle-class, two-parent heterosexual household. See Lia Karsten, "Family Gentrifiers: Challenging the City as a Place Simultaneously to Build a Career and to Raise Children," *Urban Studies* 40, no. 12 (2003): 2573–84.

73. Brentano Math and Science Academy, a community public school that is part of the Logan Square Neighborhood Association, has experienced a steady decline in enrollment; it lost more than 275 students between 1999 and 2006. Chicago Public Schools Office of Research, Education, and Accountability accessed at http://research.cps.k12.il.us/cps/accountweb/. Accessed on March 31, 2007.

74. Illinois Standard Achievement Test (ISAT) scores are posted annually and ranked in the *Chicago Tribune* (compared to all the other public schools in the city). Urban Education Scholar Pauline Lipman points out that "the historical failure to provide necessary resources and conditions to educate low-income African-American [and Latina/o] students in Chicago, when linked with accountability policies that label schools as 'failures,' also produces the rationale for closing schools, displacing residents, and gentrifying low-income areas." Pauline Lipman, "Chicago School Reform: Advancing the Global City Agenda," in *The New Chicago: A Social and Cultural Analysis*, ed. John P. Koval, et al. (Philadelphia: Temple University Press, 2006), 257.

75. David Heinzmann, "Thriving Area Still Harbors Deadliest Police Beat," *Chicago Tribune*, February 24, 2004, 1.1.

CHAPTER 4

1. For Johnson, the concept of "constellation" incorporates "an array of activities, histories, and identities" brought into alliances by distinct social actors and signifies "the mobility of many parts, as well as the ability to re-form around different nuclei." Gaye Theresa Johnson, "Constellations of Struggle: Luisa Moreno, Charlotta Bass, and the Legacy for Ethnic Studies," *Aztlán: A Journal of Chicano Studies* 33, no. 1 (2008): 157. Also see Earl Lewis, "To Turn as on a Pivot: Writing African Americans into a History of Overlapping Diasporas," *American Historical Review* 100, no. 3 (1995): 765–87.

2. See Joe Trotter, Earl Lewis and Tera W. Hunter, ed., *The African American Urban Experience: Perspectives from the Colonial Period to the Present* (New York: Palgrave Macmillian, 2004); Kenneth L. Kusmer and Joe W. Trotter, editors, *African American Urban History Since World War II* (Chicago: University of Chicago Press, 2009). Also see Arlene Dávila's *Barrio Dreams: Puerto Ricans, Latinos, and the Neoliberal City* (University of California Press, 2004).

3. Paulla Ebron and Anna Lowenhaupt Tsing, "In Dialogue? Reading Across Minority Discourses," in *Women Writing Culture: Women of Color and Western History* ed. Ruth Behar and Debra A. Gordon (Berkeley: University of California Press, 1995), 390.

4. Ruth Wilson Gilmore, "'You have Dislodged A Boulder': Mothers and Prisoners in the Post Keynesian California Landscape." *Transforming Anthropology* 8, nos. 1&2 (1999): 12–38; Ruth Wilson Gilmore, "Forgotten Places and the Seeds of Grassroots Planning" in *Engaging Contradictions: Theory, Politics, and Methods of Activist Scholarship*, edited by Charles Hale (Berkeley: University of California Press, 2008), 31–61; Lorrin Thomas, *Puerto Rican Citizen: History and Political Identity in Twentieth Century New York City* (Chicago: The University of Chicago Press, 2010); Moon-Kie Jung, *Reworking Race: The Making of Hawaii's Interracial Labor Movement* (New York: Columbia University Press, 2006).

5. Ruth Wilson Gilmore, "'You have Dislodged A Boulder': Mothers and Prisoners in the Post Keynesian California Landscape." *Transforming Anthropology* 8, nos. 1&2 (1999): 26, 27. Also see Ruth Wilson Gilmore, "Forgotten Places and the Seeds of Grassroots Planning" in *Engaging Contradictions: Theory, Politics, and Methods of Activist Scholarship*, edited by Charles Hale (Berkeley: University of California Press, 2008), 43–44.

6. In 1952 approximately 12,000 Puerto Ricans were living within eleven Chicago police districts. The census indicated 3,300 persons of Puerto Rican parentage or birth. By 1956 the census estimated 20,000 Puerto Ricans in Chicago. See Manuel Martinez, *Chicago: Historia de Nuestra Communidad Puertorriqueña—Photographic Documentary* (Chicago: privately printed, 1989), 169.

7. Henry Yu, *Thinking Orientals: Migration, Contact, and Exoticism in Modern America* (New York: Oxford University Press, 2001), 187.

8. Jacalyn D. Harden, *Double Cross: Japanese Americans in Black and White Chicago* (Minneapolis: University of Minnesota Press, 2003), 57.

9. See Jacalyn D. Harden, *Double Cross: Japanese Americans in Black and White Chicago* (Minneapolis: University of Minnesota Press, 2003).

10. Jacalyn D. Harden, *Double Cross: Japanese Americans in Black and White Chicago* (Minneapolis: University of Minnesota Press, 2003), 90.

11. Historian Charlotte Brooks writes that, "[t]he employers who turned down Nisei and the landlords who slammed doors in their faces seldom asked if they were Japanese; not being white was enough. Still, the reactions of the many Chicago residents who reconstructed their mental hierarchies of race to accommodate the Nisei revealed that not being white did not mean being black." Charlotte Brooks,

"In the Twilight Zone between Black and White: Japanese American Resettlement and Community in Chicago, 1942–1945," *The Journal of American History* 86, no. 4 (2000), 1656.

12. Felix Padilla, *Latino Ethnic Consciousness: The Case of Mexican Americans and Puerto Ricans in Chicago* (Indiana: University of Notre Dame Press, 1985), 78.

13. Elena Padilla, "Puerto Rican Immigrants in New York and Chicago: A Study in Comparative Assimilation" (master's thesis, Anthropology, University of Chicago, 1947).

14. Letter from Waitstill H. Sharp, director of Chicago Council Against Racial and Religious Discrimination, to Hazel Holm of Maryville, College, Tennessee, January 23, 1951 (Welfare Council of Metropolitan Chicago, Chicago Historical Society, Chicago Historical Society, box 148, folder 3). Also cited in Ana Yolanda Ramos-Zayas, *National Performances: The Politics of Class, Race, and Space in Puerto Rican Chicago* (Chicago: University of Chicago Press, 2003), 48.

15. Puerto Ricans, for discussion in Cabinet, February 2, 1954, Mary A. Young to Robert H. MacRae, January 28, 1954 (Welfare Council of Metropolitan Chicago, Chicago Historical Society, box 148, folder 3).

16. Minutes of the Welfare Council of Metropolitan Chicago, April 9, 1954 (Welfare Council of Metropolitan Chicago, Chicago Historical Society, box 148, folder 3).

17. Micaela Di Leonardo, *Exotics at Home: Anthropologies, Others, American Modernity* (Chicago: The University of Chicago Press, 1998).

18. It was unusual for Japanese Americans to remain in transition areas into which they had been forced originally because of their race, once those areas had become predominantly African American. Charlotte Brooks, "In the Twilight Zone between Black and White: Japanese American Resettlement and Community in Chicago, 1942–1945," *The Journal of American History* 86, no. 4 (2000), 1676.

19. American FactFinder, US Census Bureau 2000. African Americans represented approximately 18 percent of the total metropolitan population, about 1.1 million residents. See United States Department of Commerce News, US Census Bureau 2001.

20. Elena Padilla, "Puerto Rican Immigrants in New York and Chicago: A Study in Comparative Assimilation" (master's thesis, Anthropology, University of Chicago, 1947), 86.

21. Elena Padilla, "Puerto Rican Immigrants in New York and Chicago: A Study in Comparative Assimilation" (master's thesis, Anthropology, University of Chicago, 1947), 86.

22. Elena Padilla, "Puerto Rican Immigrants in New York and Chicago: A Study in Comparative Assimilation" (master's thesis, Anthropology, University of Chicago, 1947), 90.

23. Elena Padilla, "Puerto Rican Immigrants in New York and Chicago: A Study in Comparative Assimilation" (master's thesis, Anthropology, University of Chicago, 1947), 90.

24. "Editorial," *Vida Latina*, June 5, 1957.
25. The Bracero Program exclusively recruited male workers from Mexico. See Lilia Fernández, "Of Immigrants and Migrants: Mexican and Puerto Rican Labor Migration in Comparative Perspective, 1942–1964," *Journal of American Ethnic History* 29, no. 3 (2010): 25.
26. Nicholas De Genova, "'White' Puerto Rican Migrants, the Mexican Colony, 'Americanization' and Latino History," *Latino Urban Ethnography and the Work of Elena Padilla* (Urbana: University of Illinois Press, 2011), 166.
27. Although relationships between Mexican men and Puerto Rican women were not simply a matter of obtaining citizenship, the repetition of this argument among Puerto Ricans tells us something about how this relationship has been framed and imagined.
28. Report on Project to Aid Spanish Speaking People Hull House Association, November 20, 1958, p. 12 (Welfare Council of Metropolitan Chicago, Chicago Historical Society, box 330, folder 4).
29. Elena Padilla, "Puerto Rican Immigrants in New York and Chicago: A Study in Comparative Assimilation" (master's thesis, Anthropology, University of Chicago, 1947), 91–92.
30. Elena Padilla, "Puerto Rican Immigrants in New York and Chicago: A Study in Comparative Assimilation" (master's thesis, Anthropology, University of Chicago, 1947), 98–99.
31. Elena Padilla, "Puerto Rican Immigrants in New York and Chicago: A Study in Comparative Assimilation" (master's thesis, Anthropology, University of Chicago, 1947), 94.
32. Nicholas De Genova, "'White' Puerto Rican Migrants, the Mexican Colony, 'Americanization' and Latino History," *Latino Urban Ethnography and the Work of Elena Padilla* (Urbana: University of Illinois Press, 2011), 169.
33. Frances Aparicio, "Reading the 'Latino' in Latino Studies: Towards Reimagining Our Academic Location," *Discourse* 21, no. 3 (1999): 3–18; Mérida M. Rúa, "*Colao* Subjectivities: PortoMex and MexiRican Perspectives on Language and Identity," *Centro: Journal of the Center for Puerto Rican Studies* 13, no. 2 (2001): 116–33; Nicholas De Genova and Ana Yolanda Ramos-Zayas, *Latino Crossings: Mexicans, Puerto Ricans and the Politics of Race and Citizenship* (New York: Routledge, 2003); Arlene Dávila's *Barrio Dreams: Puerto Ricans, Latinos, and the Neoliberal City* (University of California Press, 2004).
34. Mérida M. Rúa, "*Colao* Subjectivities: PortoMex and MexiRican Perspectives on Language and Identity," *Centro: Journal of the Center for Puerto Rican Studies* 13, no. 2 (2001): 116–33.
35. Frances Aparicio and Susana Chávez-Silverman, eds., *Tropicalizations: Transcultural Representations of Latinidad* (Hanover: University Press of New England, 1997).
    Cuban Anthropologist Fernando Ortiz took exception to ethnographic and US sociological preconceptions of cultural exchange as a simple unilateral acquisition

of a dominant culture over a subordinate one, as entailed in the concept of acculturation. Thus, he coined the term "transculturation" as an intervention in exploring sociocultural change as the unremitting influence cultures exert upon one another and, in consequence, the powerful potential to create new cultural forms and practices. See Fernando Ortiz, *Cuban Counterpoint* (1947; reprint, Durham: Duke University Press, 1995), 97–103. Expanding on Ortiz's work, Aparicio and Chavez-Silverman use *tropicalizations* to explore transculturations between dominant and subordinate cultures in the same colonial context. They propose *tropicalizations* as an analytical tool with the potential to transcend the binary of self/other. I use their theoretical framework to examine groups that are considered part of the subordinate sector in relation to a "dominant culture" in the United States. Elsewhere, I have introduced the term *colao* to think about how ordinary people theorize and negotiate fluid identities and cultural practices grounded in daily life experience and in the materiality of history. Mérida M. Rúa, "*Colao* Subjectivities: PortoMex and MexiRican Perspectives on Language and Identity," *Centro: Journal of the Center for Puerto Rican Studies* 13, no. 2 (2001): 116–33.

36. Ien Ang, "Identity Blues," in *Without Guarantees In Honour of Stuart Hall*, ed. Paul Gilroy, Lawrence Grossberg and Angela McRobbie (New York: Verso, 2000), 2. Working with Stuart Hall's notion that identity "is a matter of 'becoming' as well as of 'being,'" Cultural Studies scholar Ien Ang examines theoretical debates concerning cultural identity as dynamic and future-oriented or as inert and historically fixed. Simply put, he seeks to address "both the necessity and 'impossibility' of identities." Ang employs the phrase "absolute antagonism" to explore the extreme manner relationships are supposedly played out between those who seek Australia to be perceived as multicultural and cosmopolitan versus those who struggle to uphold an "old-fashioned" traditional (white) Australian national identity.

37. Chicana cultural theorist Angie Chabram Dernersesian proposes ways to begin theorizing latinidad through the recognition of inter-Latino subjects in her seminal article "'Chicana! Rican? No, Chicana-Riqueña!' Refashioning the Transnational Connection." See Angie Chabram Dernersesian, "'Chicana! Rican? No, Chicana-Riqueña!' Refashioning the Transnational Connection," in *Multiculturalism: A Critical Reader*, ed. David Theo Goldberg (Oxford: Blackwell, 1994).

38. Nicholas De Genova and Ana Yolanda Ramos-Zayas. *Latino Crossings: Mexicans, Puerto Ricans and the Politics of Race and Citizenship* (New York: Routledge, 2003).

39. Gerald Suttles' work on race, ethnicity, and territoriality briefly mentioned the presence of Puerto Ricans and Mexicans in this area of the Near West Side. Gerald Suttles, *The Social Order of the Slum: Ethnicity and Territory in the Inner City* (Chicago: University of Chicago Press, 1968), Chapter 2.

40. George Lipsitz, "The Possessive Investment in Whiteness: Racialized Social Democracy and the 'White' Problem in American Studies." *American Quarterly* 47, no. 3 (1995): 369–87.

41. Latino Institute, "*Al Filo*/The Cutting Edge: The Empowerment of Chicago's Latino Electorate," (Chicago: Latino Institute, 1986), 7.

42. For a more detailed analysis of the Vieques debate, consult Pedro Cabán's "Bombs, Ballots and Nationalism: Vieques and the Politics of Colonialism," paper presented at XXIII International Congress of the Latin American Studies Association, Washington, DC, September 2002. Cabán provides a critical political and historical perspective on the struggle for peace in Vieques.

43. Katherine T. McCaffrey, "Forging Solidarity: Politics, Protest, and the Vieques Support Network," in *The Puerto Rican Movement: Voices from the Diaspora*, ed. Andés Torres and José R. Velázquez (Philadelphia: Temple University Press, 1998), 334–36. Also see, Katherine T. McCaffrey, *Military Power and Popular Protest: The U.S. Navy in Vieques, Puerto Rico* (New Brunswick: Rutgers University Press, 2002).

    The solidarity network lost ground with the death of Angel Rodríguez Cristóbal, a socialist activist arrested for trespassing on the military property during an ecumenical protest service in Vieques (November 1979). He was found beaten and hanged in his jail cell in a federal prison in Tallahassee, Florida. In 1983 Governor Romero Barceló had signed an accord with the navy wherein the navy agreed to "be a good neighbor" and bring industry to Vieques. These promises were never fully met, but the accord was defused by the local movement and by extension the network. While they did not achieve their aim, activists read their efforts as providing important political lessons for other activists, namely a Puerto Rican movement working toward coalition-building between divergent factions (focus was on winnable goals).

44. William Harrell and Linda Backiel, "Rosselló and Clinton's Vieques Agreement," *NACLA Report on the Americas* 33, 5 (March/April 2000), 2.

45. For more context and analysis on the significance of Elián González for Cubans and Cuban Americans, see Sarah Banet-Weisner, "Elián González and 'The Purpose of America': Nation, Family, and the Child-Citizen," *American Quarterly* 55, no. 2 (2003): 149–78.

46. Teresa Puente, "City's Puerto Ricans Unite Against Navy's Target Practice on Island," *Chicago Tribune*, May 4, 2000, 8.

47. Ian James, "Rep. Gutierrez Arrested in Protest on Vieques," *Chicago Sun-Times*, April 29, 2001, 23.

48. Amílcar Antonio Barreto, *Vieques, the Navy, and Puerto Rican Politics* (Gainesville: University of Florida Press, 2002).

49. Pedro Cabán, "Bombs, Ballots and Nationalism: Vieques and the Politics of Colonialism," paper presented at XXIII International Congress of the Latin American Studies Association, October 2002, Washington, DC.

50. Pedro Cabán, "Give Puerto Rico Its Independence," *Newsday*, June 15, 2001, A51.

51. Jorge Duany, *The Puerto Rican Nation on the Move: Identities on the Island and in the United States* (Chapel Hill: University of North Carolina Press, 2002), 172.

52. Marvette Pérez, "The Political 'Flying Bus': Nationalism, Identity, Status, Citizenship and Puerto Ricans," *Critique of Anthropology* 22, no. 3 (2002): 305–22. Marvette Pérez asserts that there are island-born Puerto Ricans who have inquired about naturalization as a means to secure a "constitutional" US citizenship. See Ana Yolanda Ramos-Zayas, "Delinquent Citizenship, National Performances: Racialization, Surveillance, and the Politics of 'Worthiness' in Puerto Rican Chicago," *Latino Studies* 2, no. 1 (2004): 26–44.

53. In February 2002 Martin Castro's campaign sent out a glossy four-page mailing to the more gentrified sections of Logan Square attacking Gutierrez's record on terrorism. The mailing cited Gutierrez's support of the release of Puerto Ricans who were part of the FALN (radical advocates for Puerto Rican independence jailed for bombing what they identified as sites of US capitalism and colonial administration; some members had been pardoned by President Clinton at the end of his second term). Although the campaign office claimed that the mailing was to make public Gutierrez's voting record and statements, it directly linked Puerto Ricans to terrorist activities in a moment of national mourning and heightened fears of enemies within. Castro's campaign office was flooded with telephone calls from Puerto Ricans and Mexicans disturbed by the mailing and its implications for Puerto Ricans in the city.

54. In early October 2001 a group traveled from Chicago to Orlando, Florida, to assist in the voter registration drives promoted by Calderón and the Puerto Rican Federal Affairs Administration.

55. Ana Yolanda Ramos-Zayas, *National Performances: The Politics of Class, Race, and Space in Puerto Rican Chicago* (Chicago: University of Chicago Press, 2003); Michel S. Laguerre, *Diasporic Citizenship: Haitian Americans in Transnational America* (New York: St. Martin's Press, 1998).

56. In the fall of 1979, the corner of Division Street and Western Avenue was the site of a rally for the freed Puerto Rican Nationalists Lolita Lebrón, Irving Flores, and Rafael Cancel Miranda. President Jimmy Carter granted Lebrón and her comrades clemency the fall of 1979 as a result of an intensive campaign for amnesty to free the jailed Nationalists.

57. After the downtown parade, many floats head to Humboldt Park for a second procession that takes place in the Puerto Rican barrio. Many consider this the parade of *los independentistas* (those who advocate for the Puerto Rican independence from the US). The June 2001 parade was dedicated to the fishermen of Vieques, with Jesse Jackson serving as the grand marshal with the mayor of Vieques. For a more in-depth analysis of nationalism among Chicago Puerto Ricans, see Ana Yolanda Ramos-Zayas, *National Performances: The Politics of Class, Race, and Space in Puerto Rican Chicago* (Chicago: University of Chicago Press, 2003).

58. For a more in-depth analysis of *plena* see Frances Aparicio, *Listening to Salsa: Gender, Latin Popular Music, and Puerto Rican Cultures* (Hanover: University Press of New England, 1998); Juan Flores, "Bumbún and the Beginnings of la Plena," in *Divided Borders: Essays on Puerto Rican Identity* (Houston: Arte Público Press,

1993); Ruth Glasser, *My Music is My Flag: Puerto Rican Musicians and Their New York Communities 1917–1940* (Berkeley: University of California Press, 1995).

59. National Boricua Human Rights Network, Union for Puerto Rican Students (UPRS) at NEIU, Activist Student Union (DePaul), Latin American and Latino Studies Program (UIC), *A Call to Action: A Mini-Conference on the Violations of the Human Rights of the Puerto Rican People*, Program, Chicago: National Boricua Human Rights Network, April 19, 2001.

60. The FALN, founded in Chicago's Puerto Rican neighborhoods and comprised of working-class and poor diasporic Puerto Ricans, built upon the legacy of armed struggle by Puerto Rican nationalists; the US civil rights movement and international anticolonial national liberation movements of the 1960s and 1970s further inspired it. Denouncing US imperialism, the FALN took armed actions against centers of US power: military, government, and economic sites, chiefly in Chicago and New York. Actions taken by the FALN in the 1970s and 1980s reassociated Puerto Ricans in Chicago with terrorism and anti-American sentiments. See Jan Susler, "Unreconstructed Revolutionaries: Today's Puerto Rican Political Prisoners/Prisoners of War," in *The Puerto Rican Movement: Voices from the Diaspora*, ed. Andrés Torres and José Velásquez (Philadelphia: Temple University Press, 1998); Ana Yolanda Ramos-Zayas, *National Performances: The Politics of Class, Race, and Space in Puerto Rican Chicago* (Chicago: University of Chicago Press, 2003), 26.

61. Unpublished letter to the *Chicago Defender* in author's possession.

62. Pedro Cabán, "Bombs, Ballots and Nationalism: Vieques and the Politics of Colonialism," paper presented at XXIII International Congress of the Latin American Studies Association, Washington, DC, September 2002.

63. Tamara Lytle, "Bush's Vieques Decision Riles GOP, He Defends Pulling Navy from Island," *Chicago Tribune*, June 15, 2001, 13.

64. Arian Campo-Flores et al., "On Vieques, No Hispanic Is an Island," *Newsweek*, June 2001. Pedro Cabán suggests that Vieques "highlights the emergence of national political mobilization based on an ethnically constituted notion of Latinidad." Pedro Cabán, "Bombs, Ballots and Nationalism: Vieques and the Politics of Colonialism," paper presented at XXIII International Congress of the Latin American Studies Association, Washington, DC, September 2002; Also see Pedro Cabán, "Give Puerto Rico Its Independence," *Newsday*, June 15, 2001, A51.

65. Puerto Rican Federal Affairs Administration, *Boricua, ¡Inscríbete Y Vota! Que Nada Nos Detenga!*, pamphlet, Washington, DC: Puerto Rican Federal Affairs Administration, 2001. In addition to the voter registration campaign to promote Puerto Ricans in the continental United States to support island issues like Vieques, Governor Calderón hired Charles Black, a Republican strategist, to lobby for the interests of the Puerto Rican Government in Washington. Arian Campo-Flores et al., "On Vieques, No Hispanic Is an Island," *Newsweek*, June 2001.

66. Arian Campo-Flores et al., "On Vieques, No Hispanic Is an Island," *Newsweek*, June 2001.

The last general amnesty was granted in 1986. In 1996 Congress imposed harsh immigration laws making it more difficult for the undocumented to become legal residents and facilitating deportation processes. In the Illegal Immigration Reform and Immigrant Responsibility Act (1996), anti-immigration stipulations were part of the Personal Responsibility and Work Reconciliation Act (1996)—commonly referred to as "Welfare Reform"—passed a few weeks earlier. This legislation, directed against the poor, reveals intense aggression toward "welfare" and "immigrants," deeply implicating not only Mexicans, but also Puerto Ricans and African Americans, especially women from these populations. See Nicholas De Genova and Ana Yolanda Ramos-Zayas. *Latino Crossings: Mexicans, Puerto Ricans and the Politics of Race and Citizenship* (New York: Routledge, 2003).

67. Felix M. Padilla, *Puerto Rican Chicago* (Notre Dame, Ind.: University of Notre Dame Press, 1987); Manuel Martinez, *Chicago: Historia De Nuestra Comunidad Puertorriqueña—Photographic Documentary* (Chicago: Privately printed, 1989); Mérida M. Rúa, "Colao Subjectivities: PortoMex and MexiRican Perspectives on Language and Identity," *Centro: Journal of the Center for Puerto Rican Studies* 13, no. 2 (2001): 116–33; Ana Yolanda Ramos-Zayas, *National Performances: The Politics of Class, Race, and Space in Puerto Rican Chicago* (Chicago: University of Chicago Press, 2003); Gina M. Pérez, *The Near Northwest Side Story: Migration, Displacement, and Puerto Rican Families* (Berkeley: University of California Press, 2004).

68. Making these associations, however, was tricky, and on occasion triggered acrimonious public debate between African Americans and Latinos. This tended to occur when the immigrants' rights movements used African American civil rights history and icons as a frame of reference for their cause. (I did not encounter an instance of mass public backlash with the comparison of the Vieques campaign and the civil rights movement.) Such was the case of Elvira Arellano, an undocumented immigrant and mother of an eight-year-old US citizen, who in August of 2006 defied a final order to report to the US Department of Homeland Security for deportation to Mexico. Instead, she took refuge in a church on *Paseo Boricua* in Chicago's Humboldt Park community, galvanizing a "new sanctuary movement" of interfaith religious leaders and participating congregations pledging the support "families suffering from unjust immigration laws." Her actions attracted national and international media attention. But comments she made in one interview caused a firestorm of controversy in Chicago. Arellano asserted, "I'm strong, I've learned from Rosa Parks—I'm not going to the back of the bus. The law is wrong." Her use of Rosa Parks as inspiration for her actions was read by some as Arellano comparing herself to "the mother of the modern day civil rights movement." *Chicago Sun-Times* Columnist Mary Mitchell blasted the correlation, insisting that Parks "wasn't a law-breaker," unlike Arellano who was described as "pimping the system." "Her chutzpah makes her a folk hero to some," Mitchell maintained, "but her blatant exploitation of Parks' legacy undermines the fragile coalition between some blacks

and Hispanics that has formed around the immigration issue." For weeks African Americans, Latinos, and whites expressed their opinions on the streets, in editorial pages of newspapers, on the *Chicago Sun-Times* website, and in academic journals. Although a number of black readers supported Mitchell's point of view, Arellano did receive public support from African Americans. Days after Mitchell's column appeared, nine influential black ministers prayed with Arellano and insisted that she was "contesting an immoral government policy as Parks did." Within six months, more than a dozen activists heralded the establishment of the Faith and Justice Leadership Alliance, "a coalition of Latino and African American groups that will try to join immigration reform with issues the two communities have more in common, such as crime, education and housing." Thus, out of controversy began an attempt at "critical engagement that would recognize differences and our common stakes." See Mary Mitchell, "Blacks know Rosa Parks and you, Arellano, are no Rosa Parks," *Chicago Sun-Times* August 22, 2006, 14; Oscar Avila, "Black-Clergy Group Backs Immigrant Fighting Deportation," *Chicago Tribune*, August 25, 2006, 2C.1; Suzanne Oboler, "It's Time to Brush Up and to Make History: A Response to Mary Mitchell," *Latino Studies Journal* 4, no. 4 (2006): 353–55; http://www.newsanctuarymovement.org/ (accessed June 24, 2011); Antonio Olivo, "Latino, Black Activists Form Coalition; Immigrant Leaders Act to Defuse Tension as New Marches Near," *Chicago Tribune*, February 21, 2007, 2C.2; Antonio Olivo, "Immigration Activist Will Leave Church; with D.C. Trip, She Risks Deportation," *Chicago Tribune*, August 16, 2007, 2C.1; Claudia Sandoval, "Citizenship and the Barriers to Black and Latino Coalitions in Chicago," *NACLA Report on the Americas* 43, no. 6 (2010): 36–45.

69. US Congress, House of Representatives, Office of Congressman Luis V. Gutierrez, "Gutierrez Receives Verdict, Sentence for Peaceful Protest on Vieques," press release, August 29, 2001.

70. Nuyorican Journalist Juan Gonzalez made references to the civil rights movement as well in his coverage of the Vieques struggle: "When movie stars, ministers and politicians start lining up to get arrested in support of a cause, it's a sure sign that the cause is heading to victory. This was true of the civil rights movement in the 1950s, of the peace movement during the Vietnam War and of South Africa's anti-apartheid movement. It is equally true of the movement to end nearly 60 years of Navy bombing on the Puerto Rican island of Vieques." Juan González, "Vieques Protest Victory-Bound," *Daily News*, May 1, 2001, 24. In another article, Gonzalez wrote, "Not since the sit-ins over Jim Crow and the anti-war movement of the '60s has a human rights issue stirred a whole segment of the U.S. population in this way." Juan González, "No mercy for Vieques protesters," *In These Times*, June 25, 2001, 11. Juan Guisti Cordero, "Vieques: Message from Camp García," *Centro: Journal of the Center for Puerto Rican Studies* 11, no. 2 (2000): 115–21.

To a great degree, the congressman tied the fortunes of Puerto Ricans to US ideals of liberal individualism and democratic capitalism, to borrow from

American Studies scholar Nikhil P. Singh's insightful reading of King's 1963 March on Washington speech. Vieques could now be free to pursue capitalist dreams as an exotic tourist destination. Nikhil Pal Singh, *Black is a Country: Race and the Unfinished Struggle for Democracy* (Cambridge, MA: Harvard University Press, 2004), 3.

71. Julio Ghigliotty, "Alega Vieques Se Ha Ganado El Respaldo Internacional," *El Nuevo Día Interactivo*, Junio 26, 2001.

72. Salim Muwakkil, "Changing of the Guard," *In These Times*, July 23, 2001, 3. A series of articles and commentaries discuss the political rift between Jesse Jackson and Al Sharpton vying over the leadership of a new civil rights movement. These articles question the political strategies and self-promoting personal agendas of both men in protesting on behalf of Vieques—Sharpton looked for Latino support for his future political aspirations as Jackson sought to deflect attention from his personal escapades that could have compromised his public life. See Rod Dreher, "Jessie vs. Al." *National Review Online*, June 25, 2001; Don Terry and Sabrina Miller, "Struggle for Power," *Chicago Tribune*, July 1, 2001, 2.1. For a perspective that supported Jackson's and Sharpton's involvement in the Vieques struggle, see Salim Muwakkil, "The Division Potential: Blacks Need to Form Political Coalition with Hispanics," *Chicago Tribune*, July 2, 2001, 1.13. Muwakkil believes that such a coalition is "on the leading edge of a new approach to issues of racial disadvantage." He pointed to the results of the 2000 census as a historic change that will alter the dichotomous way race has been defined in the United States since this nation's beginnings. Robert Kennedy, Jr.'s motives for supporting Vieques were never questioned as Jackson's and Sharpton's had been.

73. Rodolpho Gonzales, José Jimenez, and Karen Wald, *Tierra y Libertad: Two Interviews with Corky Gonzales & Cha Cha Jimenez* (Detroit: Radical Education Project, 1970), 13.

74. Rodolpho Gonzales, José Jimenez, and Karen Wald, *Tierra y Libertad: Two Interviews with Corky Gonzales & Cha Cha Jimenez* (Detroit: Radical Education Project, 1970), 16.

75. Michael T. Kaufman, "Black Panthers Join Coalition With Puerto Rican and Appalachian Groups," *New York Times*, November 9, 1969, 1.

76. Bruce Franklin, *From the Movement Toward the Revolution* (New York: Van Nostrand Reinhold Company, 1971), 112. The flyer described the Breakfast for Children Program of the Illinois Black Panther Party, and the free clinic on the West Side; the Young Lord's People's Church with a day care center for Spanish-speaking people; and the Young Patriots distribution of food and alternative school in Uptown.

77. See Andrew Diamond, *Mean Streets: Chicago Youths and the Everyday Struggle for Empowerment in the Multiracial City, 1908–1968* (Berkeley: University of California Press, 2009), chapter 5 and epilogue; Jeffrey O.G. Ogbar, "Puerto Rico in My Heart: The Young Lords, Black Power and Puerto Rican Nationalism in the US, 1966–1972." *Centro Journal* 18, no. 1 (2006): 148–69; Jon Rice, The World of the

Illinois Panthers, in *Freedom North: Black Freedom Struggles Outside of the South, 1940–1980* ed. Jeanne F. Theoharis and Komozi Woodard (New York: Palgrave Macmillan, 2003), 55–56.

78. Jon Rice, The World of the Illinois Panthers, in *Freedom North: Black Freedom Struggles Outside of the South, 1940–1980* ed. Jeanne F. Theoharis and Komozi Woodard (New York: Palgrave Macmillan, 2003), 55–56.

79. Lorrin Thomas, *Puerto Rican Citizen: History and Political Identity in Twentieth Century New York City* (Chicago: The University of Chicago Press, 2010), 227.

80. Carlos Alamo, "Dispatches From a Colonial Outpost: Puerto Rico as Schema in the Black Popular Press, 1942–1951" *The Du Bois Review: Social Science Research on Race* 8, no. 2 (2011): 7. The *Defender* sent staff correspondent Denton Brooks to Puerto Rico to write a series of articles, from early July until mid-September 1943, on the social and political situation in the island.

81. Jon Rice, The World of the Illinois Panthers, in *Freedom North: Black Freedom Struggles Outside of the South, 1940–1980* ed. Jeanne F. Theoharis and Komozi Woodard (New York: Palgrave Macmillan, 2003), 56. After the death of Mayor Richard J. Daley—known as the last "boss" of the city— in 1976, Harold Washington made an unsuccessful bid in the 1977 Democratic primary for mayor, but, with the support of a strategic alliance of multiracial and divergent class communities, African Americans, Mexican Americans, Puerto Ricans, and white lakefront liberals, won election in 1983 intending to represent all Chicago communities through redistribution of resources.

82. See Paul Kleppner, *Chicago Divided: The Making of a Black Mayor* (DeKalb, Illinois: Northern Illinois University Press, 1985), 229–31; Gary Rivlin, *Fire on the Prairie: Chicago's Harold Washington and the Politics of Race* (New York: Henry Holt and Company, 1992), 182, 188; Ira Glass, "Harold, Episode 84," *This American Life* (Chicago: WBEZ Chicago, National Public Radio, 1997).

83. Teresa Córdova, "Harold Washington and the Rise of Latino Electoral Politics in Chicago, 1982–1987," in *Chicano Politics and Society in the Late Twentieth Century*, ed. David Montejano (Austin: University of Texas Press, 1999), 38–40.

84. See Gary Rivlin, *Fire on the Prairie: Chicago's Harold Washington and the Politics of Race* (New York: Henry Holt and Company, 1992); Sharon D. Collins, *The Rainbow Challenge: The Jackson Campaign and the Future of U.S. Politics* (New York: Monthly Review Press, 1986).

85. Peter J. Boyer, "A Man of Faith: Can Jesse Jackson Save Himself?" *The New Yorker*, October 22, 2001, 61. It has been suggested that Jackie Jackson's participation in the Vieques campaign and subsequent arrest were a means to reconcile the Jackson marriage. Gutierrez had put forth the idea of sending Mrs. Jackson to Vieques "as a way of directing the spotlight away from Sharpton." Then again, Jesse Jackson has had a history of supporting peace in Vieques dating back to the 1980s. In 1999 he visited Vieques as part of a campaign to urge Clinton to change US policy. See Rod Dreher, "Jessie vs. Al." *National Review Online*, June 25, 2001;

Don Terry and Sabrina Miller, "Struggle for Power," *Chicago Tribune*, July 1, 2001, 2.1; Peter J. Boyer, "A Man of Faith: Can Jesse Jackson Save Himself?" *The New Yorker*, October 22, 2001. For a perspective that supported Jackson's involvement in the Vieques struggle, see Salim Muwakkil, "The Division Potential: Blacks Need to Form Political Coalition with Hispanics," *Chicago Tribune*, July 2, 2001, 1.13.

86. Lucio Guerrero, "Freedom Comes Thursday for Jacqueline Jackson," *Chicago Sun-Times*, June 27, 2001, 10.
87. Linda Backiel, "The People of Vieques, Puerto Rico vs. the United States Navy," *Monthly Review* 54, no. 9 (February 2003).
88. David Gonzalez, "Vieques Advocate Turns from Violence of Her Past," *The New York Times*, June 18, 2001, A14.
89. Juan Andrade, "Latino-Black Alliance Is Greatly Exaggerated," *Chicago Sun-Times*, July 15, 2001, 33.
90. Ana Mendieta, Fran Speilman, and Gary Wisby, "Hunger Strikers Keep up Push for School," *Chicago Sun-Times*, May 30, 2001.
91. Juan Andrade, "Latino-Black Alliance Is Greatly Exaggerated," *Chicago Sun-Times*, July 15, 2001, 33.
92. Avery Gordon, *Ghostly Matters: Haunting and the Sociological Imagination* (Minnesota: University of Minnesota Press, 1997).

CHAPTER 5

1. "*Sociales*," *Vida Latina*, October 1955, 24.
2. The most influential study of rites of passage is Arnold Van Gennep, *The Rites of Passage* (Chicago: University of Chicago Press, 1960).
3. Meredith S. Chesson, "Social Memory, Identity and Death: An Introduction," *Social Memory, Identity and Death: Anthropological Perspectives on Mortuary Rituals* (Arlington, VA: American Anthropological Association, 2001), 8, n1. Also see Susan D. Gillespie, "Personhood, Agency, and Mortuary Ritual: A Case Study from the Ancient Maya," *Journal of Anthropological Archaeology* 20, no. 1(2001): 78.
4. Maria G. Cattel and Jacob J. Climo, "Introduction: Meaning in Social Memory and History: Anthropological Perspectives," in *Social Memory and History: Anthropological Perspectives* ed. Jacob J. Climo and Maria G. Cattell (Walnut Creek, CA: AltaMira Press, 2002).
5. Steven Gregory, *Black Corona: Race and the Politics of Place in an Urban Community* (Princeton: Princeton University Press, 1998), 13.
6. Maria G. Cattel and Jacob J. Climo, "Introduction: Meaning in Social Memory and History: Anthropological Perspectives," in *Social Memory and History: Anthropological Perspectives* ed. Jacob J. Climo and Maria G. Cattell (Walnut Creek, CA: AltaMira Press, 2002).

7. Karla F.C. Holloway, *Passed On: African American Mourning Stories* (Durham: University of North Carolina Press, 2003), chapter 1.
8. St. Clair Drake and Horace R. Cayton, *Black Metropolis: A Study of Negro Life in a Northern City*, revised and enlarged ed. (New York: Harcourt, Brace and Company, 1945; Chicago: The University of Chicago Press, 1993), 457.
9. Roberto Suro, "Humboldt Park: 'Community Without Dreams,'" *Chicago Tribune*, June 4, 1978, 1, 8; Charles Leroux and Rogers Worthington, "Arson: The Fears Still Flicker Long After the Flames Are Out," *Chicago Tribune*, June 5, 1978, Tempo Section 1, 3. The *Chicago Tribune* ran a three-part series on arson and its effects on neighborhoods. Also see Charles Leroux and Rogers Worthington, "Who is to Blame for Arson's Ashes?" *Chicago Tribune*, June 6, 1978, Tempo Section 1, 4; Charles Leroux and Rogers Worthington, "It's a Crime Against Property, But Arson Hurts People the Most," *Chicago Tribune*, June 6, 1978, Tempo Section 1–2.
10. Robert Unger, "Cody Sends Condolences: Long Goodbye to 6 Near N.W. Side Fire Victims," *Chicago Tribune*, January 5, 1977, B10. Also see Patricia Leeds, "Task Force Patrols in Arson Crackdown," *Chicago Tribune*, August 7, 1976; Richard Phillip, "Federal Probe of Arsons on N.W. Side Under Way," *Chicago Tribune*, November 25, 1976.
11. Carlos Flores, "Photo Essay of Puerto Rican Chicago," *Centro: Journal of the Center for Puerto Rican Studies* 13, no. 2 (2001): 158.
12. "Slain When Cop Is Wounded: Suspect Is Identified as Youth Worker," *Chicago Tribune*, July 30, 1973, 2; "Special Jury for Latin Death Denied," *Chicago Tribune*, August 30, 1973, A6; "Victim was First to Fire, Cop Testifies," *Chicago Tribune*, November 24, 1973, A10.
13. Eric Herman, "Woman Lived to Age 107," *The Chicago Sun-Times*, June 8, 2006, 66.
14. Reymundo Sanchez, *My Bloody Life: The Making of a Latin King* (Chicago: Chicago Review Press, 2000), 212–13.
15. In the Islamic tradition the body of the deceased is neither embalmed nor is there a wake; bodies are washed with water and wrapped in white cloth shrouds, with the burial taking place soon thereafter. The Muslim Community Center of Chicago referred families to Caribe Funeral Home, which offered a special rate for Islamic burial preparations. Monifa Thomas, "Center Plans to Open First Muslim Funeral Home Here," *The Chicago Sun-Times*, October 24, 2007, 6.
16. Obituary, *Chicago Tribune*, June 15, 2008, 6.
17. Felix Padilla dedicated a chapter in *Puerto Rican Chicago* to *Los Caballeros de San Juan*. See Felix M. Padilla, *Puerto Rican Chicago* (Notre Dame, Indiana: University of Notre Dame Press, 1987).
18. Carol Stack, *All Our Kin: Strategies for Survival in a Black Community* (New York: Harper & Row, 1974), 58.
19. Although Our Lady of Guadalupe on the South Side was the first church to serve Mexicans in Chicago, the church building was erected in the 1950s. See Gerald

Suttles, *The Social Order of the Slum: Ethnicity and Territory in the Inner City* (Chicago: The University of Chicago Press, 1968); Sandra Cisneros, *Caramelo* (New York: Alfred A. Knopf, 2002).

20. The Latin American and Latino Studies program at the University of Illinois has copies of various issues of *Vida Latina*. The US Latino Recovery Project, the University of Houston, has a more expansive collection of *Vida Latina* but I have yet to locate a complete collection of the magazine.

21. "The League of United Latin American Citizens, Chicago Council No. 288," *Vida Latina*, Enero 1957, 32; "The League of United Latin American Citizens, Chicago Council No. 288," *Vida Latina*, Febrero 1957, 30; Martin Ortiz, "Casos tipicos de ayuda proporcionada por el Concilio Mexico-Americano en Chicago," *Vida Latina*, Junio 1953, 14; "Mexican American Council Accepted as Community Fund Agency and Is Granted Funds by Two Foundations," *Vida Latina*, Enero 1954, 34; "Los Caballeros de San Juan," *Vida Latina*, Junio 1954, 6.

22. Arturo Vargas Medel, "Editorial," *Vida Latina*, Febrero 1952, 2.

23. Dr. Olimpio Galindo, "Editorial," *Vida Latina*, Marzo 1952, 5.

24. "Alicia Alonso aplaudida en Chicago," *Vida Latina*, Abril 1953, 29; "Pedro Infante Triunfo en Chicago," *Vida Latina*, Julio 1953, 13; "Artista Portorriqueña [*sic*] en Chicago: Se Trata de Ruth Fernandez, *Vida Latina*, Noviembre 1953, 23, "Desbordante Júbilo de los Latinoamericanos Cuando KID GAVILAN Conservo el Campeonato de Mundo," *Vida Latina*, Diciembre 1953, 26–27.

25. "Gavilan Beats Bratton; Keeps Welter Title," *Chicago Daily Tribune*, November 14, 1953, 1.

26. "Desbordante Júbilo de los Latinoamericanos Cuando KID GAVILAN Conservo el Campeonato de Mundo," *Vida Latina*, Diciembre 1953, 26.

27. Arturo Vargas Medel, "Al Margen de un Tercer Aniversario—José Noemí Gomez y Su 'Hora Hispana,'" *Vida Latina*, Mayo 1953, 9–10.

28. *Vida Latina*, Noviembre 1954, 16. Two years later, the Chicago City Council would proclaim June 19 to 24 as San Juan week in honor of Puerto Rico's patron saint, a week full of festivities, both sacred and secular. "Activities for San Juan Day 1957, *Vida Latina*, Junio 1957, 36; "Graphics of 'San Juan Day' 1956," *Vida Latina*, Junio 1957, 37. A "Souvenir Issue" of *Vida Latina* dedicated to Puerto Ricans had been published in June 1957, highlighting the upcoming celebration of San Juan week in Chicago. A section of the magazine reflected on its coverage of "San Juan Day" festivities in 1956 with photographs of San Juan's mayor Doña Felisa Rincón's visit to the city, and the full to capacity mass that had been celebrated at Holy Name Cathedral, where civic and political leaders had joined the Puerto Rican community. Photographs of the contestants for "*Reina de las Fiestas de San Juan*" (Queen of the San Juan Festivities) were also included.

29. *Vida Latina*, Noviembre 1956.

30. "Solemne misa" *Vida Latina*, February 1954, 19; "Asistentes a la misa por la salud y bienestar del Glmo. Rafael Leonidas Trujillo Molina, benefactor de la R. Dominicana,"

Vida Latina, February 1957, 17. Trujillo ruled the Dominican Republic from 1930 until he was assassinated in 1961. His regime was considered the most tyrannous and brutal dictatorship in Latin America at the time. For a literary take on the haunting presence of Trujillo on Dominican identity see Junot Díaz, *The Brief and Wondrous Life of Oscar Wao* (New York: Riverhead Books, 2007).

31. "Editorial," *Vida Latina*, Mayo 1953.

32. "Carta Abierta," *Vida Latina*, Febrero 1953.

33. It is important to recognize that the images found in the society pages of *Vida Latina* are reflective of a celebration of heteronormative notions of family and community.

34. "Topicos Sociales," *Vida Latina*, Agosto 1954, 21.

35. Elena Padilla, "Puerto Rican Immigrants in New York and Chicago: A Study in Comparative Assimilation" (master's thesis, Anthropology, University of Chicago, 1947), 44.

36. Confirmation is the other sacrament when a sponsor is chosen to guide and witness the receipt of the Holy Ghost to those already baptized. The individual confirmed recommits to the Catholic Church. The seven Catholic sacraments are baptism, reconciliation, Holy Communion, confirmation, marriage, holy orders, and anointing of the sick. The idea of godparenthood as a form of social obligation and social celebration are assigned in other rites of passage such as *quinceañeras* and marriage.

37. Sidney Mintz and Eric Wolf, "An Analysis of Ritual Co-Parenthood (Compadrazgo)," *Southwestern Journal of Anthropology* 6, no. 4 (1950): 341–68; Elena Padilla, *The People of Puerto Rico*; Elena Padilla, *Up from Puerto Rico* (New York: Columbia University Press, 1958), 121–22; Ruth Behar, *Translated Woman: Crossing the Border with Esperanza's Story* (Boston: Beacon Press, 1993).

38. In her contemporary study of Latina adolescent sexuality in Chicago, Lorena Garcia observed the significance of the *comadre* relationship, as a source of support as well as judgment. Some mothers confided in their comadres of their daughter's sexual activity while others kept quiet because they felt ashamed or believed they would be criticized for their daughter's behavior. This became even more complicated when it was discovered that the daughter was involved in a same-sex relationship. See Lorena Garcia, *Respect Yourself, Protect Yourself: Latina Girls and Sexual Identity* (New York: New York University Press, 2012), Chapter 2.

39. "Enlace Religioso," *Vida Latina*, Julio 1953, 19; Rudolph Bush, "JOSE NOEMI GOMEZ, 84; Spanish-language Radio Broadcast Pioneer (Sports Final, CN Edition)," *Chicago Tribune*, July 22, 2002, 7.

40. "Enlace Religioso," *Vida Latina*, Julio 1953, 19.

41. "Sociales," *Vida Latina*, Junio 1959, 22.

42. "Pagina Infantil," *Vida Latina*, Mayo 1962, 9.

43. In the sixty-two available issues, of the 362 weddings announced in *Vida Latina*, San Francisco was named ninety-four times and Holy Name Cathedral, the second most mentioned church, was named forty-eight times. The Recovering the US

Hispanic Literary Heritage Project at the University of Houston has the most complete collection of *Vida Latina* from 1952 to 1962, holding sixty-two issues out of a possible 120.

44. Paul Gilroy, "Roots and Routes: Black Identity as an Outernational Project," in *Racial and Ethnic Identity: Psychological Development and Creative Expression*, ed. Herbert W. Harris, Howard C. Blue, and Ezra E. H. Griffith (London: Routledge, 1995), 26. Also see Paul Gilroy, *The Black Atlantic: Modernity and Double Consciousness* (Cambridge, MA: Harvard University Press, 1993). For a discussion on the significance of visiting to African American identity and community formation, see Earl Lewis, *In Their Own Interests: Race, Class, and Power in Twentieth-Century Norfolk, Virginia* (Berkeley: University of California Press, 1991), 101–09.

45. Earl Lewis, *In Their Own Interests: Race, Class, and Power in Twentieth-Century Norfolk, Virginia* (Berkeley: University of California Press, 1991), 109.

46. For a poetic exploration of the significance of *café* to Puerto Rican identity formation see Tato Laviera, "*café*," in *AméRican* (Houston: Arte Público Press, 1985), 39.

47. Proceeds of the profits of the festival were to be donated to the Logan Square YMCA. City Council of the City of Chicago, *Journal of the Proceedings of the City Council of the City of Chicago, Illinois* (Chicago, September 8, 1986), 33566. The city also sponsored Festa Italiana, Festival Polonaise, and Irish Fest Chicago as part of its lakefront ethnic festivals.

48. For an analysis of festivals and identity formation see Lorena Garcia and Mérida M. Rúa, "Processing Latinidad: Mapping Latino Urban Landscapes through Chicago Ethnic Festivals," *Latino Studies Journal* 5, no. 3 (2007): 317–39.

49. Roberto Clemente, right fielder for the Pittsburgh Pirates, was killed in a plane crash on December 31, 1972. He had chartered a plane to deliver aid to earthquake victims in Nicaragua. He was the first Puerto Rican and Latino selected into the Baseball Hall of Fame and has been commemorated in song, literature, a stamp, and the built environment. (Robert Clemente Community Academy High School in Humboldt Park, built in 1974, and the Logan Square US Post Office are also named in his honor.) See Miguel Algarin and Tato Laviera, "Olú Clemente," in *The Prentice Hall Anthology of Latino Literature* (NJ: Prentice Hall, 2001); Tony Pabon y La Protesta's "Clemente" *Tony Pabon y La Protesta: Introducing Nestor Sanchez* (Rico Records, 1973).

50. Rina Benmayor, "For Every Story There is Another Story which Stands Before It," in *Stories to Live By: Continuity and Change in Three Generations of Puerto Rican Women*, Rina Benmayor, Ana Juarbe, Celia Alvarez, Blanca Vázquez (New York: Oral History Task Force Centro de Estudios Puertorriqueños, 1987), 2.

51. Avery Gordon, *Ghostly Matters: Haunting and the Sociological Imagination* (Minnesota: University of Minnesota Press, 1997), 8.

52. Rachel Buff, *Immigration and the Political Economy of Home: West Indian Brooklyn and American Indian Minneapolis, 1945–1992* (Berkeley: University of California Press, 2001), 2–3.

53. Carl Sandburg, "Chicago" In *Selected Poems of Carl Sandburg*, ed. Rebecca West (New York: Harcourt, Brace and Company, 1926), 29–30.

54. The first Palmer House Hotel ("The Palmer"), a wedding present for his bride Bertha Honoré, burned to ground, along with much of the city, in the Chicago Fire of 1871. Palmer, without delay, borrowed money to rebuild State Street and an even more spectacular hotel, which opened in 1875. Barbara Lanctot, *A Walk Through Graceland Cemetery* (Chicago: Chicago School of Architecture Foundation, 1977), 30.

    When Sol Tax was in the planning stages of a study of Puerto Ricans in Chicago in 1948 based on Elena Padilla's work, she had informed him, "As to the follow-up of the informants I suggest the cards be mailed to them ... [at] the CYO, Palmer House Hotel, Stevens Hotel, Hotpoint, etc., the main employers of Puerto Ricans in the city." See Letter from Elena Padilla to Sol Tax, 3 January 1948 (Sol Tax Papers, Box 256, Folder 4, Special Collections Research Center, University of Chicago Library).

55. Daniel H. Burnham and Edward H. Bennett, *Plan of Chicago*, ed. Charles Moore (New York: Princeton Architectural Press, 1993); Carl Smith, *The Plan of Chicago: Daniel Burnham and the Remaking of the American City* (Chicago: The University of Chicago Press, 2006).

56. Barbara Lanctot, *A Walk Through Graceland Cemetery* (Chicago: Chicago School of Architecture Foundation, 1977), 1.

57. Here I am drawing from historian Vincent Brown's discussion of the limitations and potential of Orlando Patterson's concept of "social death." See Vincent Brown, "Social Death and Political Life in the Study of Slavery," *The American Historical Review* 14, no. 5 (2009): 1231–1249; Vincent Brown, "History Attends to the Dead," *Small Axe 31* 14, no. 1 (2010): 219–27. Orlando Patterson, *Slavery and Social Death: A Comparative Study* (Cambridge, MA: Harvard University Press, 1982).

58. Stuart Hall, "Cultural Identity and Diaspora," in *Identity: Community, Culture, Difference*, ed. Jonathon Rutherford (London: Lawrence & Wishart Ltd, 1990).

CHAPTER 6

1. Mérida M. Rúa, "Claims to 'The City': Puerto Rican Latinidad amid Labors of Identity, Community, and Belonging in Chicago" (PhD diss., American Culture, University of Michigan, 2004), 17.

2. John L. Jackson, *Real Black: Adventures in Racial Sincerity* (Chicago: The University of Chicago Press, 2005), 162–65. Also see Ruth Behar, *The Vulnerable Observer: Anthropology that Breaks Your Heart* (Boston: Beacon Press, 1996).

3. Ethnographers who have asked similar questions include Carol Stack, *All Our Kin: Strategies for Survival in a Black Community* (New York: Harper & Row, 1974); Sudhir Venkatesh, "'Doin' the hustle': Constructing the Ethnographer in the American Ghetto," *Ethnography* 3, no. 1 (2002): 91–111; John L. Jackson, *Real Black: Adventures in Racial Sincerity* (Chicago: The University of Chicago Press, 2005).

4. Virginia R. Dominguez, "For a Politics of Love and Rescue," *Cultural Anthropology* 15, no. 3 (2000): 363–64.

5. Virginia R. Dominguez, "For a Politics of Love and Rescue," *Cultural Anthropology* 15, no. 3 (2000): 365–66. Also see Avery Gordon, "Her Shape and His Hands," in *Ghostly Matters: Haunting and the Sociological Imagination* (Minneapolis: University of Minnesota Press, 1996), 3–28.

6. See John Jackson's *Real Black* for an example of a work that discusses the role of the researcher as a central part of the ethnography. John L. Jackson, *Real Black: Adventures in Racial Sincerity* (Chicago: The University of Chicago Press, 2005).

7. Johnnetta B. Cole, "John Langston Gwaltney (1928–1998)," *American Anthropologist* 101, no. 3 (1999): 614.

8. John Langston Gwaltney, *Drylongso: A Self-Portrait of Black America* (New York: Random House, 1980), xxiii.

9. Faye V. Harrison, *Outsider Within: Reworking Anthropology in the Global Age* (Urbana: University of Illinois Press, 2008).

10. See Ruth Behar, "Panel Comments: Challenging Disciplinary Acts through and within a Politics of Love and Rescue," comments presented at American Anthropological Association 100th Annual Meeting, Washington D.C., 2001; John Langston Gwaltney, *Drylongso: A Self-Portrait of Black America* (New York: Random House, 1980).

11. Mérida M. Rúa, ed., *Latino Urban Ethnography and the Work of Elena Padilla* (Urbana: University of Illinois Press, 2011).

12. John Langston Gwaltney, *Drylongso: A Self-Portrait of Black America* (New York: Random House, 1980); John Langston Gwaltney, "Common Sense and Science: Urban Core Black Culture," in *Anthropologists at Home in North America: Methods and Issues in the Study of One's Own Society*, ed. Donald A. Messerschmidt (New York: Cambridge University Press, 1981).

13. John Langston Gwaltney, *Drylongso: A Self-Portrait of Black America* (New York: Random House, 1980), xxii.

14. Iris Marion Young, "Asymmetrical Reciprocity: On Moral Respect, Wonder, and Enlarged Thought," *Constellations* 3, no. 3 (1997): 340–63.

15. Earl Lewis, "Connecting Memory, Self, and the Power of Place in African American Urban History," *Journal of Urban History* 21, no. 3 (1995): 366.

16. Faye V. Harrison, *Outsider Within: Reworking Anthropology in the Global Age* (Urbana: University of Illinois Press, 2008), 21. Also see Sudhir Venkatesh, "'Doin' the hustle': Constructing the Ethnographer in the American Ghetto," *Ethnography* 3, no. 1 (2002): 91–111.

17. Historians are rarely reflective about the sources that they use or the condition under which their narratives are produced, oral historians notwithstanding. Antoinette Burton's edited collection *Archive Stories* is an exception. Taking an ethnographic approach, here the contributors contemplate the archive, what constitutes

an archive, and how that has mattered in terms of how histories are written. Antoinette Burton, "Introduction: Archive Fever, Archive Stories," in *Archive Stories: Facts, Fiction, and the Writing of History*, ed. Antoinette Burton (Durham: Duke University Press, 2005).

Anthropologist Michel-Rolph Trouillot asked similar questions of the archive, archival practices, and the production of history in his masterful, and brilliantly slim, work *Silencing the Past*, but Burton is the first collection by historians to examine this dynamic. Michel-Rolph Trouillot, *Silencing the Past: Power and the Production of History* (Boston: Beacon Press, 1995).

18. Horacio N. Roque Ramirez, "A Living Archive of Desire: Teresita La Campesina and the embodiment of Queer Latino Community Histories," in *Archive Stories: Facts, Fiction, and the Writing of History*, ed. Antoinette Burton (Durham: Duke University Press, 2005), 116.

19. "Rafael Arjona Siaca: Con la participación de Dra. Gloria Arjona," interview by Ángel Collado Schwarz, *La Voz del Centro* #110, January 30, 2005, http://www.vozdelcentro.org/?p=180. Accessed on September 1, 2010.

20. Historian Durba Ghosh notes, "In processing the so-called primary sources of the archives into the secondary sources used by other scholars and students of history, it is a largely inadmissible secret that our work is often shaped by archival conditions beyond our control, conditions such as whether the archivist or librarian is sympathetic or drawn to the project." Durba Ghosh, "National Narratives and the Politics of Miscegenation, Britain and India," in *Archive Stories: Facts, Fiction, and the Writing of History*, ed. Antoinette Burton (Durham: Duke University Press, 2005), 27.

21. Report to the Joyce Foundation, August 30, 2002–August 29, 2003, Frances R. Aparicio, author's possession.

22. Gina M. Pérez, ed. Centro: Journal of the Center for Puerto Rican Studies 13, no. 2 (2001).

23. "Un siglo de puertorriqueñidad en Chicago," *Nuestro directorio anuario* (privately published, n.d.). Private collection of Georgina Bishop.

24. "*Centro de Estudios Puertorriqueños*: Marixsa Alicea and Mérida M. Rúa," interviewed by Carlos Flores, *Eight Forty-Eight*, Chicago Public Radio, April 12, 2002. Marixsa Alicea, "Cuando Nosotros Vivíamos . . .: Stories of Displacement and Settlement in Puerto Rican Chicago," *Centro: Journal of the Center for Puerto Rican Studies* 13, no. 2 (2001): 167–95; Mérida M. Rúa, "*Colao* Subjectivities: PortoMex and MexiRican Perspectives on Language and Identity." *Centro: Journal of the Center for Puerto Rican Studies* 13, no. 2 (2001): 116–33.

25. Lani Guinier, "Prologue," in *The Miner's Canary: Enlisting Race, Resisting Power, Transforming Democracy*, Lani Guinier and Gerald Torres (Cambridge, MA: Harvard University Press, 2002), 4.

26. Earl Lewis, In Their Own Interests: Race, Class, and Power in Twentieth-Century Norfolk, Virginia (Berkeley: University of California Press, 1991), 90.

27. Steven Gregory, *Black Corona: Race and the Politics of Place in an Urban Community* (Princeton: Princeton University Press, 1998), 10–11.

ESSAY ON METHODOLOGY AND SOURCES

1. See Barney G. Glaser and Anselm L. Strauss, *The Discovery of Grounded Theory: Strategies for Qualitative Research* (New York: Aldine De Gruyter, 1967).
2. Ruben A. Buford May and Mary Patillo McCoy, "Do You See What I See? Examining a Collaborative Ethnography," *Qualitative Inquiry* 6, no. 1 (2000): 65–87; Ana Yolanda Ramos-Zayas, *National Performances: The Politics of Class, Race, and Space in Puerto Rican Chicago* (Chicago: University of Chicago Press, 2003); John L. Jackson, *Real Black: Adventures in Racial Sincerity* (Chicago: The University of Chicago Press, 2005); Faye V. Harrison, *Outsider Within: Reworking Anthropology in the Global Age* (Urbana: University of Illinois Press, 2008).

BIBLIOGRAPHY

Abu-Lughod, Janet L. *New York, Chicago, Los Angeles: America's Global Cities.* Minneapolis: University of Minnesota Press, 1999.

Alamo, Carlos. "Dispatches from a Colonial Outpost: Puerto Rico as Schema in the Black Popular Press, 1942–1951." *Du Bois Review: Social Science Research on Race* 8, no. 2 (2011): 1–25.

———. "Racializing the Research Laboratory: Puerto Rico and the African American Intellectual Imaginary 1940–1950." Paper presented at the 8th International Congress of the Puerto Rican Studies Association, San Juan, PR, October 3, 2008.

Algarin, Miguel, and Tato Laviera. "Olú Clemente." In *The Prentice Hall Anthology of Latino Literature*, by Eduardo del Río, 494–521. Upper Saddle River, NJ: Prentice Hall, 2001.

Alicea, Marixsa. "Cuando nosotros vivíamos . . .: Stories of Displacement and Settlement in Puerto Rican Chicago." *Centro: Journal of the Center for Puerto Rican Studies* 13, no. 2 (2001): 167–95.

Ang, Ien. "Identity Blues." In *Without Guarantees: In Honour of Stuart Hall*, edited by Paul Gilroy, Lawrence Grossberg, and Angela McRobbie, 1–13. New York: Verso, 2002.

Aparicio, Frances R. "Cultural Twins and National Others: Allegories of Intralatino Subjectivities in U.S. Latino/a Literature." *Identities* 16, no. 5 (2009): 622–41.

———. *Listening to Salsa: Gender, Latin Popular Music, and Puerto Rican Cultures.* Hanover: University Press of New England, 1998.

———. "Reading the 'Latino' in Latino Studies: Towards Reimagining Our Academic Location." *Discourse* 21, no. 3 (1999): 3–18.

Aparicio, Frances R, and Susana Cháez-Silverman, eds. *Tropicalizations: Transcultural Representations of Latinidad.* Hanover: University Press of New England, 1997.

Appadurai, Arjun. "The Production of Locality." Chap. 9 in *Modernity at Large: Cultural Dimensions of Globalization.* Minneapolis: University of Minnesota Press, 1996.

Arredondo, Gabriela F. *Mexican Chicago: Race, Identity, and Nation, 1916–39.* Urbana: University of Illinois Press, 2008.

Avila, Oscar "Black-Clergy Group Backs Immigrant Fighting Deportation." *Chicago Tribune* August 25, 2006, 2C.1.

Backiel, Linda. "The People of Vieques, Puerto Rico vs. the United States Navy." *Monthly Review* 54, no. 9 (2003): 1–13.

Banet-Weiser, Sarah. "Elían González and 'The Purpose of America': Nation, Family, and the Child-Citizen." *American Quarterly* 55, no. 2 (2003): 149–78.

Barkley Brown, Elsa. "Negotiating and Transforming the Public Sphere: African American Political Life in the Transition from Slavery to Freedom." *Public Culture* 7, no.1 (1994): 107–46.

Barreto, Amílcar Antonio. *Vieques, the Navy, and Puerto Rican Politics*. Gainesville: University of Florida Press, 2002.

Behar, Ruth. "Panel Comments: Challenging Disciplinary Acts through and within a Politics of Love and Rescue." Comments presented at American Anthropological Association 100th Annual Meeting, Washington DC, 2001.

———. *Translated Woman: Crossing the Border with Esperanza's Story*. Boston: Beacon Press, 1993.

———. *The Vulnerable Observer: Anthropology that Breaks Your Heart*. Boston: Beacon Press, 1996.

Benmayor, Rina. "For Every Story There is Another Story which Stands Before It." In *Stories to Live By: Continuity and Change in Three Generations of Puerto Rican Women*, edited by Rina Benmayor, Ana Juarbe, Celia Alvarez, and Blanca Vázquez, 1–13. New York: Oral History Task Force, Centro de Estudios Puertorriqueños, 1987.

Bernabe, Rafael, and César J. Ayala. *Puerto Rico in the American Century: A History Since 1898*. Chapel Hill: University of North Carolina Press, 2007.

Betancur, John J., Teresa Córdova, and María de los Ángeles Torres. "Economics Restructuring and the Process of Incorporation of Latinos into Chicago." In *Latinos in a Changing US Economy: Comparative Perspectives on Growing Inequalities*, edited by Rebecca Morales and Frank Bonilla, 109–32. New York: SAGE Publications, 1993.

Betancur, John J. "The Politics of Gentrification: The Case of West Town in Chicago." *Urban Affairs Review* 37, no. 6 (2002): 780–814.

Blanc, Suzanne, Matthew Goldwasser, and Joanna Brown. "From the Ground Up: The Logan Square Neighborhood Association's Approach to Building Community Capacity." Research for Action. http://www.researchforaction.org/publication-listing/?id=9.

Bourdieu, Pierre. *Outline of a Theory of Practice*. Translated by Richard Nice. Cambridge: University of Cambridge Press, 1998.

Briggs, Laura. *Reproducing Empire: Race, Sex, Science, and the U.S. Imperialism in Puerto Rico*. Berkeley: University of California Press, 2002.

Brooks, Charlotte. "In the Twilight Zone between Black and White: Japanese American Resettlement and Community in Chicago, 1942–1945." *The Journal of American History* 86, no. 4 (2000): 1655–87.

Brown, Vincent. "Social Death and Political Life in the Study of Slavery." *The American Historical Review* 14, no. 5 (2009): 1231–49.

Bruegmann, Robert. "Built Environment of the Chicago Region." In *The Encyclopedia of Chicago*, edited by James R. Grossman, Ann Durkin Keating, and Jeff L. Reiff, 101–05. Chicago: University of Chicago Press, 2004.

Buff, Rachel. *Immigration and the Political Economy of Home: West Indian Brooklyn and American Indian Minneapolis, 1945–1992*. Berkeley: University of California Press, 2001.

Burnett, Christina Duffy, and Burke Marshall. "Between the Foreign and the Domestic: The Doctrine of Territorial Incorporation, Invented and Reinvented." In *Foreign in a Domestic Sense: Puerto Rico, American Expansion, and the Constitution*, edited by Christina Duffy Burnett and Burke Marshall, 1–38. Durham: Duke University Press, 2001.

Burnham, Daniel H., and Edward H. Bennett. *Plan of Chicago*. New York: Princeton Architectural Press, 1993.

Burton, Antoinette, ed. *Archive Stories: Facts, Fiction, and the Writing of History*. Durham, Duke University Press, 2005.

———. "Introduction: Archive Fever, Archive Stories." In Burton, *Archive Stories: Facts, Fiction, and the Writing of History*, 1–24. Durham, Duke University Press, 2005.

Cabán, Pedro. "Bombs, Ballots, and Nationalism: Vieques and the Politics of Colonialism." Paper presented at XXIII International Congress of the Latin American Studies Association, Washington DC, September 2002.

———. "Subjects and Immigrants During the Progressive Era." *Discourse* 23, no. 3 (2001): 24–51.

Cabranes, José A. "Citizenship and the American Empire: Notes on the Legislative History of the United States Citizenship of Puerto Ricans." *University of Pennsylvania Law Review* 127, no. 2 (1978): 391–492.

Carrasco, Gilbert Paul. "Latinos in the United States: Invitation and Exile." In *Perea, Immigrants Out: The New Nativism and the Anti-Immigrant impulse in the United States*, 190–204. New York: New York University Press, 1996.

Cattell, Maria G., and Jacob J. Climo. "Introduction: Meaning in Social Memory and History: Anthropological Perspectives." In *Social Memory and History: Anthropological Perspectives*, edited by Jacob J. Climo and Maria G. Cattell, 1–38. Walnut Creek, CA: AltaMira Press, 2002.

Chabram-Dernersesian, Angie. "'Chicana! Rican? No, Chicana-Riqueña!' Refashioning the Transnational Connection." In *Multiculturalism: A Critical Reader*, edited by David Theo Goldberg, 269–95. Oxford: Blackwell, 1994.

Chesson, Meredith S. "Social Memory, Identity, and Death: An Introduction." In *Social Memory, Identity, and Death: Anthropological Perspectives on Mortuary Rituals*. Arlington, VA: American Anthropological Association, 2001.

Centro de Estudios Puertorriqueños. *Labor Migration Under Capitalism: The Puerto Rican Experience*. New York: Monthly Review Press, 1979.

Chicago Fact Book Consortium, ed. *Local Community Fact Book Chicago Metropolitan Area Based on the 1970 and 1980 Censuses*. Chicago: The University of Illinois at Chicago, 1984.

Chicago Public Schools Office of Research, Education, and Accountability. http://research.cps.k12.il.us/resweb/qt.

Cisneros, Sandra. *Caramelo*. New York: Knopf, 2002.

Cole, Johnetta B. "John Langston Gwaltney (1928–1998)." *American Anthropologist* 101, no. 3 (1999): 614–16.

Collins, Sharon D. *The Rainbow Challenge: The Jackson Campaign and the Future of U.S. Politics*. New York: Monthly Review Press, 1986.

Córdova, Teresa. "Harold Washington and the Politics of Race." In *Chicano Politics and Society in the Late Twentieth Century*, edited by David Montejano, 31–57. Austin: University of Texas Press, 1999.

Coudert Jr., Frederic R. "Our New Peoples: Citizens, Subjects, Nationals or Aliens." *Columbia Law Review* 3, no.1 (1903): 13–32.

Cuff, Dana. "The Figure of the Neighbor: Los Angeles Past and Future." *American Quarterly* 56, no. 3 (2004): 559–82.

Dávila, Arlene. *Barrio Dreams: Puerto Ricans, Latinos, and the Neoliberal City*. Berkeley: University of California Press, 2004.

Davis, Julie Lynn, and David F. Merriman. "One and a Half Decades of Apartment Loss and Condominium Growth: Changes in Chicago's Residential Building Stock." Loyola University Center for Urban Research and Learning. http://www.luc.edu/curl/pdfs/one_and_a_half_decades.pdf

De Genova, Nicholas, and Ana Yolanda Ramos-Zayas. *Latino Crossings: Mexicans, Puerto Ricans, and the Politics of Race and Citizenship*. New York: Routledge, 2003.

De Genova, Nicholas. "White Puerto Rican Migrant, the Mexican Colony, 'Americanization' and Latino History." In Rúa, *Latino Urban Ethnography and the Work of Elena Padilla*, 157–77. Urbana: University of Illinois Press, 2011.

———. *Working the Boundaries: Race, Space, and Illegality in Mexican Chicago*. Durham: Duke University Press, 2005.

Diamond, Andrew. *Mean Streets: Chicago Youths and the Everyday Struggle for Empowerment in the Multiracial City, 1908–1968*. Berkeley: University of California Press, 2009.

Díaz, Junot. *The Brief and Wondrous Life of Oscar Wao*. New York: Riverhead Books, 2007.

Di Leonardo, Micaela. *Exotics at Home: Anthropologies, Others, American Modernity*. Chicago: University of Chicago Press, 1998.

Dominguez, Virginia R. "For a Politics of Love and Rescue." *Cultural Anthropology* 15, no. 3 (2000): 361–93.

Donato, Katharine M., Donna Gabaccia, Jennifer Holdaway, Martin Manalansan, IV, and Patricia R. Pessar "A Glass Half Full? Gender in Migration Studies," *International Migration Review* 40, no. 1 (2006): 3–26.

Drake, St. Clair, and Horace R. Cayton. *Black Metropolis: A Study of Negro Life in a Northern City*. 1945. Rev. ed., Chicago: University of Chicago Press, 1993.

Duany, Jorge. *The Puerto Rican Nation on the Move: Identities on the Island and in the United States*. Chapel Hill: University of North Carolina Press, 2002.

Duncan, Ronald, ed. *The Anthropology of the People of Puerto Rico*. Puerto Rico: Inter American University of Puerto Rico, 1979.

Ebron, Paulla, and Anna Lowenhaupt Tsing. "In Dialogue? Reading Across Minority Discourses." In *Women Writing Culture: Women of Color and Western History*, edited by Ruth Behar and Debra A. Gordon, 390–411. Berkeley: University of California Press, 1995.

Erman, Sam. "Meanings of Citizenship in the U.S. Empire: Puerto Rico, Isabel Gonzalez, and the Supreme Court, 1898 to 1905." *Journal of American Ethnic History* 27, no. 4 (2008): 5–33.

Fernández, Lilia. "Of Immigrants and Migrants: Mexicans and Puerto Rican Labor Migration in Comparative Perspective, 1942–1964." *Journal of American Ethnic History* 29, no. 3 (2010): 6–39.

Flores, Carlos. "Photo Essay of Puerto Rican Chicago; Capturing the Images of Chicago's Puerto Rican Community." *Centro: Journal of the Center for Puerto Rican Studies* 13, no. 2 (2001): 134–65.

Flores, Juan. "'Bumbún' and the Beginnings of Plena Music." In *Divided Borders: Essays on Puerto Rican Identity*, 85–91. Houston: Arte Público Press, 1993.

Fox Piven, Frances, and Richard A. Cloward. *Regulating the Poor: The Functions of Public Welfare*. New York: Pantheon Books, 1971.

Friedenberg, Judith, ed. *The Anthropology of Lower Income Urban Enclaves: The Case of East Harlem*. New York: The New York Academy of Sciences, 1995.

Garcia, Lorena, and Mérida M. Rúa. "Processing Latinidad: Mapping Latino Urban Landscapes through Chicago Ethnic Festivals." *Latino Studies Journal* 5, no. 3 (2007): 317–39.

Garcia, Lorena. *Respect Yourself, Protect Yourself: Latina Girls and Sexual Identity*. New York: New York University Press, 2012.

Gillespie, Susan D. "Personhood, Agency, and Mortuary Ritual: A Case Study from the Ancient Maya." *Journal of Anthropological Archaeology* 20, no. 1 (2001): 73–112.

Gilmore, Ruth Wilson. "Forgotten Places and the Seeds of Grassroots Planning." In *Engaging Contradictions: Theory, Politics, and Methods of Activist Scholarship*, edited by Charles Hale, 31–61. Berkeley: University of California Press, 2008.

———. *Golden Gulag: Prisons, Surplus, Crisis, and Opposition in Globalizing California*. Berkeley: University of California Press, 2007.

———. "'You have Dislodged A Boulder': Mothers and Prisoners in the Post Keynesian California Landscape." *Transforming Anthropology* 8, nos. 1&2 (1999): 12–38.

Gilroy, Paul. *The Black Atlantic: Modernity and Double Consciousness*. Cambridge, Mass: Harvard University Press, 1993.

———. "Roots and Routes: Black Identity as an Outernational Project." In *Racial and Ethnic Identity: Psychological Development and Creative Expression*, edited by Herbert W. Harris, Howard C. Blue, and Ezra E.H. Griffith, 15–30. London: Routledge, 1995.

Glasser, Ruth. *Aquí Me Quedo: Puerto Ricans in Connecticut/Los Puertorriqueños en Connecticut*. Connecticut: Connecticut Humanities Council, 1997.

———. *My Music is My Flag: Puerto Rican Musicians and Their New York Communities 1917–1940*. Berkeley: University of California Press, 1995.

Ghosh, Durba. "National Narratives and the Politics of Miscegenation, Britain and India." In *Burton, Archive Stories: Facts, Fiction, and the Writing of History*, 27–44. Durham: Duke University Press, 2005.

Goings, Kenneth W., and Raymond A. Mohl. "Toward a New African Urban History." *Journal of Urban History* 21, no. 3 (1995): 283–95.

Gonzales, Rodolpho, José Jiménez, and Karen Wald. *Tierra y Libertad: Two Interviews with Corky Gonzales & Cha Cha Jimenez*. Detroit: Radical Education Project, 1970.

Gordon, Avery. *Ghostly Matters: Haunting and the Sociological Imagination*. Minnesota: University of Minnesota Press, 1997.

Gregory, Steven. *Black Corona: Race and the Politics of Place in an Urban Community*. Princeton: Princeton University Press, 1998.

Grossman, James. *Land of Hope: Chicago, Black Southerners and the Great Migration*. Chicago: University of Chicago Press, 1989.

Guglielmo, Thomas A. *White on Arrival: Italians, Race, Color, and Power in Chicago, 1890–1945*. New York: Oxford University Press, 2003.

Guinier, Lani. "Prologue." In *The Miner's Canary: Enlisting race, Resisting Power, Transforming Democracy*, edited by Lani Guinier and Gerald Torres, 1–36. Cambridge, MA: Harvard University Press, 2002.

Guisti Cordero, Juan. "Vieques: Message from Camp García." *Centro: Journal for Puerto Rican Studies* 11, no. 2 (2000): 115–21.

Gwaltney, John Langston. "Common Sense and Science: Urban Core Black Culture." In *Anthropologists at Home in North America: Methods and Issues in the Study of One's Own Society*, edited by Donald A. Messerschmidt, 46–61. New York: Cambridge University Press, 1981.

——. *Drylongso: A Self-Portrait of Black America*. New York: Random House, 1980.

Harden, Jacalyn D. *Double Cross: Japanese Americans in Black and White Chicago*. Minneapolis: University of Minnesota Press, 2003.

Harrell, William, and Linda Backiel. "Rosselló and Clinton's Private Vieques Agreement." *NACLA Report on the Americas* 33, no. 5 (2000): 2, 51.

Harrison, Faye V. *Outsider Within: Reworking Anthropology in the Global Age*. Urbana: University of Illinois Press, 2008.

Harrison, Faye V., and Ira E. Harrison. "Introduction: Anthropology, African Americans, and the Emancipation of a Subjugated Knowledge." In *African-American Pioneers in Anthropology*, edited by Ira E. Harrison and Faye V. Harrison, 1–36. Urbana: University of Illinois Press, 1999.

Harvey, David. *Social Justice and the City*. Baltimore: Johns Hopkins University Press, 1973.

Henri, Florette. *Black Migration: Movement North, 1900–1920*. Garden City, New York: Anchor Press/Double Day, 1975.

Hernández, Carmen Dolores. *Ricardo Alegría: Una Vida*. Puerto Rico: Centro de Estudios Avanzados de Puerto Rico y el Caribe, Fundación Puertorriqueña de las Humanidades, Instituto de Cultura Puertorriqueña, Academia Puertorriqueña de Historia, 2002.

Hernández, David. "Armitage Street." In *Unsettling America: An Anthology of Contemporary Multicultural Poetry*, edited by Maria Mazziotti Gillan and Jennifer Gillan, 271–72. New York: Viking Press, 1994.

Hill Collins, Patricia. *Black Feminist Thought: Knowledge, Consciousness, and the Politics of Empowerment*. rev. ed. New York: Routledge, 2009.

Hirsch, Arnold. *Making the Second Ghetto: Race and Housing in Chicago, 1940–1960*. Chicago: University Press, 1983.

Holloway, Karla F.C. *Passed On: African American Mourning Stories*. Durham: University of North Carolina Press, 2003.

Hooks, Bell. *Yearning: Race, Gender, and Cultural Politics*. Boston, MA: South End Press, 1990.

"Housing Set-Asides." Chicago Rehab Network. http://www.chicagorehab.org/.

Houstoun, Marion F., Roger G. Kramer, and Joan Mackin Barrett. "Female Predominance in Immigration to the United States Since 1930: A First Look." *International Migration Review*, Special Issue: Women in Migration 18, no. 4 (1984): 908–963.

Jackson, John L. *Real Black: Adventures in Racial Sincerity*. Chicago: The University of Chicago Press, 2005.

Johnson, Gaye Theresa. "Constellations of Struggle: Luisa Moreno, Charlotta Bass, and the Legacy for Ethnic Studies." *Aztlán: A Journal of Chicano Studies* 33, no. 1 (2008): 155–172.

Karsten, Lia. "Family Gentrifiers: Challenging the City as a Place Simultaneously to Build a Career and to Raise Children." *Urban Studies* 40, no. 12 (2003): 2573–84.

Katz, Michael. "Reframing the 'Underclass' Debate." In *The "Underclass" Debate: Views from History*, edited by Michael Katz, 440–78. Princeton: Princeton University Press, 1993.

Kelley, D.G., and Earl Lewis, eds. *To Make Our World Anew: A History of African Americans*. New York: Oxford University Press, 2000.

Kleppner, Paul. *Chicago Divided: The Making of a Black Mayor*. DeKalb, Ill.: Northern Illinois University Press, 1985.

Kusmer, Kenneth L., and Joe W. Trotter, eds. *African American Urban History Since World War II*. Chicago: University of Chicago Press, 2009.

Laguerre, Michel S. *Diasporic Citizenship: Haitian Americans in Transnational America*. New York: St. Martin's Press, 1998.

Lanctot, Barbara. *A Walk Through Graceland Cemetery*. Chicago: Chicago School of Architecture Foundation, 1977.

Lapp, Michael. "Managing Migration: The Migration Division of Puerto Rico and Puerto Ricans in New York City, 1948–1968." PhD Diss., History, Johns Hopkins University, 1990.

———. "The Rise and Fall of Puerto Rico as a Social Laboratory, 1945–1965." *Social Science History* 19, no. 2 (1995): 169–199.

Latino Institute. *Al Filo/The Cutting Edge: The Empowerment of Chicago's Latino Electorate*. Chicago: Latino Institute, 1986.

Lauria-Perricelli, Antonio. "A Study in Historical and Critical Anthropology: The Making of 'The People of Puerto Rico.'" PhD Diss., New School for Social Research, 1989.

Laviera, Tato. "café." In *AmeRícan*, 39. Houston: Arte Público Press, 1985.

Lewis, Earl. "Connecting Memory, Self, and the Power of Place in African American Urban History." *Journal of Urban History* 21, no. 3 (1995): 347–71.

———. In *Their Own Interests: Race, Class, and Power in the Twentieth-Century Norfolk, Virginia*. Berkeley: University of California Press, 1991.

———. "To Turn as on a Pivot: Writing African Americans into a History of Overlapping Diasporas." *American Historical Review* 100, no. 3 (1995): 765–67.

Lewis, Oscar. *La Vida: A Puerto Rican Family in the Culture of Poverty—San Juan and New York*. New York: Random House, 1966.

Lipman, Pauline. "Chicago School Reform: Advancing the Global City Agenda." In *The New Chicago: A Social and Cultural Analysis*, edited by John P. Koval, et al., 248–58. Philadelphia: Temple University Press, 2006.

Lipsitz, George. "The Possessive Investment in Whiteness: Racialized Social Democracy and the 'White' Problem in American Studies." *American Quarterly* 47, no. 3 (1995): 369–87.

Logan, John R. and Harvey Molotch, *Urban Fortunes: The Political Economy of Place*. Berkeley: University of California Press, 1987.

Maldonado, Edwin. "Contract Labor and the Origins of Puerto Rican Communities in the United States." *International Migration Review* 13, no.1 (1979): 103–21.

Martínez, Manuel. *Chicago: Historia de Nuestra Comunidad Puertorriqueña-Photographic Documentary*. Chicago: privately printed, 1989.

McCaffrey, Katherine T. "Forging Solidarity: Politics, Protest, and the Vieques Support Network." In Torres and Velázquez, *The Puerto Rican Movement: Voices from the Diaspora*, 329–40. Philadelphia: Temple University Press, 1998.

———. *Military Power and Popular Protest: The U.S. Navy in Vieques, Puerto Rico*. New Brunswick: Rutgers University Press, 2002.

Mills, C. Wright, Clarence Ollson Senior, and Rose Kohn Goldsen. *The Puerto Rican Journey: New York's Newest Migrants*. New York: Harper & Row, 1950.

Mintz, Sydney, and Eric Wolf. "An Analysis of Ritual Co-Parenthood (Compadrazgo)." *Southwestern Journal of Anthropology* 6, no. 4 (1950): 341–68.

Mitchell, Mary. "Blacks know Rosa Parks and you, Arellano, are no Rosa Parks." *Chicago Sun-Times* August 22, 2006, 14.

Moraga, Cherri, and Gloria Anzaldúa, eds. *This Bridge Called My Back: Writings by Radical Women of Color*. Watertown, MA: Persephone Press, 1981.

Morales, Iris. "¡Palante, Siempre Palante! The Young Lords." In Torres and Velázquez, *The Puerto Rican Movement: Voices from the Diaspora*, 210–27. Philadelphia: Temple University Press, 1998.

Muñiz, Vicky. *Resisting Gentrification and Displacement: Voices of Puerto Rican Women of the Barrio*. New York: Garland Publishing, 1998.

Murra, John V. Review of The Puerto Rican Journey: New York's Newest Migrants, by C. Wright Mills, et al. *The Hispanic American Historical Review* 31, no. 4 (1951): 680–81.

Naples, Nancy. "Activist Mothering: Cross-Generational Continuity in the Community Work of Women from Low-Income Urban Neighborhoods." *Gender and Society* 6, no. 3 (1992): 441–63.

Nyden, Philip, Emily Edlynn, and Julie Davis. *The Differential Impact of Gentrification on Communities in Chicago*. Chicago: Loyola University Center for Urban Research and Learning, 2006.

Oboler, Suzanne. *Ethnic Labels, Latino Lives: Identity and the Politics of (Re) Presentation in the United States*. Minneapolis: University of Minnesota Press, 1995.

———. "It's Time to Brush Up and to Make History: A Response to Mary Mitchell." *Latino Studies Journal* 4, no. 4 (2006): 353–355.

Olivo, Antonio. "Immigration Activist Will Leave Church; with D.C. Trip, She Risks Deportation," *Chicago Tribune* August 16, 2007,

———. "Latino, Black Activists Form Coalition; Immigrant Leaders Act to Defuse Tension as New Marches Near." *Chicago Tribune* February 21, 2007,

Ortiz, Fernando. *Cuban Counterpoint: Tobacco and Sugar*. 1947. Reprint, Durham: Duke University Press, 1995.

Padilla, Elena. "Looking Back and Thinking Forward: Puerto Ricans in Chicago and in New York." In Rúa, *Latino Urban Ethnography and the Work of Elena Padilla*, 25–30. Urbana: University of Illinois Press, 2011.

———. "Nocorá: An Agrarian Reform Sugar Community." PhD Diss., Columbia University, 1951.

———. "Puerto Rican Immigrants in New York and Chicago: A Study in Comparative Assimilation." Master's thesis, University of Chicago, 1947.

———. *Up from Puerto Rico*. New York: Columbia University Press, 1958.

Padilla, Felix M. *Latino Ethnic Consciousness: The Case of Mexican Americans and Puerto Ricans in Chicago*. South Bend, IN: University of Notre Dame Press, 1985.

———. *Puerto Rican Chicago*. Notre Dame, Ind.: University of Notre Dame Press, 1987.

———. "The Quest for Community: Puerto Ricans in Chicago." In *In the Barrios: Latinos and the Underclass Debate*, edited by Joan Moore and Raquel Pinderhughes, 129–48. New York: Russell Sage Foundation, 1993.

Pardo, Mary S. *Mexican American Women Activists: Identity and Resistance in Two Los Angeles Communities*. Philadelphia: Temple University Press, 1998.

Park, Robert E., and Ernest W. Burgess. *The City*. *1925*. Reprint, Chicago: The University of Chicago Press, 1968.

Parenti, Christian. *Lockdown America: Police and Prisons in the Age of Crisis*. New York: Verso, 1999.

Patterson, Orlando. "Migration in Caribbean Societies: Socioeconomic and Symbolic Resource." In *Human Migration: Patterns and Policies*, edited by William McNeil and Ruth S. Adams, 106–143. Bloomington: University of Indiana Press, 1978.

———. *Slavery and Social Death: A Comparative Study*. Cambridge, MA: Harvard University Press, 1982.

Perea, Juan F., ed. *Immigrants Out: The New Nativism and the Anti-Immigrant impulse in the United States*. New York: New York University Press, 1996.

Pérez, Gina M. *The Near Northwest Side Story: Migration Displacement and Puerto Rican Families*. Berkeley: University of California Press, 2004.

———. "The Other 'Real World': Gentrification and the Social Construction of Place in Chicago." *Urban Anthropology* 31, no. 1 (2002): 37–69.

———. "Puerto Ricans in Chicago." *Centro: Journal of the Center for Puerto Rican Studies* 13, no. 2 (2001): 4–5.

Pérez, Marvette. "The Political 'Flying Bus': Nationalism, Identity, Status, Citizenship and Puerto Ricans." *Critique of Anthropology* 22, no. 3 (2002): 305–22.

Ramos-Zayas, Ana Yolanda. "Delinquent Citizenship, National Performances: Racialization, Surveillance, and the Politics of 'Worthiness' in Puerto Rican Chicago." *Latino Studies* 2, no. 1 (2004): 26–44.

———. "Gendering 'Latino Public Intellectuals' Personal Narratives in the Ethnography of Elena Padilla." In Rúa, *Latino Urban Ethnography and the Work of Elena Padilla*, 178–206. Urbana: University of Illinois Press, 2011.

———. *National Performances: The Politics of Class, Race, and Space in Puerto Rican Chicago*. Chicago: University of Chicago Press, 2003.

Reina Pérez, Pedro A. *La Semilla Que Sembramos: Autobiografía del Proyecto Nacional*. San Juan, P.R.: Centro de Estudios Avanzados y El Caribe, 2003.

Rice, Jon. "The World of the Illinois Panthers." In *Freedom North: Black Freedom Struggles Outside of the South, 1940–1980*, edited by Jeanne F. Theoharis and Komozi Woodard, 41–64. New York: Palgrave Macmillan, 2003.

Ritchie, Donald A. *Doing Oral History: A Practical Guide*. New York: Oxford University Press, 2003.

Rivera Ramos, Efrén. *The Legal Construction of Identity: The Judicial and Social Legacy of American Colonialism in Puerto Rico*. Washington, DC: American Psychological Association, 2001.

Rivlin, Gary. *Fire on the Prairie: Chicago's Harold Washington and the Politics of Race*. New York: H. Holt, 1992.

Rodríguez, Néstor P. "Social Construction of the US-Mexico Border." In Perea, *Immigrants Out: The New Nativism and the Anti-Immigrant Impulse in the United States*, 223–43. New York: New York University Press, 1996.

Roque Ramirez, Horacio N. "A Living Archive of Desire: Teresita La Campesina and the Embodiment of Queer Latino Community Histories." In Burton, *Archive Stories: Facts, Fiction, and the Writing of History*, 111–35. Durham, Duke University Press, 2005.

———. "'That's My Place!': Negotiating Racial, Sexual, and Gender Politics in San Francisco's Gay Latino Alliance, 1975–1983," *Journal of the History of Sexuality*, Special Issue: Sexuality and Politics since 1945, 12, no. 2, (2003): 224–258.

Royko, Mike. *Boss: Richard J. Daley of Chicago*. New York: Plume, 1971.

Rúa, Mérida M. "Claims to 'The City': Puerto Rican Latinidad amid Labors of Identity, Community, and Belonging in Chicago." PhD Diss., University of Michigan, 2004.

———. "Colao Subjectivities: PortoMex and MexiRican Perspectives on Language and Identity." *Centro: Journal of the Center for Puerto Rican Studies* 13, no. 2 (2001): 117–33.

———, ed. *Latino Urban Ethnography and the Work of Elena Padilla*. Urbana: University of Illinois Press, 2011.

Sánchez, Reymundo. *My Bloody Life: The Making of a Latin King*. Chicago: Chicago Review Press, 2000.

Sánchez Korrol, Virginia E. "Latinismo among Early Puerto Rican Migrants in New York City: A Sociohistoric Interpretation." In *The Hispanic Experience in the United States: Contemporary Issues and Perspectives*. edited by Edna Acosta-Belén and Barbara R. Sjostrom, 151–62. New York: Praeger, 1988.

Sandburg, Carl. "Chicago." In *Selected Poems of Carl Sandburg*, edited by Rebecca West, 29–30. New York: Harcourt, Brace and Company, 1926.

Sandoval, Claudia. "Citizenship and the Barriers to Black and Latino Coalitions in Chicago." *NACLA Report on the Americas* 43, no. 6 (2010): 36–45.

Senior, Clarence. "Migration and Puerto Rico's Population Problem." *Annals of the American Academy of Political and Social Science* 285, Puerto Rico a Study in Democratic Development (1953), 130–136.

———. *Puerto Rican Emigration*. Río Piedras, PR: Social Science Research Center, University of Puerto Rico, 1947.

Singh, Nikhil Pal. *Black is a Country: Race and the Unfinished Struggle for Democracy*. Cambridge, MA: Harvard University Press, 2004.

Smith, Carl. *The Plan of Chicago: Daniel Burnham and the Remaking of the American City*. Chicago: University of Chicago Press, 2006.

Squires et al., Gregory. *Chicago: Race, Class, and the Response to Urban Decline*. Philadelphia: Temple University Press, 1987.

Stack, Carol. *All Our Kin: Strategies for Survival in a Black Community*. New York: Harper & Row, 1987.

———. *A Call Home: African Americans Reclaim the Rural South*. New York: Basic Books, 1996.

Steward, Julian, Robert A. Manners, Eric R. Wolf, Elena Padilla Seda, Sidney W. Mintz, and Robert L. Scheele. *The People of Puerto Rico: A Study in Social Anthropology*. Urbana: University of Illinois Press, 1956.

Stuart, Guy. "Integration or Segregation: Metropolitan Chicago at the Turn of the Century." Paper Presented at the Race, Place, and Segregation: Redrawing the Color Line in Our Nation's Metros Symposium, The Civil Rights Project, Harvard University, May 2002.

Suarez, Ray. *The Old Neighborhood: What We Lost in the Great Suburban Migration, 1966–1999*. New York: The Free Press, 1999.

Susler, Jan. "Unreconstructed Revolutionaries: Today's Puerto Rican Political Prisoners/Prisoners of War." In Torres and Velázquez, *The Puerto Rican Movement: Voices from the Diaspora*, 144–54. Philadelphia: Temple University Press, 1998.

Suttles, Gerald D. *The Social Order of the Slum: Ethnicity and Territory in the Inner City.* Chicago: University of Chicago Press, 1968.

Taylor, D. Garth, and Sylvia Puente. "Immigration, Gentrification, and Chicago: Race Ethnic Relations in the New Global Era." Chapin Hall Center for Children at the University of Chicago. http://www.about.chapinhall.org/uuc/presentations/Taylor PuentePapaer.pdf.

Thomas, Lorrin. *Puerto Rican Citizen: History and Political Identity in Twentieth Century New York City.* Chicago: University of Chicago Press, 2010.

Toro-Morn, Maura I. "Boricuas en Chicago: Gender and Class in the Migration and Settlement of Puerto Ricans." In Whalen and Vázquez-Hernández, *The Puerto Rican Diaspora: Historical Perspectives*, 128–51. Philadelphia: Temple University Press, 2005.

———. "The Gender and Class Dimensions of Puerto Rican Migration to Chicago." PhD Diss., Loyola University of Chicago, 1993.

———. "Género, Trabajo y Migración: Las Empleadas Domésticas Puertorriqueñas en Chicago." *Revista de Ciencias Sociales* 7 (1999): 102–25.

Torres, Arlene. "Re-Articulating Hidden Histories: Puerto Rican Ethnography in the Late Twentieth Century." Paper Presented at New Perspectives in Latino/Latina Studies Lecture Series, University of Michigan, February 1999.

Torres, Andrés, and José Velázquez. *The Puerto Rican Movement: Voices from the Diaspora.* Philadelphia: Temple University Press, 1998.

Trías Monge, José. *Puerto Rico: The Trials of the Oldest Colony in the World.* New Haven: Yale University Press, 1997.

Trotter, Joe, Earl Lewis, and Tera W. Hunter, eds. *The African American Urban Experience: Perspectives from the Colonial Period to the Present.* New York: Palgrave Macmillan, 2004.

Trouillot, Michel-Rolph. *Silencing the Past: Power and the Production of History.* Boston, Beacon Press, 1995.

Tuttle, William M. *Race, Riot: Chicago in the Red Summer of 1919.* New York: Atheneum, 1970.

Van Gennep, Arnold. *The Rites of Passage.* Chicago: University of Chicago Press, 1960.

Vega, Bernardo. *Memoirs of Bernardo Vega: A Contribution to the History of the Puerto Rican Community in New York.* Edited by César Andreu Iglesias. Translated by Juan Flores. New York: Monthly Press, 1984.

Venkatesh, Sudhir Alladi. "Chicago's Pragmatic Planners: American Sociology and the Myth of Community." *Social Sciences History* 25, no. 2 (2001): 275–317.

———. "'Doin' the hustle': Constructing the Ethnographer in the American Ghetto." *Ethnography* 3, no. 1 (2002): 91–111.

Venkatesh, Sudhir Alladi, and Alexandra K. Murphy. "Policing Ourselves: Law and Order in the American Ghetto." In *Youth, Globalization, and the Law*, edited by Sudhir Alladi Venkatesh and Ronald Kassimir, 124–62. Stanford: Stanford University Press, 2007.

Villa, Raúl. *Barrio-Logos: Space and Place in Urban Chicago Literature and Culture.* Austin, TX: University of Texas Press, 2000.

Vincent, Joan. *Anthropology and Politics: Visions, Traditions, and Trends.* Tucson: The University of Arizona Press, 1990.

Von Hoffman, Alexander. *House by House, Block by Block: The Rebirth of American Urban Neighborhoods.* New York: Oxford University Press, 2003.

Whalen, Carmen Teresa. "Bridging Homeland and Barrio Politics: The Young Lords in Philadelphia." In Torres and Velázquez, *The Puerto Rican Movement: Voices from the Diaspora,* 107–23. Philadelphia: Temple University Press, 1998.

———. "Colonialism, Citizenship, and the Making of the Puerto Rican Diaspora: An Introduction." In Whalen and Vázquez Hernández, *The Puerto Rican Diaspora: Historical Perspectives,* 1–42. Philadelphia: Temple University Press, 2005.

———. *From Puerto Rico to Philadelphia: Puerto Rican Workers and Postwar Economies.* Berkeley: University of California Press, 2002.

Whalen, Carmen Teresa and Víctor Vásquez-Hernández, eds. *The Puerto Rican Diaspora: Historical Perspectives.* Philadelphia: Temple University Press, 2005.

Williams, Raymond. *Marxism and Literature.* Oxford: Oxford University Press, 1977.

Young, Iris Marion. "Asymmetrical Reciprocity: On Moral Respect, Wonder, and Enlarged Thought." *Constellation* 3, no. 3 (1997): 340–63.

Yu, Henry. *Thinking Orientals: Migration, Contact, and Exoticism in Modern America.* New York: Oxford University Press, 2001.

INDEX